SCRIPTURE TEXTBOOKS FOR CATHOLIC SCHOOLS

VOLUME IV

THE CHURCH IN THE NEW TESTAMENT

THE LIBERATION OF ST PETER, AFTER A PAINTING BY
DOMENICHINO

(*Acts* 12)

SCRIPTURE TEXTBOOKS FOR CATHOLIC SCHOOLS

General Editor:
The Very Reverend Monsignor JOHN M. T. BARTON, D.D., L.S.S., F.S.A.
English Consultor of the Pontifical Biblical Commission

THE CHURCH IN THE NEW TESTAMENT

by the Reverend Father
SEBASTIAN BULLOUGH, O.P.,
M.A.(Cantab.), S.T.L.
Senior Scripture Master at Blackfriars School, Laxton

With a Foreword by His Eminence
THE CARDINAL ARCHBISHOP OF WESTMINSTER

LONDON
BURNS OATES AND WASHBOURNE
Publishers to the Holy See

Nihil Obstat : EDUARDUS CAN. MAHONEY
Censor deputatus
Imprimatur : E. MORROGH BERNARD
Vic. Gen.
WESTMONASTERII
die 29 Septembris 1944

Nihil Obstat : FR. RICARDUS KEHOE, O.P., S.T.L., S.S. Lic.
FR. VICTOR WHITE, O.P., S.T.L.
Imprimatur : FR. BERNARDUS DELANY, O.P.
Prior Provincialis
LONDINI
die 12 Martii 1941

First published 1945
Second impression 1948

THIS BOOK WAS MADE IN GREAT
BRITAIN AND PRINTED BY WILLIAM
CLOWES AND SONS, LIMITED,
AT LONDON AND BECCLES

FOREWORD

THE present series of Scripture textbooks for schools is both welcome and opportune. The books ought to arouse a more intelligent interest in the minds of the children in the unspeakable treasures which God unfolds in His written word to mankind.

It is our fervent hope that through the study of the books the children will be encouraged to read the Scriptures themselves. So many people are taught all about the Scriptures but few are taught to read them. St Jerome tells us that to be ignorant of the Scriptures means to be ignorant of Christ. This point is stressed by our Holy Father in his encyclical letter on the Bible. His Holiness explains that our Divine Lord will be better known, more ardently loved and more faithfully imitated, in as far as men know and meditate on the sacred Scriptures, and especially the New Testament.

Scripture lessons should teach children not only about the Scriptures, not only about the facts of our Lord's life, but about our Lord Himself. They should be taught to know our Lord through the reading of the New Testament. " Everything in the Scripture ", says St Paul, " has been divinely inspired, and has its uses ; to instruct us, to expose our errors, to correct our faults, to educate us in holy living " (II Tim. 3. 16).

May the devout and frequent reading of the Scriptures inspire us to a greater love of our Blessed Lord.

✠ BERNARD,
Cardinal Archbishop of Westminster.

INTRODUCTION

By the GENERAL EDITOR

IT is a genuine pleasure to write a few lines by way of introduction to Fr. Sebastian Bullough's able volume on "The Church in the New Testament". The book (it might almost be called the library) known as the Acts of the Apostles is one of the most stimulating and enthralling of narratives in any language or literature, but for its proper understanding a good deal of explanation is necessary. Without some knowledge of the Roman world at the time of the Apostles' adventures (this is surely the correct word), of Greek culture and civilisation, and of Judaism in the New Testament period, there is likely to be a whole succession of gaps in a reader's appreciation of the book. And, not least for a Catholic student, there are many questions of deep significance for the history and growth of the early Church which cannot easily be explained in footnotes to a verse-by-verse commentary.

In the present volume Fr. Bullough has made what seems to me to be a wise selection of topics and has duly stressed all that is most important. In a book of this size it would be impossible (even if it were not undesirable) to include all the myriad details of criticism, history, and archaeology that may be found in such works as the Abbé Jacquier's voluminous commentary and the learned (though almost consistently unorthodox and frequently perverse) series entitled "The Beginnings of Christianity". Here, the main issues have been happily combined with a sufficient quantity of other useful, if less vital, information, and the frequent interludes are an agreeable reminder that *Acts* as a history of Apostolic times is a jewel with many facets.

I may conclude with the remark that I should have found this book precious beyond all others of the kind in the days when I was privileged to prepare young Edmundians for the School Certificate Examination in Holy Scripture. It would have replaced or supplemented the somewhat uninspired manuals that my class and I studied together in those days, and its use would have eliminated entirely the laborious dictation of notes and preparation of mimeographed sheets, both of them in my experience wretched substitutes for a really efficient textbook.

JOHN M. T. BARTON.

St Catherine the Martyr,
West Drayton, Mddx.

Feast of the Conversion of
St Paul, 1944

AUTHOR'S PREFACE

THIS is the fourth volume of a series of six intended to cover the requirements of the six years of normal secondary education. This book is written as a basis for Scripture Study in a Fourth Form, where boys or girls may be expected to be round 14 years of age. In all this series an attempt has been made to present Scripture as a living reality, and especially as one of the main *channels of Revelation* by which God makes known to us the Divine Truth. Since the idea of the Church is central in the whole of Revelation, we have felt that at this stage a special study should be made of the Church as reflected in the New Testament, and of course the chief text is the history of the *Acts*. The *Epistles* will later receive fuller treatment in Vol. VI, but here also they are constantly referred to, and there are special sections devoted to their contents.

In order to see the Bible as a revelation, and particularly in relation to the Church, it is important that the student should see the links between the Bible and the present living organism of the Church, hence we have made frequent mention of liturgical practice and doctrines as understood both in New Testament times and now, and we have constantly amplified our biblical study with the examination of history and tradition outside the inspired books. Part of what we know of the beginnings of Christianity is from the Bible, and part is from the Tradition of the Church: all goes to build up the living reality which is the Church, in which "we live and move and have our being".

THIS BOOK

This book is not a commentary: but its object is to acquaint those who study it, with the living Church, the Mystical Body of Christ, in its beginnings among men in the Apostolic Age. Yet almost the whole text of the *Acts* is examined, and not many points of history or revelation connected with the life of the Church as shown in the *Acts* have been left aside. The text (Rheims Version) has been taken in sections, and studied rather in the style of the patristic commentaries, with a mixture of text (always in "inverted commas" and referenced), paraphrase, précis and explanation. In each such section the significance or value of the facts related is briefly analysed, and many of the classical biblical difficulties are alluded to if not fully explained, though a laboured study of minutiae has been specially avoided. The older reader will require a fuller treatment, and for this he must go to the commentaries or to the sources quoted in the Index of References to Authors. A working knowledge of Latin is supposed, though passages are normally translated. Similarly some knowledge of Greek (or at least a capacity to read the words) is more than helpful in the attempts made at elementary exegesis of the text.

USE IN SCHOOL

1. *Division of work.* The year's work is divided into sections representing the work of about 50 classes (at two classes a week devoted to Scripture), including Introductions, Background, Exegetical Sections, and Interludes. A normal school year will actually have rather more than 50 classes. These divisions are shown by the bracketed numbers, *e.g.* (50), at the head of each section, and are intended only as "normae directivae" or guiding lines to the master, to help him to marshall all his material throughout the year. There is no doubt that such a schedule in a textbook is a great boon to the teacher. At the same time he is left entirely free to adapt this syllabus to his own arrangements. The same should be said of the suggested pauses for Christmas and Easter: it may be found more useful to pause elsewhere, and various Interludes may well be shifted to other positions in order to serve as Introductions or Conclusions to a term.

2. *Teaching.* This book could be used in various ways as a help to Scripture Study at School, but it always presumes a text of the New Testament handy. If all the class have the book, the sections could be read over beforehand and then explained in class; otherwise it could serve as a basis for the master's explanations. The New Testament itself could either be read over beforehand, or read and explained in class. The master is expected of course to supplement the material of this book with his own thought and reading, and for this purpose the references at the back may be useful. Madame Cecilia's commentary in particular will provide much valuable material. We have used Greek fairly freely, because in practice this, as well as the use of the less familiar characters of Hebrew or Arabic, is often found to stimulate interest in a point of exegesis.

3. *References.* We have entirely avoided the use of foot-note-references to authors for the support of statements made, since these would distract or bore the IV Form pupil, but they have been grouped according to pages at the back of the book (Index I), so that the schoolmaster may feel no discomfort for lack of the support of scholarship.

4. *Indices.* For the purpose of pedagogy we have distributed our material through the year, so that biblical, doctrinal, liturgical or historical matters are raised as the New Testament text is studied, on the Rabbinic principle of "a word by the side of the road". When therefore the book is not being worked through in class, this deliberate scattering of the material would make it particularly trying to look up or confirm a particular point. So special attention has been paid to the Indices, to make them complete and easy of reference.

We hope and pray therefore that a book of this kind may help the boys and girls in our schools to a deeper understanding of the Truths of our Holy Religion, and to a greater awareness of the position of the Bible in God's plan for the instruction of Christians.

Lastly, the author asks his readers for a short prayer to God and to the Blessed Mother for him: his great desire has been to bring them to a greater knowledge and love of the things of God, so that both his and their service of God may be the more perfect.

LAXTON.

Feast of the Epiphany, 1941.

I want here to add my thanks to those who helped me in my attempt to find suitable illustrations, especially Fr. Walter Weld, S.J., of Stonyhurst.

I also want to record my gratitude to Gerald Simblett of Form VI here at Laxton, for all his assistance in the labour of proof-reading and indexing, and for his competent compilation of the Greek Index.

LAXTON.

Passion Week, 1945.

CONTENTS

CONTENTS

CONTENTS

xiv

CONTENTS

LIST OF ILLUSTRATIONS

MAPS

INTRODUCTION

1. A GENERAL SURVEY

In the prayer *Te igitur* at the beginning of the Canon of the Mass, a prayer that goes back in its present form to a very great antiquity, perhaps as far as the second century (A.D. 100–200) and certainly is not later than the fourth century (A.D. 300–400), we pray that God may accept and bless these gifts, this holy and pure Sacrifice: "imprimis, quae tibi offerimus pro Ecclesia tua sancta catholica: quam pacificare, custodire, adunare, et regere digneris toto orbe terrarum": "which we offer thee in the first place for thy holy catholic Church, that thou wouldst deign to give her peace, protection, unity, and guidance all the world over". The first concern then of the priest and people as they stand daily before the altar to offer their sacrifice, their greatest prayer, to God, is to pray for the Church. And this concern for the welfare of the Church goes back to the earliest ages of the Christian era.

Similarly in the Creed which we call the Apostles' Creed, the expression of our Catholic Faith which we learn in our youth and which will remain for us always its simplest formulation, there is the mention of the "Holy Catholic Church". It is not certain whether this Creed goes back as it stands to the Apostles themselves, but what is certain is that as far as we can trace it back, to the end of the Second Century in its simplest form, it has the article which expresses belief in the "Holy Catholic Church".

At the very roots, then, of our Christian Life lies the idea of the Church, the consciousness that we belong to the Catholic Church, to the Church founded by Christ. Now by the Christian Life is meant that Spiritual Life which we lead as Christians: for it is by a Spiritual Life that we are marked off from the pagans and those who do not believe in Christ. We are not distinguished from them by any bodily mark, as the races of the world are distinguished one from another by the colour of their skin, the shape of their head, and such like; but we are distinguished from them because we can think of and love something that they cannot think of or love. And thinking and loving are affairs of the spirit, even though our thought and our love will have results in our exterior actions: for very many of the things we do require previous thought and desire. Hence when the Christian has Christian principles of thought and love, he will act in external things in a Christian way. Now in the *Catechism* (which is an excellent manual of simple Theology or Science about God) we learn (n. 141) that Prayer is "the raising up of the mind and heart to God". Raising the mind means thinking, and raising the heart is a way of saying loving or desiring: and so the Catechism definition of Prayer simply means "thinking about God and loving him". But we Christians, by the grace of God, know also that Jesus Christ is the Second Person of the Blessed Trinity, and that he is True God and True Man: and so we can raise our minds and hearts to him also, and pray to him, as when we say after Benediction "Blessed be Jesus Christ, True God and True Man", we are saying what we know and believe about him, and also that we love him. Similarly in the great Christian prayer of the *Hail Mary* we say "Blessed is the fruit of thy womb, Jesus", and we call Mary the "Mother of God" to show that we know that he is really God, and at the same time really Man because he is her Son.

It is then our knowing Our Lord Jesus Christ, and our loving him, that makes that "Spiritual Life", that life of thought and love, that distinguishes us as Christians from those men who do not think about Christ or love him.

And in our greatest Christian Prayer which is the Mass, and in the very expression of our Faith, our Christian thinking, we have the idea of the Church. We read in the Acts (11. 26) how the body of men who were followers of Christ were first called Christians (χριστιανοί) in the Greek speaking city of Antioch. It was St Paul (Rom. 12. 5; 1 Cor. 12. 12–13) who first called the body of Christians the Body of Christ: and this has since been called the doctrine of the "Mystical Body". The Church is looked upon as a Body, one with the Head who is Christ: hence as members of the Church we are members of Christ's Body; and our devotion to the Church is a devotion to Christ himself.

It is therefore as followers of Christ, as Christians, united to Christ by Faith and Charity, that is to say by our belief in him or knowledge of him (Faith) which enables us to think of him, and by our love of him (Charity), that we are members of that body, the Church, which is the "mystical" Body of Christ. And as members of the Church we have that "spiritual life" of thought and love, that is of prayer to Christ, that distinguishes us as Christians.

This year's work will now be a study of the growth of the Church from the time of its foundation by Christ when he was upon this earth to the time when historical documents show us clearly that the Church was in existence with the main features of its present organisation. And this means a study of the period from the end of the Gospel-age to the time when the last books of the New Testament were written. We have therefore called this section of Biblical study "The Church in the New Testament".

2. THE SOURCES OF OUR STUDY

Man of himself could not have known that Our Blessed Lord was True God: he needed to be told. And it is the same with many truths of our holy Religion: man needs to be told of them, and to be told on a divine authority. God has therefore *revealed* to man certain things: and explanation to man on the part of God of certain things about himself is called *Divine Revelation*.

Now God has chosen various ways of making things known to man: that is, there are different kinds of Revelation. But the main channels of Revelation are two, namely:

Scripture
Tradition.

By Scripture is meant those books, written with divine authority and under divine inspiration, which teach men things about God, which God intended to reveal, and which are collected together into one book called the Bible.

By Tradition is meant the handing down (Traditio in Latin) of truths revealed by God through the Apostles to the later writers of the Church, not put into writing until later, and reflected in the practice of the Church and especially also in the Liturgy. Thus for instance the prayer of the *Hail Mary* we receive partly from Scripture and partly from Tradition. The words "Hail, full of grace, the Lord is with thee" are recorded in Scripture by St Luke (1. 28), and the words "Blessed art thou among women, and blessed is the fruit of thy womb" similarly come from Lk. 1. 42. The rest of the prayer comes from the Tradition of the Church.

Similarly with our present study of the origins and growth of the Church, we depend partly upon Scripture and partly on Tradition for what we know. But since this part of our school training is concerned primarily with Scripture rather than with Doctrine or with Church History, our inquiry in this book will be chiefly to find out what Scripture tells us of this part of Divine Revelation which deals with the beginnings of the life of the Church. We are assuming that we have already a familiarity with the Gospel history and teaching, that is with the life and teaching of Our Lord on earth, which is the ground covered by the Four Gospels (and would correspond to the study with Volumes II and V of this series); and we also assume some acquaintance with the contents of the Bible in general, with the notions of the first Revelations of God to mankind in the Old Testament, and the continued Revelation through the history of the Jewish people in preparation for the Coming of Our Lord (and this would correspond to Biblical study with Vol. III of this series).

Following therefore upon the history of Our Lord as told in the Gospels, the Gospel-age, we proceed to study the latter part of the New Testament, that is, the continuation of Revelation to the Apostles after the Ascension of Our Lord, the Apostolic age. This part of the New Testament, beginning with the *Acts of the Apostles*, is a little longer than the first part which is the Gospels. It is composed of the *Acts*, which is a sort of chronicle of the spread of the Church through SS. Peter and Paul, ending up in Rome which was to become the Mother of all the Churches, the centre of Christendom, and of a series of no less than twenty-one *Letters* or *Epistles* from various Apostles to different groups of the first Christians who came under their care. The last book of this latter part of the New Testament is an account of a wonderful vision granted by God to St John the Evangelist as a Revelation of many heavenly things. Revelation is in Greek ἀποκάλυψις from ἀπο-καλύπτω to un-cover: hence this book of the vision is called the *Apocalypse*.

Now all these books, the *Acts*, the *Epistles* and the *Apocalypse*, will come into this year's work, as they all show something of the beginnings of the life of the Church. But as the Epistles and the Apocalypse will receive a special year of study later on (Vol. VII), we will only use them to help us to understand the account which is given us in the *Acts*.

A great part of our study this year will therefore be devoted to the book of the *Acts*, in which we read of the spread of the Church first among the Jews of Jerusalem, and then gradually further afield (chaps. 8–9) in Palestine, and finally, especially through St Paul, to the Gentile world of Greeks and Romans. Meanwhile we shall note something of the *Epistles* that were written during this period. And alongside we shall supplement our study of these Biblical sources with facts that we know from tradition, and features of the present-day organisation of the Church which can be traced back to those times.

We shall conclude this year's work at the close of the Apostolic age, that is, about the year A.D. 100, the end of the first century from the birth of Christ, when the last of the Apostles was dead; and we shall glance into the so-called Sub-apostolic age, the period of the generation after the Apostles, when we shall find the Church as we know it now firmly established in its origins.

3. THE APOSTOLATE AND THE FOUNDATION OF THE CHURCH

St Paul (Eph. 2. 19–20) writing to some of his own disciples and encouraging them in their new Faith says: "Now therefore you are no more strangers and foreigners; but you are fellow-citizens with the saints, and the domestics of God *built upon the foundation of the apostles* and prophets, Jesus Christ himself being the chief corner stone". This passage is used in the Divine Office in the Common of Apostles for the Chapter at Vespers and Lauds. It was chosen because it shows how the Apostles are the very foundations of the Church, the foundations laid in the Gospel-age, with Jesus Christ himself as the corner stone, the foundations on which the structure of the Church was built during our period, the Apostolic age.

The Collect or Prayer for the Feast of SS Peter and Paul (June 29) goes even further, asking that the Church may "in everything follow the teaching of *those through whom she received the beginnings of her Faith*" ("in omnibus sequi praeceptum, per quos religionis sumpsit exordium").

In the Masses of the Apostles, again, we find words used from the Psalms, which have become thereby very familiar, and which also emphasise the very special place of the Apostles in the Church. The Introit of several Apostles' Feasts (for instance St James, July 25): "Mihi autem nimis honorati sunt amici tui, Deus: nimis confortatus est principatus eorum" from Ps. 138. 17 ("How honourable are thy friends to me, O God: how mighty is their leadership!"). The Gradual from the same Mass is from Ps. 44. 17: "Constitues eos principes super omnem terram: memores erunt nominis tui, Domine" ("Thou shalt make them princes over all the earth: they shall remember thy name, O Lord"). And the Offertory from Ps. 18. 5: "In omnem terram exivit sonus eorum: et in fines orbis terrae verba eorum" ("Their sound hath gone forth into all the earth: and their words unto the ends of the world").

But it is in the Gospels themselves that we see the real privileged position and authority of the Apostles. In the account of their being chosen we read (Lk. 6. 13): "He called unto him his disciples and he chose twelve of them (whom he also named *apostles*)". The word ἀπόστολος from ἀποστέλλω to send away, which corresponds exactly with the Aramaic שליחא (sheliha), is Our Lord's own word, and means one who is specially sent by another. (The Greek word meant originally a messenger, or ambassador, and in later Greek a naval officer.) The first great quality of the Apostles is that they were *chosen by Christ*, and the second that they are *sent by him*.

St Mark in the account of their choosing tells us for what they were chosen (Mk. 3. 14–15): "And he made that the twelve should *be with him*, and that he might send them to *preach*. And he gave them power to *heal* sicknesses, and to cast out devils". When they had been with him and got to know him and his teaching, they were able to be sent out to preach, and then, in order to confirm their preaching with miracles, they received the power of healing.

But Our Lord also gives them special power (Mt. 18. 18): "Amen I say to you, whatsoever you shall bind upon earth, shall be bound also in heaven: and whatsoever you shall loose upon earth, shall be loosed also in heaven". This power is a partaking of Christ's own divine authority to forgive sin; and the exercise of this power, which is called jurisdiction, is reserved to Peter, when Our Lord says specially to Peter (Mt. 16. 19): "And I will give *to thee* the keys of the kingdom of heaven". Thus all the Apostles have this power from Christ, but exercise it under the authority of Peter.

Further, towards the end, at the Last Supper, in the long talk recorded by St John, during which he suddenly breaks into a prayer for these very chosen ones of his, who are the Apostles, he speaks more precisely of the way they are to continue his work, sharing in his very own authority, so that as he founded the Church, so they share in his work (they are to "be with him") and with him found the Church and teach his doctrine even after he is gone. (Jn. 17. 14, 17–18, 20) "I have given them thy word, and the world hath hated them, because they are not of the world. . . . Sanctify them in truth. Thy word is truth. As thou hast sent me (ἀπέ-στειλας) into the world, I also have sent (ἀπέστειλα) them into the world. . . . And not for them only do I pray, but for them also who through their word shall believe in me". Here is the continuing of Christ's mission through the Apostles.

And just before Our Blessed Lord ascended into Heaven, he crowned his gifts of his power to the Apostles with a fulness of power to continue his work upon earth (Mt. 28. 18–20) "All power is given to me in heaven and in earth. Going therefore teach ye all nations: baptizing them in the name of the Father, and of the Son, and of the Holy Ghost. Teaching them to observe all things whatsoever I have commanded you: and behold I am with you all days, even to the consummation of the world". Here we see the Apostles as the real foundations of the Church, with Christ himself as the corner stone, prepared to receive the full structure of the Church. It is the rearing of this structure on the foundations of the Apostles that is to be our study.

(3) # HISTORICAL BACKGROUND

1. Roman Empire
2. Greek culture and trade
3. Judaism in the Roman Empire

In order adequately to understand a series of events like the spread of the Church during the first century A.D. it is important to know something of the background of the land and people among whom the events are to be enacted. It is like a play, in which we have to receive some indication of where the scene is laid before we can fully understand the action of the play.

First we must understand that all round the Mediterranean, the land wherein took place the events of the *Acts* and *Epistles*, Palestine, Asia Minor, Greece and Italy, was all Roman territory, territory forming part of the great Roman Empire, and that throughout the lands mentioned there was a more or less uniform system of government, a uniform official language, and all the facilities of intercommunication afforded by the unity of the Empire. Hence the Roman Empire has been considered to be the instrument arranged by God in his Providence for the spread of the Church, by providing a unity in the world which enabled the Gospel to be preached without too much hindrance from distance, difference of custom, or official interference.

But behind this Roman unity there was already a unity in the East and Mediterranean Europe provided by that treasure of civilisation which is the Greek language and the culture it brought with it. Greek had long been the "lingua franca" (or language which could be understood everywhere) of the Mediterranean lands, it was the language used by writers and by merchants, and it became the language of the Missionaries of Christ as well. Hence it is that the whole New Testament was written in Greek, and in the type of Greek called κοινή or "common", which was used at the time by the merchants and all the Mediterranean folk. This will be the subject of the second background in this section.

Yet Christ was born into the Chosen People of the Jews, chosen by God from antiquity to receive the Saviour of the world, and prepared for this through the ages of Hebrew history represented by the classical Hebrew literature which is the Old Testament. Greek was indeed spoken in Palestine, the country of the Jews, and Latin by the officials, but the language of the people was Aramaic, a "Semitic" language like their own liturgical language which was Hebrew. Our Blessed Lord was a Jew, and all the first Christians were Jews or Palestinians, and so the language of Our Lord and his first followers was Aramaic. The learned class among the Jews were the priests and Rabbis (meaning "greater" or "chief" people) who had a Hebrew "Rabbinic" culture that was all their own. From the Gospels we are familiar with the Rabbis, and in Roman times the Jews retained most of their own customs and institutions, and the Rabbinic system continued to flourish. St Paul in his early days had been a keen adherent of the Rabbinic school, and much of the material of his Epistles deals with the attitude that a Jew, with all his Hebrew and Rabbinic background, should take up to the new doctrine, the New Testament, preached by Christ.

This life of Judaism within the Empire will be the subject of our third background. These three cultures, then, Latin, Greek, and Hebrew are the scene upon which the life of the Apostles was to be played, their life of preaching Christ, preaching Christ crucified (as St Paul says, 1 Cor. 1. 23), on whose very Cross (so that all might read) (Lk. 23. 38) "there was also a superscription written over him in letters of Greek, and Latin, and Hebrew".

1. ROMAN EMPIRE

In such a place as this we cannot devote more than a glance to the earlier history of Rome until the Empire: we shall then see briefly something of the extent and organisation of the Empire under Augustus: then a note on the later Emperors: and finally an observation on Roman rule in Palestine.

a. OUTLINE OF EARLIER ROMAN HISTORY

An outline such as this is only intended to indicate the gradual growth of Rome as a world power: naturally we see this history in proper detail in our classical studies. We can however see from this plan how the power of Rome extended almost concentrically from Italy, if we look at the same time at the accompanying map of the Provinces of the Empire.

YEARS	B.C.	
	753.	The traditional date of the Founding of Rome (the starting point of the dates
700		A.U.C. "Ab Urbe Condita").
600		Rome governed by *Kings*.
		Rome a small city-state.
500	509.	Rome becomes a *Republic*.
		Rome gets increasing power in *Italy*.
400		Wars with Gauls, and with Greeks under
300		Pyrrhus.
	275.	Pyrrhus leaves Italy: Roman domination in *Italy* is complete.
200	264–202.	Punic Wars: Rome overcomes *Carthage*. Power in the *Mediterranean*.

YEARS	B.C.	
100		Power grows in *Greece and Asia Minor*. Civil Wars.
	70.	Consulship of Pompey: conquests in the *East*.
50	58–51.	Caesar's Gallic Wars: conquests of *Gaul* and *Britain*.
	44.	Death of Caesar.
27		Octavian becomes AUGUSTUS: EMPIRE ESTABLISHED.

(4)   *b*. THE EXTENT AND ORGANISATION OF THE EMPIRE

In the accompanying map we see the Roman Empire as it was administered by Augustus, about 27 B.C., and such it remained more or less for the succeeding 100 years, *i.e.* right into our period. Many of the outlying provinces first became parts of the Empire as autonomous but vassal kingdoms, and their gradual incorporation into the Empire proper is an historical study of its own. There were many and varying degrees of dependence upon Rome. Judea was at one time a vassal kingdom under Herod, and at another time a province under a Procurator.

Augustus further divided the provinces into Senatorial and Imperial Provinces. The Imperial Provinces were, generally speaking, the more outlying and consequently less settled and orderly, and in these provinces the Emperor would keep military forces present under his own orders. The Senatorial Provinces were governed by Proconsuls, and the Imperial Provinces by either Legati or else by Prefects or Procurators who personally represented the Emperor, and there were more soldiers stationed in these provinces to keep order. Of the provinces which are our concern here, the remoter ones, Judea, Syria, Cilicia, Cappadocia, Galatia, Pamphylia, Lycia, and Thracia were Imperial Provinces, governed by Legati or Prefects or Procurators; while Macedonia, Achaia, Asia, Bithynia, Pontus, and Cyprus were Senatorial Provinces, governed on a non-military basis by Proconsuls.

While a territory was no more than a vassal kingdom, naturally all justice and administration was carried out within the kingdom itself; but even when such a territory became a province, the local laws were often respected and even enforced by the new Roman authority, although without that authority they now carried no weight. This situation is obvious in case of the trial of Our Blessed Lord; and both here and in the arrests of St Paul we have this mixture of the two rights, although the ultimate judgment necessarily comes from the Roman governor.

Further, in the matter of religion, it was a Roman principle to tolerate the local religion, and this very fact, as long as Christianity was being preached to Jews in the Empire, protected Christianity along with Judaism which was a religion officially accepted as that of the people of Palestine. But also the Jewish communities in the cities of Asia Minor and Greece and even Rome were similarly tolerated, and this greatly facilitated the work of the Apostles in those cities, for they naturally went first to the Jews in those cities. In Rome itself, where there were subjects from all the provinces, there was much freedom of worship, and the big circular temple which was called the Pantheon, the sanctuary of all the gods, built to honour all the various gods worshipped by the various peoples of the Empire, and now converted into a Christian Church in honour of Our Lady and all the Martyrs, still stands in Rome as a witness to the broad view taken by the Roman authorities. It is worth noting in passing that the Feast of All Saints (November 1) was instituted in connexion with the consecration of this temple as a Christian church in the year 610.

Lastly it should be noted that the organisation of the

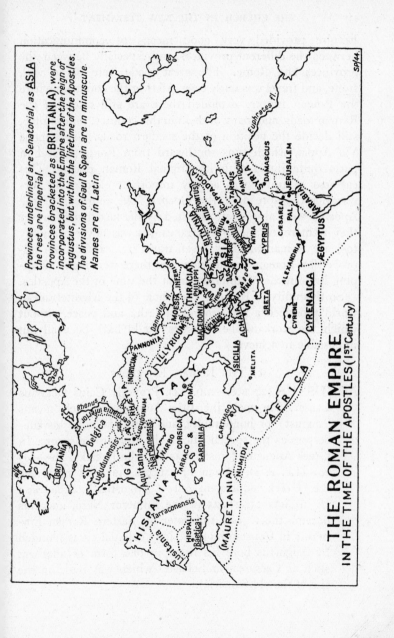

Provinces underlined are Senatorial, as <u>ASIA</u>. the rest are Imperial.

Provinces bracketed, as (BRITTANIA), were incorporated into the Empire after the reign of Augustus, but within the lifetime of the Apostles.

The divisions of Gaul & Spain are in Latin

Names are in Latin

SP/44.

THE ROMAN EMPIRE
IN THE TIME OF THE APOSTLES (1ST Century)

Empire provided very good means of communication between the different provinces, and especially between the provinces and Rome. The great roads were paved with stone, and travel was fairly easy. All over the countries where the Roman Empire extended there are still traces of the Roman roads, and many of them in this country, for example, still decide the position of the modern roads. The famous Via Appia, which runs southward from Rome, is still in parts quite intact with its original Roman paving. This easiness of travel was a very important element in forwarding the spread of the Gospel. The journeys of the Apostles were also greatly assisted by the fact that wherever they went round the Meriterranean, it was never necessary to leave Roman territory. Even travel by sea had been improved by Roman organisation, and there were regular shipping lines in the Mediterranean at the time of the Apostles.

So this unity of Rome in the whole of the Mediterranean world produced a background of order and peace without which the work of the Apostles would have been all but impossible to achieve.

c. THE ROMAN EMPERORS

AUGUSTUS (27 B.C.—A.D. 14). Properly Caius Octavius Caesar. He took the title Augustus (which means "august" or honourable), and it was kept by his successors as the special title of the Roman Emperors. In Greek Augustus himself was apparently called Αὐγούστος (Lk. 2. 1), though his successors used in Greek the Greek equivalent of "Augustus" Σεβαστός : cf. in Acts 25. 21, 25 of the Emperor Nero, and this became the regular title later of Eastern Roman Emperors in Constantinople. Many colonial cities founded by Augustus bore his name in one form or another: such as Caesarea, or Sebaste (which was built on the site of the old Samaria).

TIBERIUS (A.D. 14–37). Attempts made, and finally abandoned, to extend the Empire into Germany. The City of Tiberias, founded by King Herod about the year 26, was named after him. He sent Pontius Pilate as Procurator of Judea, when it once more became a Province. He was Emperor at the time of the Public Life and Death of Our Lord.

CALIGULA (37–41). Disturbances in the East and in Palestine, because of Caligula's desire to have statues of himself put up for veneration.

CLAUDIUS (41–54). Final conquest of Britain. Conquests in Africa. Careful provision for the administration of justice in the provinces. Most of St Paul's travels took place during his reign. Claudius did much to improve the City of Rome, and his famous aqueducts still in part remain.

NERO (54–68). Extension of the Empire in the East towards Armenia. First Persecution of Christians 64. Martyrdom of SS Peter and Paul. Revolt of Judea 66: Vespasian sent to quell the revolt, which finally resulted in the fall of Jerusalem in the reign of Vespasian himself.

GALBA, OTHO, VITELLIUS all had short reigns during a disturbed period in Rome, called the "Year of the Four Emperors" (68–69).

VESPASIAN (69–79). Proclaimed Emperor while fighting in Judea. The war there was concluded by Titus with the fall of Jerusalem in 70. He began the famous Colosseum in Rome. He developed the organisation of the provinces.

TITUS (79–81). At the beginning of his reign took place the famous eruption of the volcano Vesuvius, which buried Pompeii. During this and the preceding reign the Christians enjoyed liberty.

3

DOMITIAN (81–96). Progress in Britain and in Germany. The rule of the Emperor was becoming more absolute. Second Persecution of Christians 91–93. Ordeal of St John the Evangelist, his exile to Patmos.

NERVA (96–98). Release of many victims of Domitian and recall of exiles, including St John.

TRAJAN (98–117). Conquests in Dacia (across the Danube, in what is now Hungary) and in the East beyond the Euphrates right down to Mesopotamia. Other desert conquests included the Province of Arabia, the area now known as Transjordan to the east of the Dead Sea and Jordan. The reign of Trajan is often regarded as one of the most prosperous periods of the Empire as a whole. Trajan himself was the first Emperor to come from the provinces (his home was in the Province of Baetica in Spain). The famous historian Tacitus lived and wrote during the reign of Trajan. The martyr St Ignatius (with whom our book will conclude) suffered under Trajan. Although he was in general a very just ruler, the practice of Christianity was forbidden because of its appearance of secrecy and the loyal obedience to the Bishops. The Catacombs in Rome were much developed at this time.

Lastly, it should be noted in general that very many of the remains which still stand in Rome date from the period of these Emperors.

d. ROMAN RULE IN PALESTINE

We have seen how a Roman province often began as a vassal kingdom, and later became a province under a Procurator. The case of Judea is complicated because at one period the House of Herod was restored to the kingship for a short time.

It was in 63 B.C. under Pompey's conquest that the Jews

first became vassals of the Romans. The Romans appointed the High Priest and also a local king, Antipater from Idumea. It was his son, Herod (the Great) who began to reign in 40 B.C., dying just after our Lord's birth, in 4 B.C.,[1] who succeeded him, and at his death divided his kingdom between his sons, to whom, however, the Roman authorities denied the title of kings. They were to be called Tetrarchs (Ethnarch in Judea), and Archelaus became Ethnarch of Judea, and his brother Herod Antipas, Tetrarch of Galilee (which he still was at the time of John the Baptist's preaching (Lk. 3. 1) and Our Lord's Passion (Lk. 23. 7)).

Archelaus was however deposed in A.D. 6, and Judea became a Roman province with a Procurator. Pontius Pilate was the Procurator A.D. 26–36.

The kingdom was restored by the Emperor Claudius under King Herod Agrippa I, A.D. 41–44, but after this was once more a province under Procurators until the end in A.D. 70 when Jerusalem was destroyed. After the destruction of Jerusalem, Judea of course continued as a Roman province under Procurators, with a garrison built on the ruins of the ancient capital.

Summary

63–4 B.C.	Judea a vassal kingdom (Kings of the House of Herod).
4 B.C.–A.D. 6	Judea an ethnarchy.
A.D. 6–41	Judea a province under Procurators.
41–44	Judean kingdom restored (vassal kingdom).
after 44	Judea a province again with Procurators.

[1] The calculation on which we base our years as A.D. (Anno Domini) from the Birth of Our Lord is generally now held to be inaccurate by about 4 years. This is the more understandable when we realise that no one used the "A.D." system until the monk Dionysius Exiguus, over 500 years after Christ, fixed it (though incorrectly).

(5)   2. GREEK CULTURE AND TRADE

It was not a Greek who spread Greek culture throughout the East, but it was Alexander the Great, the Macedonian, son of Philip of Macedonia who had conquered Greece. Alexander had had all the opportunities of Greek education, and as he spread his vast Empire, he spread Greek civilisation with it.

And further, when eventually it came to the Romans to be heirs of Alexander's conquests, it was the Romans who protected and fostered the Greek civilisation which had remained established throughout the East.

a. GREEK CULTURE

It is generally considered that although Greek art and literature had its origins in the remotest past—Homer had probably lived round 800 B.C. or earlier—the highest point of perfection was reached in Athens at the time of Pericles, who became leader of the Athenian Republic in 461 B.C. It was at this time that there flourished in Athens the great tragedians Aeschylus, Sophocles, and Euripides, the greatest historian of antiquity Herodotus, and the great sculptor Phidias. The year 403, however, marks a supremacy in Greece of the rival state of Sparta, and a very disturbed period followed. The historians Thucydides and Xenophon have related to us many details of this time.

In the mid-fourth century, however (round 350 B.C.) we again find a very fruitful period in Athenian culture: it is the time of the great philosophers, Socrates, Plato, and Aristotle, and the greatest, perhaps, of all the Greek sculptors, Praxiteles, lived at this time. It was at this time too, that Philip, king of the neighbouring Macedonia, sent his son Alexander to the University at Athens.

Before long, however, war had broken out between Macedonia and Greece, and in 336 Philip conquered the country. He was succeeded after two years by his son Alexander.

b. ALEXANDER THE GREAT

Alexander, brought up with all the refinement of Greek culture, and having, it is said, Aristotle the great philosopher, as his tutor, now that he was lord of Greece, wished to spread Greece to the ends of the earth.

Before long he had the whole of the East under his control: he had spread his Empire right into Egypt and Persia; and with his Empire went all that Greece had to give to the world. Alexander reigned for only 13 years, and died in the midst of his furthest conquests at Babylon in 323 B.C. He was then only 33 years old.

But his conquests had left their mark: wherever he went he founded Greek cities, he left behind him Greek scholars, Greek colonists and traders. He quickly established communications, roads, and seaways: trade and exchange soon became regular between the Mediterranean and the distant parts of the Empire in Persia, India, and Egypt. Alexandria, one of his cities and named after him, soon became the most cosmopolitan city of the world.

Alexander, although he had brought to all his Empire the fruits of Greek thought, had yet carefully respected local customs and rights, and hence the people of his Empire all contributed to its richness. At his death his Empire was divided among his generals, and the main parts were the Seleucid Empire of Persia and the Ptolemaic Empire of Egypt. But both these remained essentially Greek. Palestine lay between the two, and from the time of Alexander onwards was definitely Hellenic in culture, though the Hebrew element always remained. Yet the Jews of Palestine were now

Greek-speaking, as the books of the Old Testament of the period show, beginning with Ecclesiasticus which was first known to us only in its Greek translation; and the books of the Maccabees were of course written in Greek.

c. Greek Civilisation in the Roman Empire

From round the year 150 B.C. the influence of the Romans began to be felt in the East, as we have seen, and one by one the provinces of the Empires that succeeded Alexander's were absorbed into the Roman Empire. Alexander had paved the way for Rome: the East was already united by the Greek culture which he had given it: Greek was already the "lingua franca" of the East as well as of the Eastern Mediterranean: there were already the trade-routes established by the Greek colonists: Alexandria, which was to become the second city of the Empire, was already a centre of learning and of trade. The Jews had also settled as Greek-speaking colonists in this Greek-speaking world, and we find important settlements of Jews in many of the great cities, and especially in Alexandria.

Thus we see how the influence of Greek culture, and especially of the Greek language, this influence brought originally by Alexander the Great, facilitated the uniting of the Roman Empire, and was therefore not overruled by the Latin of the Romans, but on the contrary encouraged. Greek gradually became very generally spoken even in Italy, and in Rome itself, especially by the foreign elements there. The early Christian writers all wrote in Greek: indeed the first Christian writer to use Latin was the North-African Tertullian at the beginning of the third century. We have relics of the almost universal use of Greek in the early Church in our Roman Liturgy, in the words "Kyrie eleison" and a few other phrases, notably the "Agios o Theos" in Holy Week.

[*Photo by courtesy of the Very Rev. Mgr. Barton*

STREET OF LOW ARCHES, JERUSALEM

(6)   3. JUDAISM IN THE ROMAN EMPIRE

We have been studying the background to the labours of the Apostles which was the Roman Empire: we have been considering the cultural background which was chiefly Greek. This was the background of the Gentile world in which they moved. Yet scattered throughout this world were the Communities of Jews, the Diaspora (from διασπείρω to scatter through), and this was the first scene of the preaching of the Apostles. They always first visited the Jewish quarter, and it was indeed a momentous decision when the time came to preach the word equally to those other men who had not had the preparation for the Word of Christ that was a Jewish upbringing. The religious background of these other men did not lead them close to Christ: but for the Jew it was otherwise: we have seen men in the Gospel cry out (Jn. 1. 45): "We have found him of whom Moses in the law, and the prophets did write". This was the preparation that Judaism could give. Christ was (Lk. 2. 32: the "Nunc dimittis") "a light to the revelation of the gentiles", but to the Jews "the glory of thy people Israel".

a. THE HEBREW BACKGROUND

From the time of Moses until the Captivity: that is for about 700 years before 586 B.C., the Jews had remained a people very much apart. They had lived in the midst of barbaric peoples and had preserved the laws that God had given them and kept their race pure; they had lived among men who practised hideous idolatrous rites and they had kept clean their worship of the One true God, according to the revelation that he had given them. And all this they achieved by being a nation apart, by remaining united and together in their little land of Palestine.

They produced during this period a literature that was all

their own. Their own language was Hebrew, a language at once simple in its resources (its vocabulary and variety of syntax is relatively small) but rich in its possibility of expression. The Hebrew Literature they produced, as far as it remains to us, is a unique Literature: it is the Old Testament, the Hebrew Bible. They were a people conscious that they alone in the ancient world knew the true God, and their whole literary output was religious. This very fact, that the only books of theirs which have been preserved are the Sacred Books, only serves to show the religious character of the people of Israel.

And the people was a religious people, because it was the Chosen People of God: chosen from among the races of the earth to receive the Revelation of the Personal God, the One God. The great foundation of the Jewish Faith was, and still is, this unity of the one God. The great prayer of the Jews, recited daily by every pious Jew, was, and still is, the verse from Deuteronomy (6. 4): "Hear, O Israel: the Lord our God is one Lord". This is called the "Shema" from the opening word שְׁמַע "Hear". The Jews were also ever conscious of the words of God to Abraham their father (Gen. 12. 2–3): "I will make of thee a great nation, and I will bless thee, and magnify thy name: and thou shalt be blessed. I will bless them that bless thee, and curse them that curse thee; and in thee shall all the kindred of the earth be blessed". Here we have a hint of the other great treasure of the Jewish people, the hope of the Saviour to come, and to come for certain to be born into their own people.

So the Jews were the Chosen People, and chosen by God to receive this double revelation: that of the One God, who is Lord of All; and that of the Saviour of the world, who would come to redeem them and all the nations of the earth from sin.

God had indeed revealed himself in a personal way to the first man he created, Adam, and spoke with him as would a father; but men in their wickedness "changed the glory of the incorruptible God into the likeness of a corruptible man and of birds, and of fourfooted beasts and of creeping things" (as St Paul puts it in Rom. 1. 23). Men corrupted this first revelation, and then invented false gods and idols in an attempt to satisfy their need for religion: but of all the people of antiquity Israel alone remained faithful to the revelation. Israel, the Chosen People, was gradually taught more about God, and what Man's relation to God should be, and that Man was made in the image of God. The Greeks, like the faithless ones among the Jews of whom we read in the Psalms (Ps. 105. (Heb. 106.) 21) "forgot God", and groping for the divine, made for themselves instead gods in the image of man.

Now all this religious background which was the Hebrew culture was gradually building up for many centuries, and gradually producing meanwhile the greatest religious literature of all time. But in 586 B.C. came the destruction of Jerusalem by the Babylonians and the exile of Israel in Babylon. Was this then the end of the Hebrew culture? No, indeed; but here it took a new turn.

Israel had so far been a nation apart: now, sufficiently strengthened in its religious background, it found itself mixed with the various elements of the ancient world. The days of the little religious principality in Palestine were really over: the company that returned after the fifty years in exile were only a part of the original community. Many had stayed in Babylon, others had begun to spread to various places. Israel was no longer "a garden enclosed, a garden enclosed" (Cant. 4. 12).

b. THE HELLENIC INFLUENCE

The Hebrew Literature of the time after the exile has a different tone: the language was ceasing to be commonly spoken, and its place was being taken by Aramaic, a language of the same stock. The colonies of Jews in various parts of the ancient world began to take on a character of their own, no longer in close contact with Jerusalem, the Holy City.

When, at the time of Alexander, Greek culture was spreading throughout the East (as we have seen), the Jews naturally came under this influence like everyone else. The Jewish communities outside Palestine of course became Greek more rapidly: and it was at Alexandria, where there were many devout Jews, that the Old Testament, the Hebrew Bible, was first translated into Greek in order that the people might read the Bible in what had become their own tongue. This is the famous version known as the "Septuagint" (usually written LXX, *i.e.* 70, in Roman figures), so called because it was said to have been made by a group of seventy scholars. The later parts of the Old Testament were even (as we have seen) written in Greek, like the Books of the Maccabees. Other books, even if they were originally composed in Hebrew, were published in Greek, like the Book of Ecclesiasticus. Many Jews began to take Greek names.

Yet all the time these Greek-speaking Jews did not forget that they were the Chosen People, they did not forget their "Hebrew Background". There remained at certain places centres of Hebrew learning, notably at Babylon and in Palestine itself. These were beginnings of the great Rabbinic Colleges: here Hebrew, though by now in most places a dead language, and heard by most people only in the Scriptures and in the Liturgy, continued to be used and cultivated; much as Latin is used and cultivated in the big Ecclesiastical Universities at the present day. And thus a New Hebrew Literature grew up, with the language developing the while (with many "modern" Aramaic elements); much as there is at the present day a vast Latin Literature, which continues to grow, among the theologians of the Church.

In this way there began to grow, alongside the Greek element in Judaism, the Rabbinic tradition with its own methods and its own literature. By the time of Our Lord, Rabbinic teaching and literature had begun to accumulate for about two centuries, especially at Babylon and in Palestine. The Talmud, the great legal library of the Jews, is a collection of these traditions, made at a much later date. At the time of St Paul, there were many Jews who came from Greek-speaking cities, but yet were fully instructed in their Hebrew Rabbinic literature: and St Paul himself was such a one, for he had, on his own testimony (Acts 22. 3) sat "at the feet of Gamaliel", the great Rabbinic teacher in Jerusalem, and been "taught according to the truth of the law of the fathers".

c. IN THE ROMAN EMPIRE

Such then were the men who were found in the Jewish colonies after the Romans had conquered the East: men whose speech and thought was chiefly Greek, but who had that religious background of Judaism of which we spoke earlier, whether or no they had a Rabbinic training. These were the men to whom the Apostles first brought the Gospel of Christ: the men to whom they wrote their Epistles in Greek. The Epistle to the Romans, for instance, is written to the *Jews* in Rome.

Judaism was a religion for the most part tolerated within the Empire, for it was the religion of Palestine, and on the Roman principle a local religion was to be tolerated and respected. Hence it was that, in general, the Jewish settlements in all the various cities of the Empire were allowed to practise their religion unmolested.

Thus Christ, who had come into the world by being born into the Jewish people, was first preached in the great cities of the Empire, including Rome itself, under the cover and protection of Judaism; and as the Romans at first regarded Christianity as merely a department of Judaism, they were almost unwittingly receiving Christ into their midst.

Note on the Chronological Table that follows: The dates given in any Chronological Table of this period cannot claim to be precise : there are too many elements of Roman, Jewish, and New Testament chronology to make reckoning simple. Many of the dates therefore in this table are to be taken as approximate, although the sequence or order of events as shown is for the most part entirely certain. The dates given by different scholars often vary by a few years, but those given here would receive fairly general acceptance. They are based upon the dates given by Father Hugh Pope in his "Aids" and by Dr Brownlow in his "Early History of the Church of God".

A CHRONOLOGICAL TABLE

of the Apostolic Age

(7)

YEAR A.D.	ROMAN EMPEROR	CHRISTIANS		REFS. TO ACTS	ROMAN RULE IN PALESTINE
		IN ROME	IN PALESTINE		
30 —	Tiberius since 14		32. St Stephen martyred	7	Pontius Pilate Procurator since 26
			33. Conversion of St Paul	9	
	37. Caligula				36. Marcellus
40 —	41. Claudius				37. Marullus
		42. St Peter first in Rome	42. St James the Gt martyred, St Peter arrested	12 / 12	41. King Herod Agrippa I
			47. St Paul's first Journey	13	44. Procurators again
		49. St Peter visits Jerusalem	49. Council of Jerusalem	15	
50 —			49–52. St Paul's second Journey	15	
	54. Nero		53. St Paul's third Journey	18	52. Felix Procurator
			55–57. St Paul imprisoned at Caesarea	21	
		57. St Paul arrives in Rome	57. St Paul taken to Rome	27	57. Festus Procurator

Year	Emperors	Church	Christians of Jerusalem		Judæa
60		60. St Paul is released 64. First Persecution 67. Martyrdom of SS Peter and Paul Linus succeeds	61. St James the Less is martyred: Symeon is Bp 70. Flight of Christians to Pella, with Symeon	28	62. Other Procurators 66. Revolt of Jews 70. Fall of Jerusalem
70	68–69. 4 Emps. 69. Vespasian	Earliest of the Catacombs 79. Cletus	Return of Christians to Jerusalem		Other Procurators
80	79. Titus 81. Domitian				
90		91–93. Second Persecution 91. Clement 93. St John at the Latin Gate Exiled to Patmos 96. Back to Ephesus			
100	96. Nerva 98. Trajan	100. John dies			

EXEGESIS OF ACTS

Note on the exegetical sections that follow. The word "Exegesis" means interpretation or explanation of a text, and is used specially of interpretation of the Biblical text. It is a Greek word, and comes from ἐξηγέομαι "to lead the way" or be a ἡγεμών or "leader". These sections are then intended to lead the way to understanding the text of the Acts of the Apostles. For this purpose we have divided each section into three parts:

  A. The *significance* of the event, or its importance in the whole of revelation: why it is of special interest to us who are followers of Christ and "built upon the foundation of the apostles" (Eph. 2. 20).
  B. The *story* or the description of the event.
  C. *Details* in the section of text chosen.

(8) SECTION 1: OUR LORD'S ASCENSION AND PROMISE

(Acts 1. 1–14, *cf.* Lk. 24. 44–53; Mt. 28. 16–20)

A. SIGNIFICANCE

Our Blessed Lord's active Life and Ministry was concluded at his Passion and Death: but after his Resurrection he chose to appear at intervals during forty days to his disciples, in order further to teach them and to confirm their faith. The last time that he appeared to them, he appeared to them and ascended into Heaven in order to show them that his risen Body was a heavenly Body, and that being God the Son his true place was in Heaven "at the right hand of God, the Father Almighty"; and also to show them that now it is *they* who are to continue his work upon earth.

Yet he will not leave them merely to their own human resources. The work of Christ is a divine work, and it is Christ who will work through them, though no longer with his visible presence. He promised to them his invisible help and presence: "Behold I am with you all days, even to the

32

consummation of the world" (Mt. 28. 20: the last words of
this Gospel). Now the spread of the Church is to be the
work of the Apostles.

But they were not to start straight away. They were to
wait in the City, in Jerusalem, till they be "endued with
power from on high" (Lk. 24. 49): the power of the Holy
Ghost, who will come and fortify them for their task.

So this moment is the transition from the work of Christ
carried out by himself, to the work carried on by the Apostles.

B. STORY

We learn from St John (20. 19) that after the apparent
failure of Our Lord's Mission, ending in his Death, the
disciples gathered together behind closed doors for fear of
the Jews. It was on such an occasion that Our Lord first
appeared to them after the Resurrection.

Also from St John (21. 1–23) we learn that after this they
scattered and returned for a time to Galilee to occupy themselves with earning a livelihood. We find Peter back at his
fishing-nets. Twice it is recorded that Our Lord appeared
to them in Galilee (Jn. 21. 1; Mt. 28. 16); but it was back at
Jerusalem that he bade them farewell.

But at this last meeting some apparently did not yet
understand. "Lord, wilt thou at this time restore again the
kingdom to Israel?" (Acts 1. 6). They were still thinking
of an earthly kingdom, perhaps of Israel throwing off the
Roman rule. They had not yet understood what Our Lord
meant when he said during his trial before Pilate (Jn. 18. 36)
"My kingdom is not of this world": they did not yet understand that the Kingdom of God on earth was the Church
which Christ had founded upon them, and which they were
to go out and build. It was indeed necessary that they should
yet be instructed by the Spirit of God, as indeed they were,
and transformed into fearless Apostles of the Kingdom of
God, after the outpouring of the Spirit at Pentecost.

4

But Our Lord had now only one thing to tell them: and that one thing was the Promise of the Holy Spirit, after which "you shall be witnesses unto me in Jerusalem, and in all Judea and Samaria, and even to the uttermost parts of the earth" (Acts 1. 8). He further spoke of them being about to be "baptised" with the Holy Ghost, not merely with water, but as St John the Baptist had said years before (Lk. 3. 16) "with the Holy Ghost and with fire". Of course the verb $\beta a\pi\tau i\zeta\omega$ in Greek merely means "to dip or bathe", and so here they are to be bathed in fire, in the Holy Ghost who will cleanse them as fire, and make them ready for their mission.

St Matthew also reports (28. 19) how Our Lord at the end commanded a universal apostolate: "Going, therefore, teach ye all nations": and here they are commanded to bear witness to Christ in the whole world.

Only they were to wait. Actually they had to wait ten days, until the Jewish Feast of Pentecost, fifty ($\pi\epsilon\nu\tau\eta\kappa o\sigma\tau\acute{o}s$ means 50th) days after Easter.

Then he lifted up his hands and blessed them, and "whilst he blessed them, he departed from them, and was carried up to heaven" (Lk. 24. 51) "and sitteth on the right hand of God" (Mk. 16. 19). And while they were beholding him going up to heaven, behold two men stood by them in white garments" (Acts 1. 10). The white garments seem to be a usual description of an angel, the angel at the tomb of Christ also is in white (Mk. 16. 5, "a young man, sitting on the right side, clothed in a white robe"). The words of the mysterious "two men" are words of consolation, and remind us of Our Lord's Coming at the end of the world. They have become familiar to us in the Liturgy as the Introit of the Mass of the Ascension "Viri Galilaei, quid admiramini aspicientes in caelum?" of which the music is one of the finest pieces of Plainsong in the Gradual.

"And they went back into Jerusalem with great joy"

[Photo E.N.A.

THE APOSTLES' SPRING, ON THE JERICHO ROAD, THE ONLY WATER BETWEEN BETHANY
AND THE VALLEY OF THE JORDAN. IT WAS HERE THAT THE APOSTLES BROKE THEIR
JOURNEYS ON THE WAY TO THE HOLY RIVER

(Lk. 24. 52), and not as one might expect with sorrow at the departure of the Master, but with joy, for they had received their commission to continue this work, and they had received his promise that he would be with them, and his promise of the Spirit who "will teach you all things, and bring all things to your mind, whatsoever I shall have said to you" (Jn. 14. 26).

And what were the Apostles doing during the ten days that followed? They lived in an "upper room" (since the Greek has "the" upper room, was it the upper room of the Last Supper?) and "were persevering with one mind in prayer with the women, and Mary the mother of Jesus" (Acts 1. 14). This is the last time that Our Blessed Lady is mentioned in the Bible, and in this last view we have of her we see her at prayer. She is protecting and supporting them with her prayer, as she is protecting and supporting us: daily we ask her prayer "Holy Mary, Mother of God, pray for us sinners"; in ejaculations we call on her help; in her litanies we repeat again and again "Pray for us". She is our Mother because she is Christ's Mother; and the work of Christ, the care of his Church, has scarcely been put into the human hands of the Apostles, when she is there, and praying.

C. DETAILS

v. 1   "Theophilus" to whom the Book of the Acts is dedicated. St Luke similarly dedicated his Gospel to the same "most excellent Theophilus" (Lk. 1. 3). No one knows who Theophilus was. The title "most excellent" was given to certain officials in the Empire, and St Luke's friend might be one of these. On the other hand, since the name means "Friend of God" in Greek, it may just indicate the Christian reader, whoever he may be.

v. 8   Jerusalem, Judea, Samaria, the whole world. This order was in fact preserved by the Apostles. We do not read of any preaching outside Jerusalem until the persecution in which Stephen died, when (8. 1) the Christians dispersed into Judea and Samaria, and still further afield under Philip (8. 26–40) and of course right into Europe with the preaching of St Paul.

v. 9 "a cloud received him out of their sight". That is to say he was no longer seen. Christ ascended into Heaven by his own will, both by the power of his divine will, and by the power of his human will, for since his body was glorified it obeyed his will perfectly: hence when he wished to appear on earth, then his body appeared on earth: similarly when he vanished, as on the road to Emmaus (Lk. 24. 31, "and he vanished out of their sight"), it was when he willed not to be present any longer. Here he willed to be present to the Apostles, and to be seen ascending into Heaven, and then to be present no longer; he thus vanished as into a cloud.

v. 12 "a sabbath-day's journey": the amount of walking allowed by the Rabbis without breaking the sabbath: just under a mile.

v. 13 Note Peter's name, as always, first on the list.

(9) SECTION 2: THE CHOICE OF MATTHIAS
(Acts 1. 15–26)

A. SIGNIFICANCE

At the election of this new member of the College of twelve Apostles, to replace Judas the traitor, St Peter states clearly what is necessary for an Apostle. When Our Blessed Lord chose the twelve, St Mark (3. 14) tells us that "he made that twelve should *be with him*". Here again, St Peter makes the first condition that he should have "companied with us all the time that the Lord Jesus came in and went out among us, beginning from the baptism of John until the day wherein he was taken up from us" (1. 21–22). This therefore includes the forty days after the Resurrection; and hence such a one must become with the Eleven a witness to Our Lord's Resurrection. The *witness to the Resurrection* was an essential quality of the Apostle. This of course did not mean more than having seen Our Lord some time after the Resurrection, for no one of men ever saw the actual moment of the Resurrection, as the deacon sings on Holy Saturday during the beautiful ritual of blessing the Paschal Candle: "O vere beata nox, quae sola meruit scire tempus et horam, in qua Christus ab inferis resurrexit!" ("O truly blessed night, who alone wert worthy to know the moment and hour of Christ's resurrection from the dead!") St Paul was at pains to show (1 Cor. 15. 3–9) that he was really an apostle because he had seen the Risen Christ: "and last of all, he was seen also by me, as by one born out of due time" (v. 8).

B. STORY

Peter, as the chief, stands up in the midst of the brethren (used here, as often hereafter, of the religious community of the first Christians) to propose the election of another Apostle to replace Judas the traitor. Presumably he felt that since Our Lord chose twelve, that number should be retained. The betrayal had been foretold to them at the Last Supper, and they had all feared (Mk. 14. 19): "They began to be sorrowful, and to say to him one by one: Is it I?" They had all seen him come to the garden as "the leader of them that apprehended Jesus" (Acts 1. 16). They looked upon the Psalm that says: "And his bishopric let another take" as referring to Judas. This Psalm (Ps. 108: Hebrew 109) is indeed most applicable to Judas: it is one of the strongest curses upon ungrateful treachery that has ever been written: this is the context of the passage:

O God of my praise, be not silent
For the mouth of the wicked and the mouth of deceit are opened against me;

They have spoken to me with a tongue of falsehood,
And words of hatred have surrounded me;

And they have attacked me without cause:
In place of my love they have turned against me.
                                   But I am at prayer.

And they have set on me evil for good,
And hatred instead of my love.

Put him in charge of a wicked man,
And may an enemy stand at his right hand.

When he is judged, may he come out guilty,
And may his supplication be as a crime;

May his days be few,
His charge may another take;

May his sons be fatherless and his wife a widow,
And may his sons indeed wander and want,
And beg because of their desolation.   Etc.

All this had been fulfilled of Judas, but that line in v. 8 "His charge may another take". That is "the job of which he has charge": the LXX translated the Hebrew word by ἐπισκοπή "supervision" and since ἐπίσκοπος came to be used for a "bishop" (and our English word is a corruption of the Greek one), or one who has charge of the faithful, it came to be translated here "his bishopric". Well, this had not yet been fulfilled, and Peter said "the Scripture must needs be fulfilled" (Acts 1. 16).

Everybody knew how Judas had committed suicide, and how the hanging corpse had afterwards swollen and burst, and how the field had come to be known in Aramaic as חקל דמא Haqel-dema, the field of blood.

Therefore they set about choosing someone to "take his

charge". St Peter lays down the conditions of companion-
ship with Our Lord, and witness to the Resurrection. There
must have been quite a number to choose from: of the 120
who were present (1. 15) many must have known Our Lord;
and St Paul tells us that Our Lord was seen after the Resurrection, not only by Peter and after that by the Eleven, but
also "by more than five hundred brethren at once" (1 Cor.
15. 5–6). Two, however, were chosen, Joseph Barsabas
Justus and Matthias. The historian Eusebius († 340) in his
"Historia Ecclesiastica" (1. 12) says that it was believed that
both of them were among the 72 disciples of Our Lord sent
"two and two before his face into every city and place
whither he himself was to come" (Lk. 10. 1).

To decide then between these two, they cast lots, probably
by writing the names on small tablets, putting them into a
vessel, and seeing which should be shaken out first. Thus
was St Matthias numbered among the Twelve. The New
Testament tells us no more about St Matthias. In a later
chapter we shall study the traditions that have been preserved
about the subsequent activities of the Apostles.

C. Details

v. 18   Judas "being hanged". This reading coincides with
the story as told by St Matthew (27. 5), though the
Greek just means "falling headlong".[1] The Vulgate rendering (of which ours is a translation) is
rather an explanation. St Matthew also suggests that
the reason why the field was called "the field of
blood" is that it was bought with the thirty pieces
of silver for which Judas betrayed Our Lord. Both
this and the fact that Judas committed suicide
there are good reasons for the field receiving
this name among the people.

[1] The Greek word is πρηνής, which some think may be translated
"having swelled up".

v. 20 St Peter combines two quotations from the Psalms. The first part is from Ps. 68. (Heb. 69.) 26 which runs: "Let their encampment be deserted: in their tents let no one dwell".

v. 26 On drawing lots: St Bede (quoted by Fr Pope in his "Layman's New Testament",) commenting on this passage says: "If people think . . . that God should be consulted by lots after the example of the Apostles, let them remember that the Apostles only did so in full assembly and after praying to God".

(10) SECTION 3: PENTECOST (Acts 2. 1–43)

A. SIGNIFICANCE

In the Catechism (n. 262) we learn that Confirmation is "a Sacrament by which we receive the Holy Ghost, in order to make us strong and perfect Christians and soldiers of Jesus Christ". The coming of the Holy Ghost at Pentecost was the "Confirmation" of the Church. Now at Baptism a man becomes a Christian, and receives the beginnings of Grace by which we belong to Christ: at Confirmation we receive the fulness of Grace, so that we are able to act more fully under him, and really to work for him. "The Holy Ghost is given to the Christian to strengthen him, that he may fearlessly proclaim the name of Christ" they said at the Council of Florence. Christ had said (Jn. 15. 5): "Without me you can do nothing". We can do nothing as Christians without belonging to Christ. But we need the strength of the Holy Ghost: "the Paraclete, the Holy Ghost, whom the Father will send in my name, he will teach you all things" (Jn. 14. 26).

It was obvious that until now the Apostles were not yet prepared "fearlessly to proclaim the name of Christ", and it was also obvious that they did not yet fully understand the work of Christ, as we saw in the conversation with Our Lord just before the Ascension, when they clearly did not yet understand what his Kingdom should be (Acts 1. 6). Yet the moment that the Holy Ghost came, who should teach them all things, they immediately began to preach about Christ.

St Peter, as the head, immediately preached his first great sermon: "Ye men of Judea, and all you that dwell in Jerusalem, be this known to you, and with your ears receive my words" (2. 14). He did not fear now to speak openly of Jesus, and tell his whole story. He did not now hesitate to preach penance and sorrow for sins (2. 38); and he followed straight away the last command of Christ (Mt. 28. 19): "Going therefore teach ye all nations: baptising them in the name of the Father and of the Son and of the Holy Ghost". We see him here baptising many, and these converts of the first preaching of the Apostles numbered about 3000 (Acts 2. 41).

This preaching, with the resulting conversions, was the immediate effect of the receiving of the Holy Ghost: the transformation was complete: the work had started: the building of the Church on the foundation of the Apostles had begun.

B. Story

(1) *The Coming of the Holy Ghost.* The Holy Ghost came with a sound "as of a mighty wind coming", which filled the whole house. This is what they heard. What they saw were "as it were tongues", dividing themselves (διαμεριζόμε-ναι) or distributed; tongues as it were of fire. The appearance was, it seems, as of a ball of fire that divided itself, and thus it (note the singular, not as it were a small flame for each) sat upon every one of them. The fire divided itself, and sat upon each of them. It is worth noting that these are all like-nesses: the Holy Ghost is not a wind, nor fire, any more than

he is a dove. Just as here the words "as it were" are inserted with care, so similarly at the Baptism of Jesus all three accounts say "as a dove" (Lk. 3. 22; Mk. 1. 10; Mt. 3. 16). God chose that the Holy Ghost should here be manifested with the appearance of wind and of fire, to help those present to understand his power. Wind and fire are among the great forces of nature, and together with water are the great cleansers. Water is the gentlest and commonest cleanser, and hence is used as a sign at Baptism. Fire is a violent cleanser: and we do not often realise how much the wind cleans up the countryside in the autumn. This impression of wind anyway represented the greatness of the power with which they were to be "endued from on high" (Lk. 24. 49).

(2) *Those Present*. "There were dwelling at Jerusalem Jews, devout men out of every nation" (2. 5). These were the Jews of the "Diaspora" or dispersion, which began after the return from the exile. We saw in our Historical Background (Section 3) how after this time the Jews began to scatter. The Jews were enjoined to visit the Holy City of Jerusalem on the three great feasts of the Jewish year: the Passover or Pasch (corresponding to our Easter-time), Pentecost (50 days after the Pasch), and the Feast of Tabernacles (or tents) (at the beginning of October). So now, at the Feast of Pentecost, there were many Jews who had been able to afford to make the journey to Jerusalem from the various parts of the world where they lived. Many of these will have been Jews of Jewish stock: others will have been converts to Judaism, called "proselytes", for there were always a number of pagans attracted to the Jewish religion.

The areas of the world from which these pilgrims came are of interest to us, because the first converts to the Church were among them. Madame Cecilia in her Commentary groups them according to the dispersions:

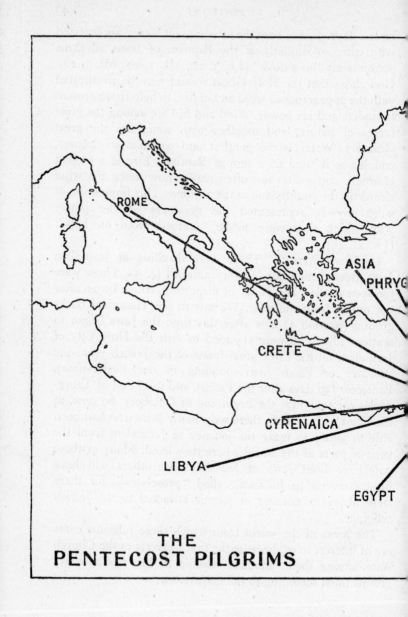

THE
PENTECOST PILGRIMS

ROME

ASIA

PHRYG

CRETE

CYRENAICA

LIBYA

EGYPT

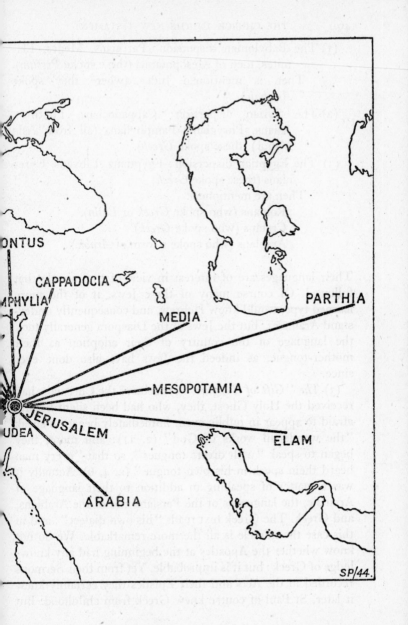

(1) The Babylonian dispersion: Parthians, Medes, Elamites, men of Mesopotamia (these spoke *Persian*).
Then is mentioned Judea (where they spoke *Aramaic*).

(2) The Syrian dispersion: Cappadocians, Pontines, Asians, Phrygians, Pamphylians (all from Asia Minor) (these spoke *Greek*).

(3) The Egyptian dispersion: Egyptians, Libyans, Cyrenians (these spoke *Greek*).
Then are mentioned:
Romans (who spoke *Greek* or *Latin*).
Cretans (who spoke *Greek*).
Arabians (who spoke a form of *Arabic*)

Their languages are of interest in view of the miracle that followed. Of course many of these Jews, if of the more learned type, would know Hebrew, and consequently understand Aramaic; but the Jews of the Diaspora generally took the language of the country of their adoption as their mother-tongue, as indeed the Jews have also done ever since.

(3) *The "Gift of Tongues"*. As soon as the Christians had received the Holy Ghost, they, who had been silent before, afraid to appear in public even, immediately began to speak "the wonderful works of God" (2. 11): and more, they began to speak "with divers tongues", so that "every man heard them speak in his own tongue" (2. 4, 6). Actually it was a matter of speaking in addition to their language of Aramaic, the languages of the Persians and of the Arabians, and Greek. The Greek text reads "his own dialect": and in this case the miracle is all the more remarkable. We do not know whether the Apostles at the beginning had any knowledge of Greek: but it is improbable. Yet from their Sermons recorded in the Acts and their Epistles they certainly knew it later. St Paul of course knew Greek from childhood. But

perhaps the Greek used in their writings by SS Peter, John, James, and Jude, was the result of the gift of tongues granted them at the first Christian Pentecost.

It should be noted that the "Gift of Tongues" implies a miracle in the speaker: a sudden capacity to speak in another language, and does not imply that the hearers heard the speech transformed into their own language. There is discussion about the purpose or use of "Gift of Tongues": some authors maintain that it was granted in order that the Apostles might be able to preach to anyone (and this was held by the ancient writers generally, and by St Thomas Aquinas in II–II 176. 1). Other writers (including many modern writers) hold that it was given as a special manner of praising God (Acts 2. 11: "We have heard them speak in our own tongues the wonderful works of God". During this first period of the life of the Church the Gift of Tongues (also called "Glossolalia") was granted on a number of occasions; again in the Acts at the conversion of Cornelius (10. 45–46), and during the ministry of St Paul at Ephesus (19. 6): "And when Paul had imposed his hands upon them, the Holy Ghost came upon them, and they spoke with tongues and prophesied". The gift seems to have been frequent at Corinth; St Paul refers to it several times in the First Epistle. On these occasions at least, it does not seem to have served the purpose of preaching. At Pentecost, however, even if it was not a set method of preaching, this "speaking the wonderful works of God" seems to have had a deep effect on the hearers, and the object of speaking a strange language would seem to be to allow hearers who were strangers to understand.

Some of the hearers were then astonished (2. 12); but others, and in any crowd there are such, mocked, and said they were drunk.

(4) *St Peter's Sermon.* Presumably he spoke in Aramaic: the common language of Jerusalem, and the pilgrims would

have enough Aramaic to understand most of it, as they would for their needs in the city.

He begins by refuting the charge of drunkenness: it is but 9 a.m., and the Jews according to the directions of the Rabbis did not take anything until after the morning prayer. Probably this would not yet have taken place. But, on the contrary, St Peter says, this is the fulfilling of the prophecy of Joel (2. 28–32) where God speaks of "pouring out the Spirit upon all flesh" and many signs are to follow: prophecies, visions, dreams.

But St Peter immediately goes on to preach the Gospel of Jesus Christ. They had all heard of him in Jerusalem, naturally. Now he witnesses to his Resurrection. And all this, he says, fulfils the Scriptures. Where David in the Psalm (15. (Heb. 16.) 10) says: "Thou shalt not leave my soul in the place of the dead, or suffer thy holy one to see corruption", he cannot refer to himself for his tomb is here, but it must refer to someone who was to come. But (Acts 2. 32) "This Jesus hath God raised again, whereof all we are witnesses"; (v. 36) "This same Jesus, whom you have crucified".

Many people then repented, and said "What shall we do?" Peter bade them do penance and be baptised.

And thus were made the first converts of the Church, about 3000: (2. 42) "and they were persevering in the doctrine of the apostles, and in the communication of the breaking of bread, and in prayers".

C. DETAILS

v. 16   Joel: one of the "minor prophets" in the Old Testament, so called because their books are short, often of only 3 chapters, though two have 14 and one 9. The prophecy of Abdias is only a single chapter. There are 12 "minor prophets".

CHRIST GIVING THE KEYS TO ST PETER, AFTER A PAINTING BY PERUGINO

5

v. 24, 27, 31   "hell" is used here, as often, in the manner
of the Hebrew language, for the place where the
dead are supposed to be. The Hebrews spoke of
"descending to Sheol (שְׁאוֹל)" for dying: the Greek
"Hades" has the same meaning.

(11) INTERLUDE ON THE PERSON OF THE HOLY GHOST AND HIS GIFTS

Whenever we bless ourselves with the Sign of the Cross,
and say: "In the Name of the Father, and of the Son, and of
the Holy Ghost", we are proclaiming our Faith in the Holy
Trinity. Indeed this Sign of the Cross with its accompanying
words is the great sign of Catholics throughout the world. In
the East they make the Sign of the Cross in the same way,
but differ in that they touch the right shoulder before the
left. But the sign and the Faith it stands for is the same.
Similarly, when we say so frequently the prayer: "Glory be to
the Father and to the Son and to the Holy Ghost", again we
are proclaiming our Faith in the Holy Trinity. This prayer
is said at the end of every Psalm in the Divine Office, and
every Hymn in the Breviary ends with a verse which conveys the same meaning: the giving of glory to the Trinity,
and hence called a "doxology" (a word of δόξα glory).

Further, our Creeds all begin with an expression of our
belief in the Holy Trinity: "I believe in God, the *Father*
Almighty . . . and in Jesus Christ his only *Son*. . . . I believe
in the *Holy Ghost*. . . ."

THE BLESSED TRINITY

In order to discuss the Person of the Holy Ghost, it is
important that we should go over our notions of the Trinity,
even though very briefly. We believe then in One God: but
this God is an entirely perfect being. And this entirely perfect being has a real life. Now with us life means change

movement, growth; and so enters in the imperfection of our life: we live in past, present, and future: we grow as we live. But it is obvious that the idea of the future, or of the yet ungrown, contains the idea of imperfection, because that which is not yet, or not yet grown, has not even the elementary perfection of existing at all. So it is even in our "spiritual life" of thought and love: our thoughts are imperfect, and necessarily so until they grow and take shape; and our love is imperfect until we know sufficiently well to be able to love.

But in God it is not so: in God all is perfect: his thought has never grown, it has always been, and always been perfect and all-embracing: "factorem caeli et terrae, visibilium omnium et invisibilium" as we sing in the Credo ("maker of heaven and earth, of all things visible and invisible"). This thought of God, God's thinking (St John called it the "Word" of God), is so perfect that it is not only exactly like God himself, but *is* God. St John in his Gospel at the very beginning says it exactly: (Jn. 1. 1) "In the beginning was the Word, and the Word was with God, and the Word *was* God". This is what we mean by God the Son, the Word of God. The Word or Thought of God indeed comes from God, like a Son comes from a Father, and that is why we use the names God the Father, and God the Son. Now because the Son is the thought of the Father, yet so perfect as to be one with the Father (Jn. 10. 30: "I and the Father are one"), it is through thought that a person acts; therefore does St John say of the Word: (1. 3) "All things were made by him", and we sing in the Credo of God the Son, "Per quem omnia facta sunt" ("through whom all things were made"). And it became much easier for us to understand when "The Word was made flesh, and dwelt among us" (Jn. 1. 14), and men could see and speak with God the Son, the Word Incarnate (that is to say "become flesh or man").

Now a similar reasoning is necessary to understand something of the Third Person. The other element in our Spiritual Life is that of love, but we cannot love unless we have first thought. Now in God's life, which is a spiritual life since he is a Spirit and not a body, his Love is also entirely perfect, his Love has never grown, but has always been; yet it necessarily depends upon his thought, since there is no love but depends upon knowledge and thought. God's love, again, is so perfect that it is not only exactly like God himself, but *is* God. And this love of God has been called the "Holy Ghost" or "Holy Spirit": and because love depends upon thought, the Holy Ghost depends on the Word or thought of God. This is why we sing in the Credo: "Qui a Patre *Filioque* procedit" ("who proceeds from the Father *and* the Son"). There was at one time in the Church much confusion over the word "Filioque" in the Creed, because some people did not understand the true relation between thought and love. Now it is love or desire that is the mainspring of our actions, we do things because in some way we want to, for some reason we desire to do them. Thus the Holy Ghost is the love between the Father and the Son, and just as we sing in the Credo, of Christ, the Second Person: "per quem omnia facta sunt" ("through whom all things are made"); so of the Third Person, the Holy Ghost, we sing: "Et in Spiritum Sanctum, Dominum et vivificantem" ("And in the Holy Ghost, the Lord and life-giver"), and in the Liturgy we frequently use the words of the Psalm (103. (Heb. 104.) 30): "Emitte spiritum tuum, et creabuntur, et renovabis faciem terrae" ("Send forth thy spirit and they shall be created, and thou shalt renew the face of the earth") of the Holy Ghost, the life-giving principle.

THE HOLY GHOST IN SCRIPTURE

The mystery of the Blessed Trinity is one that no man could have known of or attempted to understand apart from Revelation from God. And so the knowledge of the Person of the Holy Ghost depends entirely upon what God has revealed. At the very beginning of the Christian Revelation we hear of the Holy Ghost, when the Angel Gabriel announces the Incarnation to Mary: "The Holy Ghost shall come upon thee" (Lk. 1. 35). Here again the Holy Ghost is a life-giving principle; and in the Creed we say "Conceived by the Holy Ghost". And Our Lord himself speaks several times of the Holy Ghost: especially when he is speaking of the Promise of the Holy Ghost: (Jn. 14. 26) "The Holy Ghost, whom the Father will send in my name", and here indeed we see how the Holy Ghost proceeds from the Father *and* the Son. The Holy Ghost is the "Spirit of Truth" (Jn. 14. 17; 15. 26; 16. 13) who will teach them all things. As Our Lord is about to leave this earth, he tells the Apostles that they "shall receive the power of the Holy Ghost" (Acts 1. 8), as indeed at Pentecost they do. Here again we see the Holy Ghost as the "vivificans" or life-giver.

THE HOLY GHOST AND THE CHURCH

Here we only have to apply the idea of God the Holy Ghost as the life-giver, "vivificans", to the growth of the Church. We have seen in our study of the text, how historically the Church began a new life after the coming of the Holy Ghost. The Holy Ghost has by some been called the "heart of the Church", that is to say, the principle of life within the Church. The Holy Spirit is said to "inspire" the life of the Church: and it is evident that there is a hidden source of life, coming from God, that preserves and guides the Church. This is the influence of God the Holy Ghost. At Pentecost we read that "they were all filled with the Holy Ghost, and they began to speak with divers tongues, *according as the Holy Ghost gave them to speak*" (Acts 2. 4): here we have the active guidance of the Church by the Holy Ghost.

The Gifts of the Holy Ghost

Here we have an application of the idea of the life-giving principle to the individual soul. The gifts are defined by St Thomas as "certain perfections in a man, by which he is disposed to follow the movement of God". Such a man, by receiving this perfection, becomes susceptible to the inspiration of God. The so-called Seven Gifts are these perfections, given to us by the life-giving principle which is the Holy Ghost. They are all signs of spiritual growth, a growth produced by the influence of the Holy Ghost. They are usually enumerated as 1. Wisdom, 2. Understanding, 3. Counsel, 4. Fortitude, 5. Knowledge, 6. Piety, and 7. Fear of the Lord. It will be seen at once that these are all spiritual qualities by which a man becomes stronger and therefore readier in God's service. Hence it is to the Holy Ghost that we pray for guidance in difficult decisions: before the election, for instance, of a new Pope, a Mass of the Holy Ghost is celebrated; and it is to the Holy Ghost that we pray for an increase in our own personal holiness, as in the well-known Antiphon: "Come O Holy Spirit, fill the hearts of thy faithful, and kindle in them the fire of thy love".

(12) INTERLUDE ON THE UNITY OF THE CHURCH *à propos* of Acts 2. 42

In the account of the effect of St Peter's sermon at Pentecost, after the Descent of the Holy Ghost, we read that "they therefore that received his word were baptised: and there were added in that day about 3000 souls" (Acts 2. 41). Verse 42 then describes their perseverance:

ἦσαν δὲ προσκαρτεροῦντες	they were persevering
1. τῇ διδαχῇ τῶν ἀποστόλων	1. in the teaching of the Apostles
2. καὶ τῇ κοινωνίᾳ,	2. and communion,

3. τῇ κλάσει τοῦ ἄρτου   3. the breaking of bread
4. καὶ ταῖς προσευχαῖς   4. and prayers

These have been referred to as the four Marks of Unity. Our edition, based on the Vulgate, has only three notes: for the Vulgate reads: "in doctrina Apostolorum, et communicatione fractionis panis, et orationibus", combining "communion" with the "breaking of bread". It is generally understood that the "breaking of bread" here refers to the Eucharist, and the Latin reading restricts then the word "communion" to its Eucharistic sense; but the word κοινωνία which is from κοινός "common", can have the much wider sense of "fellowship" (which is how the Authorised Version (Anglican) and also the Revised Version (Anglican), and the recent (Catholic) Westminster Version translates it here). If we take the text as it is in the Greek, the Eucharistic unity is expressed already in the "breaking of bread", and the "communion" here is more of a juridical unity: i.e. that the body of Christians is one Body, under one jurisdiction or government, which is "common" to all. The word "communion" is used in modern theological language in these two senses: the one *liturgical*, that is Eucharistic Communion (as when we say: "I am going to Communion"); and the other *juridical*, which means a common relation to authority (as when we say: "We are in communion with the Maronite Church, but we are not in communion with the Nestorians", or when people say: "We do not belong to the same communion", for which some people say: "to the same jurisdiction"). In this latter sense it is usually possible to substitute the word "fellowship" and still preserve the sense, though in modern English the word "fellowship" has now received a less serious meaning: that of a loose bond between members of some society.

But the interesting thing is that the Greek usage of the early Church has the same word for the liturgical and the juridical unity: and rightly so, for they are intimately connected: so much so, that there can be no liturgical unity without the juridical. That is to say, it is not possible in normal circumstances to receive the Sacraments from those who do not recognise the same authority: for instance we are not allowed normally to receive Absolution or Holy Communion from a priest who belongs to a Church which does not recognise the authority of the Pope, such as the Orthodox Eastern Church, or the Syriac[1] Nestorian Church. With liturgical unity, and the Eucharist in the Apostolic times, we shall deal in a later interlude: here we shall study briefly the juridical unity.

The first basis of unity, as noted in this verse of the Acts, is the "teaching of the Apostles", which was no more than a continuation of the teaching of Christ. The Church was founded by Christ, upon the foundations of the Apostles, therefore unity with the Apostles in their teaching meant unity with Christ. The Body of Christians is one, because the Body of Christ is one. And Christ himself in the great prayer for unity, in the course of the long talk to the Apostles after the Last Supper, says: "That they all may be one, as thou, Father, in me, and I in thee: that they also may be one in us" (Jn. 17. 21). St Paul bids his disciples be "careful to keep the unity of the Spirit in the bond of peace. One body and one Spirit . . . One Lord, one faith, one baptism" (Eph. 4. 3–6); but all this depends, he says further on (v. 13), on the measure of the fulness of Christ. This is the famous word of St Paul, $\pi\lambda\acute{\eta}\rho\omega\mu\alpha$ "fulness" of Christ, by which he means that the Church, which he has likened to the Body of Christ, is "full" or "perfect" through the unity of its members.

Now this unity in the Church requires for its preservation

---

[1] "Syriac" in the sense that this ancient language is used in the Nestorian liturgical books, and that a modern dialect of Syriac is spoken by these people.—GENERAL EDITOR.

a "communion" of government: and this communion is unity with Christ. But after Christ's Ascension, he was no longer going to be there to lead them: he was going to give the leadership to the Apostles and especially to Peter, on whom he was going to found his Church (Mt. 16. 18), and to whom he would give the keys of the Kingdom of Heaven (v. 19). It is evident that no one who calls himself a Christian would refuse to accept the authority of Christ, or refuse the unity which the Body of Christians receives from Christ himself. But it is never so easy to accept a delegated authority: it is less easy to do what we are told by a lesser official, than if we are told by the chief in person.

Thus right at the beginning there were people who would not accept the teaching of the Apostles. Probably the first that we hear of are those mentioned by St John in his first Epistle (1 Jn. 2. 19), where he says: "They went out from us; but they were not of us. For if they had been of us, they would no doubt have remained with us". Those men would not remain "in the teaching of the Apostles, and communion" as we read of the faithful in this passage of the Acts. And so began what is called "Schism" in the Church: division among Christians on the matter of accepting the authority of the Apostles. So still now there are "Schismatics", that is Christians who accept all the doctrines that we do, but refuse the authority of the successor of Peter, who is the Pope, the Bishop of Rome. There are a number of Schismatic Churches in the East, and of these it is said that "they are not in communion with Rome". From some of these Eastern Churches have grown up groups who desired unity with Rome, and were willing to accept the authority of the Pope, and these, together with those who never broke away, are called the "Uniat" Eastern Churches, because they are united with us in Communion.

So this unity among the first Christians, which included the new converts, was first remarked here at Pentecost:

they were united in the teaching of the Apostles, in communion, that is unity of government or authority with the Apostles, and then in liturgical unity through the Eucharist and prayer. And this manifestation of the life of the Church, this living preservation of unity, is once more to be attributed to the work of the Holy Ghost, the life-giver: the Spirit of Unity: one body and one Spirit (as St Paul says): and at Pentecost at Mass, the Introit begins: "Spiritus Domini replevit orbem terrarum, alleluia": the Spirit of the Lord has filled the whole world: which happened through the Church, who receives her life itself, and so her unity, through the Holy Ghost.

(13)   SECTION 4: THE CURE OF THE LAME MAN AND ITS CONSEQUENCES (Acts 3. 1–4. 31)

A. SIGNIFICANCE

In this section we have a series of events, each of which is the first of its kind in the history of the Church.

(1) To begin with we have the first miracle worked by the Apostles, and the purpose of this miracle was so clearly to provide an opportunity of proving the power of Christ.

(2) Secondly, for the first time we have a public Apologetic, or defence of an action performed in the name of Christ. Peter has to address the crowd that had gathered, and explain.

(3) For the first time the Apostles are cited before a tribunal, and have to make a defence: but they did not "find how they might punish them, because of the people" (Acts 4. 21).

(4) Lastly, we read for the first time of the prayer made by the Church for the Apostles, in thanksgiving for their deliverance, and asking God that "with all confidence they might speak the word of God" (4. 29).

Each one of these activities has continued all through the history of the Church: there has not been an age when God has not worked miracles through the Church: the Church has continued to develop "Christian Apologetics", to defend herself: the members of the Church have continued to be persecuted by those who do not believe in Christ: and the Church has constantly prayed for the welfare of her members, and especially for those who preach the word of Christ. In the Collect of the Votive Mass for the Propagation of the Faith, the Church prays thus: "Send, we beseech thee, labourers into thy harvest, and grant to them that they may speak thy word with all confidence (these words are taken from this passage of the Acts), so that thy doctrine may spread rapidly and brilliantly, and all nations may know thee, the True God, and him whom thou didst send, Jesus Christ Our Lord". The Dominican Missal contains a special prayer for preachers, thus: "Enlighten, O Lord, the hearts of thy servants with the grace of the Holy Ghost: give them a burning word: and grant an increase of virtue to those who preach thy word".

B. Story

The disciples were continuing to attend the Jewish services in the temple at Jerusalem, and as Peter and John went in to the afternoon service they were stopped at the door by a lame beggar, who asked them for something. Peter made the famous remark (3. 6): "Silver and gold I have none; but what I have, I give thee", and he bade him be cured "In the name of Jesus Christ of Nazareth". He had no money to give him, but he had a cure in the name of Jesus. The beggar was a well-known figure, and the astonishment of the people was great when they saw him not only walking (which apparently he had never been able to do before, and he was 40 years old), but also leaping, and praising God.

But Peter took the opportunity, and asked the people

(3. 12): "Why wonder you at this? or why look you upon us, as if by our strength and power we had made this man to walk?" No, he said, it was by the power of Jesus, the Son of the God whom we all worship, and whom our fathers worshipped before us in the Old Testament (3. 15): "The author of life you killed, whom God hath raised from the dead, of which we are witnesses". Again the argument is similar to that of the Sermon at Pentecost: the Scriptures told of the Saviour who was to come, and Jesus, who rose from the dead is this Saviour, and we can witness to his resurrection. Again he insists on this witness. He then calls upon them to recognise him, and to be penitent and converted: (3. 26) "To you first, God, raising up his Son, hath sent him to bless you: that every one may convert himself from his wickedness".

Among the hearers were some of the priests of the Temple, the "officer", that is the chief of the temple-police, who were Levites, that is of priestly family, and some Sadducees. The Sadducees were a sect among the Jews of the time who did not believe in the Resurrection of the dead: and many of the priests at the time belonged to this sect. Peter's insistence upon the Resurrection of Christ naturally made all the Sadducees among the priests all the more hostile. The two Apostles were therefore arrested and put into prison for the night.

At their trial on the morrow, they were asked (4. 7) by what authority had they done this? Peter's answer is straightforward: (4. 10) "In the name of Our Lord Jesus Christ of Nazareth, whom you crucified, and whom God hath raised from the dead".

But the miracle had had its effect: the number of converts had now been raised to 5,000, that is, there were 2,000 since Pentecost. And here it would be worth making a note on the *Function of Miracles*. A miracle is not worked merely for the benefit or convenience of the person who is healed, for then one might well ask why were not all the other lame people also healed? The Vatican Council defined a miracle as "Factum divinum luculenter Dei omnipotentiam commonstrans" ("a divine action that clearly shows the all-embracing power of God"), in the course of the Third Session of the Council in the year 1870. A miracle then is done to show the power of God, or to show that the authority of the speaker through whom the miracle is worked is the authority of God. The miracle is a type of argument that the simplest mind can understand, designed to prove the divine authority of the speaker. It is more convincing than discussion, as Our Lord himself said: (Jn. 10. 25) "I speak to you, and you believe me not; the works that I do in the name of my Father, they give testimony of me", and (Jn. 10. 38) "Though you will not believe me, believe the works". So on occasion God gave the Apostles the power to work miracles in order to confirm their preaching. And this, rather than the incidental benefit to the ill person, is the real function of a miracle. And this fact is very clearly shown in the miracle which we are studying.

Because, therefore, of this strong effect upon the people the priests did not dare to keep Peter and John (4. 21, 23), and let them go.

And when they returned to the other Christians, the body of the Christians uttered their great prayer (Acts 4. 24–30), the first public prayer of the Church which has been recorded. The prayer is very Biblical and is based upon quotations from the Old Testament, and expresses two main ideas:

i. (v. 24–28) Scripture foretold persecution of Christ, and it was fulfilled in his death: therefore we Christians must expect persecution.

ii. (v. 29–30) Therefore we pray that God give us courage and perseverance, and confirm our message with further miracles.

And when they had prayed, the ground shook as with an earthquake, at the coming of the Holy Ghost upon them (4. 31).

C. Details

3. 2   "the gate of the temple which is called Beautiful": this name has not been identified, and does not occur elsewhere: it must have been a popular name for one of the gates.

3. 7   "His feet and soles received strength." αἱ βάσεις καὶ τὰ σφυδρά.[1] Although the first of these can be used merely to mean "feet", yet both were medical terms, apparently for bones at the ankle. The first seems to refer to the bone in the foot on which the tibia (or main leg-bone) rests: the astragalus: and the second seems to mean the ankles, and is used by Galen, the Greek physician, for the malleoli or bones that jut out on either side of the ankle.

    The man therefore appears to have had some deformity or weakness of the ankles which prevented him from walking, for he needed to be carried (3. 2).

4. 5   "Their princes, ancients, and scribes": we shall refer to the composition of the Sanhedrin in a later note.

4. 24   "With one voice": this probably means either (i) that they were using a form of prayer already fixed, and reciting it together; or (ii) that they all prayed in turn, and St Luke in the Acts gives us a summary of what they said.

---

[1] σφυδρά (Galen's word) is the original reading of the oldest codices, later altered to σφυρά, the usual word for "ankles". (v. Jacquier.)

(14)   SECTION 5: GOODS IN COMMON
              (Acts 2. 44–47; 4. 32–37; 5. 1–11)

A. SIGNIFICANCE

These passages give us an idea of the manner of life of the first Christians, and they seem to have acted very much as one community. They "had all things in common" (2. 44), and "neither did any one say that aught of the things which he possessed was his own, but all things were common unto them" (4. 32). Their property they sold and brought the money and gave it to the Apostles, who then arranged its distribution (2. 45; 4. 34–35).

They seem to have kept their own houses, for they "broke bread" at home (κατ' οἶκον). This may mean that each household celebrated their Eucharist privately, or else that all or many went to different houses in turn. Anyway the Eucharist took place in private houses. Public prayers continued in the Temple. (2. 46.)

Then we have the terrible punishment that came to those who, having entered on this manner of life, failed to keep it, in the story of Ananias and Saphira (5. 1–11).

The object of renouncing possessions in this way, be it among the early Christians or among religious at the present day, is to enable men to occupy themselves more freely with the things of God, and at the same time to detach them from earthly possessions which can so easily claim more of our care than they should. (See the Interlude that will follow this Section.)

B. STORY

The Community of Christians at Jerusalem decided that it would be well to have their goods in common: at least those that desired this. The fact that it was free to join in this plan is evident from St Peter's words to Ananias (5. 4),

"Whilst it remained, did it not remain to thee? and after it was sold, was it not in thy power?" That is to say: while the land remained unsold, did it not remain belonging to thee: and after it was sold, did not the money remain in thy power? They were therefore under no obligation either to part with their goods, or to surrender the money they would get from selling them.

When we read (Acts 2. 44) that "all they that believed were together and had all things in common" we must understand that this applies to the Christians at Jerusalem only, and that of the 3,000 converts of Pentecost (2. 41) very many came from the Diaspora or scattered communities of Jews in the Empire and were only pilgrim-visitors to the Holy City. The Christian community at Jerusalem, among whom was practised this common ownership, can only have been a small body.

We are given two examples of the practice of this community of goods, one good example and one bad one. The good example is that of Barnabas, who was afterwards to become the companion of St Paul, and who is honoured by the Church as an Apostle (the Collect for June 11 says: "O God, who rejoicest us by the merits and intercession of the blessed Barnabas thy Apostle"). Further it was Barnabas who introduced St Paul after his conversion to the Apostles at Jerusalem (Acts 9. 27). Barnabas, then, sold his land and brought the money to the Apostles (4. 37).

The bad example is that of the couple, Ananias and Saphira, who also sold their land, but brought only part of the price of the land (5. 1–2), though pretending at the same time to be among those who were practising the self-denial and renunciation of all worldy goods, as proposed by Our Lord when he said to the rich young man (Mt. 19. 21): "If thou wilt be perfect, go sell what thou hast, and give to the poor, and thou shalt have treasure in heaven; and come follow me". This is one of the so-called "counsels", and is not a command: so that there is no obligation on Christians to practise this. But there is a sort of sacrilege or profaning of holy things, in pretending to follow this exalted counsel or recommendation of Our Lord, and then all the time to be in possession of goods in the ordinary way. The sin of these two was not the fact that they did not give up their goods (they were free to do this or not), but that they pretended to be leading this life of special perfection whereas in reality they were not. That is why St Peter says (5. 3) that they have "lied to the Holy Ghost", because they have pretended to offer to God their worldly goods, but actually have kept some possessions: "Thou hast not lied to men, but to God" (5. 4). After this condemnation by St Peter, the judgment of God struck down Ananias, and he died there and then. Just after he was buried (in the East people have to be buried straight away and sometimes by law within twenty-four hours), his widow came in. St Peter asked her whether this money just deposited was the price of the land: she told the same lie as her husband, and said that it was. She had been given a chance of telling the truth, and had not taken it. St Peter tells her what had happened to Ananias, and she immediately fell down dead herself.

It is important to note that the punishment was inflicted upon this tragic couple by God, in order to preserve the purity of his Church, but that the condemnation of their action was made by the visible head of the Church, which was Peter.

C. Details

4. 36   "Joseph, who by the Apostles, was surnamed Barnabas (which is by interpretation, the son of consolation)." Another example of a man in the Christian community receiving an additional name, as did Justus (Acts 1. 23). The interpretation is not entirely simple: but probably represents the Ara-

maic בר־נבוא Bar-nebhu'a "Son of Prophecy",
and the connexion between prophecy and consolation may be illustrated by 1 Cor. 14. 3: "He
that prophesieth, speaketh to men unto edification
and exhortation and comfort".

5. 1 "Ananias": a common Hebrew name, meaning "the
Lord is gracious".

"Saphira": an Aramaic name, meaning "beautiful".

5. 4 Some authors hold that the death of Ananias occurred through shock at realising what he had done,
and similarly that of Saphira at learning of the fate
of her husband. Others say that this explanation
destroys the idea of God's intervention and
punishment. But whatever the immediate cause of
death, the fact of their death was a judgment of
God.

5. 11 "Fear upon the whole Church": the first use of the
word "Church" in the Acts to describe the body
of Christians.

(15) INTERLUDE UPON RELIGIOUS POVERTY

Its Practice

The practice of poverty, as we have just been studying it
in the previous section upon the community of goods among
the early Christians, is still practised by many Christians
at the present day. We have seen that at the time of the
Apostles no one was commanded to dispose of his goods,
and that if he took this decision it was free, but further, that
it was a serious decision, and did not admit of half-measures.
All this continues to exist in the Church, and in the
majority of Religious Orders strict community of goods is
observed, so that no one owns anything personally "neither
does any one say that aught of the things which he possesses

are his own" (Acts 4. 32), and the things which he uses do not belong to this or that member of the Order, but are merely reserved for his use. St Augustine, in the Rule that he wrote, and which is the basis of the manner of life of several Orders, explains it thus: "Call not anything your own, but let all things be common. Let food and clothing be distributed to each one of you by your Superior, not in equal measure to all, because you are not all of equal strength, but so as to provide for each one according to his need. For thus you read in the Acts of the Apostles, that they had all things in common, and that distribution was made to every man, according as he had need". Thus the very clothes which a religious wears do not really belong to him, but are given him by the Superior, who also has the right to change them for others should he wish. Similarly with other objects: but a Superior is bound as far as he can to supply the needs of those under him: for instance, a person who has to teach or write has to be provided with the necessary books, and the Constitutions of the Dominicans specially mention this (Constitution 554). But even so, these objects cannot be said to belong to the person, but are said to be "ad usum" or "for the use of" this person. Thus a religious who has taken vows cannot own anything, and anything that he may get or earn, he may only use with permission or make over to the common stock. This renunciation of worldly goods, or this giving-up of ownership takes place when a person has finished his period as a novice, about a year or so after joining the Order, and "takes vows". Most religious Orders have a triple vow: poverty, chastity, and obedience. The first, the so-called Vow of Poverty, means this giving-up of possessions, and the other two are also a matter of giving up certain rights: with the Vow of Chastity the religious gives up the right to marry and found a family, and with the Vow of Obedience he gives up the right to choose the work he shall do or the life he shall lead.

The Vow of Poverty is, as it were, the foundation of the others because it establishes the relation between the man and all the material things that surround him. Although this vow of Poverty is common to almost all the religious Orders, yet each has its own manner of fulfilling it. St Benedict in his Rule (chap. 33) insists upon personal poverty, namely that none shall presume to "give or receive anything without leave of the Abbot, nor to keep anything as their own", without requiring a real poverty of the community. St Francis on the other hand wished that the very community itself should own nothing. St Dominic required that apart from the personal poverty of the friars, the community itself should be poor, and the manner of the common life, according to the requirements of the work should be as that of poor people: the furniture provided for the novices should be (Const. 103) "pauper, sed sufficiens et decora".

So the tradition that began among the early Christians is continuing among Christians today. It is still free to Christians to adopt the "common life", and there are still very many who do so. The fact that they take a vow, when they enter upon this life, renders the life stable, that is it cannot be a passing desire, but is a permanent manner of life, as it obviously was at the time of the Apostles, witness the incident of Ananias and Saphira who were unfaithful.

It is interesting to note another small parallel between modern religious life and the Apostolic times in the receiving of an additional name. We have just read of Joseph who was called in addition Barnabas: in the older religious Orders a person who enters the Order usually receives an additional name by which he is commonly known, as was Barnabas by his new name.

Its Purpose

We know that we are here in this world for God, "to know him, love him and serve him" (Catechism, n. 2): and it is a matter for each of us to decide, when planning our career, not merely how to achieve success in the world or even how to make a living, nor merely how to keep out of sin; but how best to serve God. In almost every walk of life it is possible to give God most excellent service, and there have indeed been Saints (that is, people who have served God in a perfect way) among all kinds of people. But there will always be some who feel that they could serve God better if they devoted their lives entirely to his service, and freed themselves as far as possible from the cares of this world. They may be called upon later to do work in the world, but it will not be their choice: they will have taken a vow of Obedience. They may be called upon to live in very varied surroundings and circumstances, but it will not be their concern: they will have taken a vow of Poverty. It is then a desire to serve God in the most perfect way that they are able that prompts men to enter Religious Life: it is the attraction of a life that is at once a freedom from a thousand cares and troubles, and at the same time a renunciation that is often very heroic. This freedom that is gained, together with the many rights that are given up, produces a peace of mind that not only greatly assists men in serving God (and thinking of him at all), but also greatly helps them to serve other people. This peace of mind, then, is attained in Religious Life, because it is keyed to the most important thing in the world which is the service of God, and because it is protected by the vows, especially the vow of Poverty.

In the Gospel

The practice of voluntary poverty has never been an obligation or command: but it has been a recommendation from the beginning. Our Lord was asked (Mt. 19. 16): "Good master, what good shall I do that I may have life everlasting?" On being told that he must observe the commandments of God, he said (19. 20): "All these have I kept from my youth, what is yet wanting to me?" The reply of Jesus we have recently quoted: "If thou wilt be perfect, go sell what thou hast, and give to the poor, and thou shalt have treasure in heaven: and come, follow me". Our Lord did not say that to dispose of goods was the only way to follow him, but he did recommend it as a good way of following him. Again another time he was approached (Mt. 8. 19–20): "A certain scribe came and said to him: 'Master, I will follow thee whithersoever thou shalt go'. And Jesus saith to him: 'The foxes have holes, and the birds of the air nests; but the Son of man hath not where to lay his head'." From the beginning therefore there have been people who were prepared to renounce the things of this world, in order to be more perfect and in order the closer to follow Our Blessed Lord. He himself said (Mt. 19. 12): "He that can take it, let him take it": and these recommendations of a way of life are called the "Evangelical counsels".

The practice then of Religious Poverty has its roots in the Gospel itself, is seen among the early Christians in the Acts, and after the time of the Apostles appeared among those who retired into the desert to lead lives devoted to God. We then see it reflected in the great Rules of St Augustine († 430) and of St Benedict († 543), and continued in all the great religious Orders of the Church in modern times.

(16–17)   SECTION 6: FURTHER ARREST OF APOSTLES (Acts 5. 12–42)

A. Significance

This whole section conveys a vivid impression of the growing popularity of the Christians. At the same time "By the hands of the Apostles were many signs and wonders wrought among the people" (Acts 5. 12) and there continued to join them many converts.

People brought their ill people into the streets, at least to receive the shadow of Peter, by which miracles were worked.

Then, again through the Sadducees, the Apostles are arrested. For the first time they are delivered from prison by an Angel (5. 19). This happened again to Peter in Acts 12. 7. Paul is released from prison in Acts 16. 26 through an earthquake.

The last arrest was of Peter and John, and this time it seems to be all the Apostles who were arrested together.

This is also the first occasion that the Christians suffered real physical violence in persecution: for they were scourged (5. 40), "and they indeed went from the presence of the council, rejoicing that they were accounted worthy to suffer reproach for the name of Jesus" (5. 51). It is the beginning of the spirit of Martyrdom in the Church, and "the white-robed army of the Martyrs" that followed them in history, followed them also in this rejoicing.

B. STORY

The miracles worked by the Apostles were bringing them more and more converts, and such was their popularity and the eagerness of the people to benefit from their cures that ill people were brought out into the streets to them. The same thing had happened to our Lord himself only a couple of years previously (Mk. 6. 56): "And whithersoever he entered, into towns or into villages or cities, they laid the sick in the streets". The sight must have been familiar to Peter.

Then the High Priest, probably still Annas (as in 4. 6), and the Sadducees that surrounded him, had the Apostles arrested. Last time they were arrested (as related in chap. 4), it was because of their teaching to the people, and it was especially the teaching about the Resurrection that naturally annoyed the Sadducees. This time we read that it was principally envy of the popularity of the Apostles that put them against them (5. 17).

The Apostles were put into prison for the night: but when they were to be fetched by the guard in the morning, the prison was found to be empty. The council was already assembled to try them, and someone came and told them that the men they were seeking were once more in the temple, teaching, as if nothing had happened.

The temple-police went to the temple to find them, and brought them to the council "without violence", that is, they did not use force to bring them. They must have come willingly, being prepared to speak before the council, and particularly not wishing to cause a disturbance among the people, who might otherwise have begun to throw stones at the police had there been a struggle. This remark about the police fearing that the people might throw stones at them if they laid violent hands on the Apostles (5. 26), is an interesting witness to the people's favour towards the Apostles.

The Apostles were then brought in before the council. It was the same gathering as had tried them on the previous occasion. This was the supreme Jewish court of appeal, and was the "senate" of the Jewish people, but at this time, under Roman rule, they no longer had the power of life and death over those they judged, as the Jews themselves said during the Passion of Our Lord: their words are familiar to us from the Passion sung on Good Friday (Jn. 18. 31), "Nobis non licet interficere quemquam" ("It is not lawful for us to put any man to death"). This council was known as the "Sanhedrin", a word which was a Hebrew corruption of the Greek word συνέδριον meaning "council", and dating therefore from Hellenic times in Palestine. The Sanhedrin in full session consisted of 71 members, who belonged to three classes: (i) the chief priests; (ii) the "ancients" or "elders" of Israel, that is, the heads of the families; and

(iii) the "scribes" who were the lawyers. These three classes are mentioned by St Luke in Acts 4. 5: "Their princes (*i.e.* chief priests), and ancients, and scribes".

The members of the Sanhedrin would naturally belong to various religious and political parties within Israel. The Jews at that time, and indeed still now, although there are many points of the Faith held dogmatically by all, were nevertheless free to hold different opinions on many other points. There were religious differences even on so important a point as the Resurrection or life-after-death in any form, for the Old Testament itself (the one bed-rock of doctrine for all Jews) has no clear teaching on this point. There were also many differences on strictness or otherwise of the observance of the Law of Moses contained in the Old Testament, and variety in its interpretation. There was a growing "mysticism" or theory of man's spiritual relation with God in prayer, in Israel at the time, and there were different views held on these points as well. These various parties are spoken of in the Bible as "sects" (*e.g.* Acts 26. 5) or "heresies" (*e.g.* here 5. 17), the word in the Greek being αἵρεσις, which is derived from αἱρέω "to take" used in the middle voice for "to take for oneself", *i.e.* "to choose". A heresy then means an opinion that one has chosen for oneself.

Of these sects or religious opinions at this time in Israel the most important are those of the *Sadducees* and the *Pharisees*. These two parties tended in opposite directions: the Sadducees tried to simplify religion, and refused any doctrines that were not to be found in the Books of Moses in the Old Testament; whereas the Pharisees tended to develop greatly the meaning of passages of the Old Testament, and to add many new doctrines and commands. Thus we know that the Sadducees refused the doctrine of the Resurrection of the dead because it was not in the Old Testament, whereas the Pharisees held it, as being implied in the spiritual nature of man. The Pharisaic teaching, taken to excess, resulted in the burdensome legalism or over-stress on lawyers' traditions with which we are familiar in the Gospels, and this was countered by the Sadducean teaching of a plain Biblical religion unhampered by Pharisaic additions. On the other hand, the Sadducean teaching easily degenerated into mere materialism, in which the Law was only observed in its minimum requirements, and Jewish religious interest became only a matter of Jewish political views, the race-interest conquering the religious interest altogether. This again was countered by Pharisaism, in which in its good form a really spiritual view of religion was taken, and a really mystical system had begun to grow. Thus there was a good element in both parties, which would counter the degenerate element in the other: the Pharisaic spiritual outlook would make up for the Sadducean materialism, and the Sadducean refusal of all but Biblical doctrines would adjust the excessive legalism of the Pharisees.

The reactions of these two parties to Christianity is very interesting. Christianity gradually began to be regarded as another such party, or sect, or "heresy" (Acts 28. 22, where the Jews in Rome speak to St Paul of "this sect"), and thus received criticism and hostility from both the Sadducees and Pharisees: from the Sadducees for proclaiming so new a doctrine as the Resurrection, and from the Pharisees for claiming to abolish many of the Pharisaic traditions which had grown up. But the Pharisees provided the better ground for the growth of Christianity. St Paul indeed had been a Pharisee: "according to the most sure sect of our religion I lived a Pharisee", he said, when on trial at Caesarea (Acts 26. 5). But nowhere do we read of a Sadducee that was con-verted to Christianity. The material outlook of the Sad-ducees, their political views of the kingdom of Israel, and their resistance to the doctrine of the Resurrection which was the central doctrine of the Christian preaching, all put them out of sympathy with the Christian message. With the

Pharisees, however, whose degenerate element had been so often reproved by Our Blessed Lord himself, the good element, through its spiritual outlook on religion and its more spiritual idea of the Messianic hope of Israel, had a greater chance of understanding and receiving the teaching of the Apostles.

The study of these two sects is particularly relevant to our present passage: the history of the Apostles being cited before the Sanhedrin. The ruling classes in Jerusalem at the time appear to have been Sadducees, and the High Priest himself and his family seem to have been Sadducees (Acts 5. 17), and it was members of this sect who both on this occasion and on the last (chap. 4) had the Apostles arrested. But there were also Pharisees in the Sanhedrin, and it was through the words of Gamaliel, a Pharisee, that the Apostles were on this occasion released.

The accusation made here against the Apostles was that they were continuing to preach the doctrine of Christ, although they had been commanded not to do so. Further, they said, they were bringing the blame for the death of Christ upon the Jewish rulers. But we know how at the Trial of Our Lord the people had accepted the responsibility, saying (Mt. 27. 25): "His blood be upon us, and upon our children".

St Peter, replying, pleaded guilty to their accusation, but continued to claim that he was right: first, he said, we must obey God rather than men (Acts 5. 29). Here is the problem of the Martyr who is accused before the tribunal of his country. Many of the Christian Martyrs have been accused of being disloyal: and they have all replied on the same lines. When we have two obediences, the higher obedience, that to God, must come first. If we are obeying God we cannot be disloyal to our own country. Many of our own English Martyrs had to say the same thing. St Peter then repeated the outline of his preaching, in the same way as before

(4. 10), saying "*God* raised up Jesus, whom *you* put to death . . . and we are witnesses of these things" (5. 30–32).

Naturally, this was worthy of condemnation from the Sadducean accusers (5. 33), but Gamaliel, the Pharisee, rose to speak and advised caution. He quoted two examples of parties that had arisen in recent times and come to nothing. So with reference to the Christians, he said (Acts 5. 38): "If this counsel or this work be of men, it will come to nought. But if it be of God, you cannot overthrow it: lest perhaps you be found even to fight against God". It is interesting to note that the Pharisee's more spiritual outlook made him wonder whether this work was not perhaps a work of God, whereas the rougher Sadducees had condemned it outright. But the advice of Gamaliel carried weight, and the Apostles were acquitted.

They were nevertheless scourged before being allowed to go. Before Gamaliel had spoken they had wanted to have them killed, and this would have meant claiming the punishment from the Romans, as in the case of Our Lord, but now they were content with applying the official synagogue punishment, which was scourging. This was in punishment for having disregarded the Sanhedrin's prohibition of preaching the doctrine of Christ. This scourging was a violent punishment: and the Greek verb δέρω really means "to skin" or "to flay", and the victim was whipped with a leather whip thirty-nine times ("forty strokes save one", II Cor. 11. 24). The Hebrew law (Deut. 25. 2–3) prescribed the punishment thus: "And if they see that the offender be worthy of stripes: they shall lay him down, and shall cause him to be beaten before them . . . yet so, that they exceed not the number of forty: lest thy brother depart shamefully torn before thy eyes". It was therefore the custom to give thirty-nine strokes, lest the number prescribed by the Law as a limit should be exceeded. Apparently it has been known that a victim has died under this torment. But the Apostles departed "rejoicing that they were accounted worthy to suffer reproach for the name of Jesus".

They owed their freedom indeed to Gamaliel, who is an interesting figure to us Christians. Not only did he get the Apostles their freedom on this occasion, but he was the Rabbinic teacher who trained Saul, afterwards Paul, in his Pharisaism (Acts 22. 3). St Luke must have included his name with particular interest in connexion with both St Peter and St Paul later on. An ancient tradition has it that he eventually became a Christian, and it is not improbable since he may well have followed something of the activities of Paul, his former disciple, and have observed the fortunes of Peter and the other Christians in whose favour he had spoken in the Sanhedrin. There is a mysterious reference to him in the Antiphon at the Vespers of the 3rd of August, when it is told how he appeared in a vision to Lucian the priest, and indicated to him where he should find the relics both of himself and of St Stephen the First Martyr. The finding of his body at Jerusalem is commemorated in the Martyrology on this day.

C. DETAILS

v. 17   "the High Priest" probably Annas. The Roman Procurators had appointed a High Priest, and apparently intended to make it an annual office. Hence we have in Jn. 18. 13: "Caiphas, who was High Priest of that year". Yet Our Lord was first taken to Annas, who had been High Priest since A.D. 6. Perhaps the Jews still looked upon him as High Priest, and did not recognise the Roman appointment except in matters of Roman law. Hence for a trial before the Sanhedrin, it was still Annas who presided.

v. 30   "Hanging him upon a tree": more literally "wood", used again by St Peter, to refer to the Cross on which Our Lord was crucified, in Acts 10. 39 (in a speech), and in his Epistle, 1 Pet. 2. 24. The phrase "tree" for the Cross has then been often used in the liturgy.

v. 33   "Cut to the heart": literally "they were cut", the words "to the heart" having been added to show the meaning. In 7. 54, after Stephen's speech the same word is used with "as to the heart" added also in the Greek.

v. 36   "Theodas": some have identified with one Theudas who organised a revolt, of whom we hear from the Jewish historian Josephus (who wrote round about the year A.D. 90); but the facts and the dates do not fit very well.

v. 37   "Judas of Galilee": of him we hear through Josephus as well: his rising seems to have been, however, of an entirely political nature.

(18) SECTION 7: THE APPOINTMENT OF THE SEVEN DEACONS (Acts 6. 1–7)

A. SIGNIFICANCE

The appointment of these Deacons shows that the time had come when the Church needed some more definite organisation. It marks the first delegation of powers of the Apostles, even though it seems at first to have been only in matters of administration.

This need arose through the great growth in numbers of the Christians in Jerusalem: and a consequence of this increase was the unavoidable one of some dissensions and murmurings. It was in answer to a complaint that this move was taken.

Lastly it should be observed that the Greek-speaking element is to the fore in this matter. The complaint came from them, and all the Deacons have Greek names (though many Jerusalem Jews also had Greek names), but Nicolas is reported to be from Antioch.

B. STORY

At this stage St Luke no longer gives us figures for the number of Christians: and those at Jerusalem were now (Acts 6. 2) just "the multitude of the disciples". Until now the distribution of goods in the "common life" of the Christians had been done by the Apostles, presumably helped by some of the local Jews ("the Hebrews" of v. 1).

But at Jerusalem itself there were not only pilgrim-Jews from all over the world as we saw at Pentecost, but there were also Jews from the Greek-speaking world who had made their homes in Jerusalem, and had their own synagogues there, where the Jewish rites were carried on, as at Alexandria and the other Greek cities, in Greek. These are the various synagogues described in 6. 9. A number of Jews from these Greek-speaking groups in Jerusalem had obviously joined the Christians, and they were complaining that the local Jews who were helping the Apostles to distribute food and goods among the whole Christian community were somehow mismanaging things in regard to these foreign Jews, especially in the matter of providing for the widows in these groups. Among the Jews, the father of a family holds a very special position, and the women had little or no part either in the official life of the nation or in the religious services: hence it was that a widow, having no man of the household to represent her, rather easily dropped out of the organisation of the community. We therefore find all through the Bible, both in the Old and the New Testaments, special care recommended for the widows. This was obviously a case where this duty had somehow been overlooked, for the widows were evidently to be supported by the organisation of the Church, if they had no menfolk of their family to care for them. St Paul later wrote (1 Tim. 5. 16): "If any of the faithful have widows, let him minister to them, and let not the Church be charged: that there may be sufficient for them that are widows indeed" (*i.e.* that have none to look after them).

The Apostles, therefore, coming to the conclusion that they could no longer adequately look after the needs of all the community, decided to appoint seven men to look after this work. "It is not reason that we should leave the word of God and serve tables" (6. 2). The word here "to serve" is διακονεῖν, hence those who were to do this were διά-κονοι, or those who "minister" or provide. They therefore chose these seven, who came to be known as Deacons. After choosing them, they "praying imposed hands upon them" (6.6).

The imposing of hands was a symbol already recognised among the Jews for conferring a spiritual power: Moses thus consecrated Josue as leader of the people (Num. 27. 18, 23), and in Deut. 34. 9 we read: "And Josue the son of Nun was filled with the spirit of wisdom, because Moses had laid his hands upon him". Thus also were Levites consecrated. Similarly later in the Acts and in St Paul we find this rite conferring spiritual power.

So the Apostles in consecrating these Deacons were delegating to them some of their power and authority, for the management and administration in the Church had been a part of their work, that was now to be performed by Deacons; and it is also evident that at the same time they were empowered to share in the Apostles' work of preaching, as we read in the latter part of chapter 6 and chapters 7–8.

C. Details

v. 5   "Nicolas a proselyte": that is, a convert to Judaism. He was a Greek from Antioch. St Luke is believed to have been also from Antioch, and similarly to have been a proselyte or convert to Judaism before embracing Christianity: hence perhaps his record of this detail about Nicolas.

v. 5 Of Stephen's work and martyrdom we read in chapters 6–7 of the Acts. We read of Philip's preaching in chapter 8. Tradition held that Prochorus was martyred at Antioch. Of the rest we know nothing more whatever.

INTERLUDE ON THE DIACONATE

In Modern Times

The Sacrament of Holy Order is that by which the ministers of the Church are ordained and receive power and grace to perform their sacred duties (Catechism n. 305). The chief of these sacred duties is the offering of Holy Mass. There are grades or steps among the clergy or ministers, but only one who has reached the grade of Priest is able to be the principal minister at the Mass. There are in all seven grades within Holy Order: the first four are called "Minor Orders" (Porter, Reader, Exorcist, Acolyte), and carry with them no great obligations: the remaining three are called "Major Orders" and carry with them grave obligations. They are Subdeacon, Deacon, and Priest. The chief difference between all these degrees is the closeness with which they serve the Sacrifice of the Mass: the Porter, for instance, is supposed to look after the building wherein is celebrated Mass; the Acolyte corresponds to a normal "server" at Mass. The Subdeacon reads parts of the Mass (the Epistle), and the Deacon assists the Priest, handing him the chalice and even carrying the Blessed Sacrament for him on occasion. The word "Deacon", as we saw, means one who serves or provides, and in modern times the chief duty of the Deacon is to assist the Priest closely at High Mass, to expose the Blessed Sacra-

7

ment for him at Benediction, and on occasion to be delegated by the Priest to distribute Holy Communion. But
nowadays the idea that the Diaconate, or degree of Deacon,
is a step towards the Priesthood, has become in the West [1]
its principal feature, and a person hardly ever remains a
Deacon for more than a year. It is as a Deacon that a young
man begins that intimate service of Our Lord in the Eucharist, that is to be in its fulness his chief occupation when he
is a Priest. For as a Deacon he first has the Blessed Sacrament put into his hands, as a preparation for his Priesthood,
when he will consecrate the Body and Blood of Our Lord at
Mass.

IN THE EARLY CHURCH

The duties of the Deacon in the early Church were similar
to those of the modern Deacon: serving the Priest at the
altar, and especially (as now) singing the Gospel. But there
appear to have been more administrative tasks that came
into the work of the Deacon, as at the beginning of the
Diaconate in the Acts of the Apostles. The main distinction,
however, from the modern Diaconate was that the position
of Deacon was not then exclusively looked upon as a preparation for the Priesthood: the Diaconate was a permanent
career (as still now sometimes in the East), involving
capacities for administration, and also probably for singing,
since in the elaborate ritual of the early Church, the Deacon
was responsible for more musical rendering than he is now.
The chant of the "Exsultet" on Holy Saturday, to be
entirely executed by the Deacon, is one of the last remains of
his extensive musical duties. The Dalmatic, the distinctive
vestment of the Deacon, appears in Rome as the Deacon's
garment in the fourth century.

At the beginning, then, the Deacons were the close

[1] In the Eastern Churches a permanent diaconate is still to be found.—
GENERAL EDITOR.

assistants of the Priests (the Apostles) in their work of administering the goods of the early Church, and also in their work of preaching. But it was probably very soon that they also became the close assistants at the service of the altar, which then became their principal work.

ORDINATION

Deacons are still ordained by the imposition of the hands of the Bishop, who says at the same time: "Accipe Spiritum Sanctum ad robur" ("Receive the Holy Ghost for strength"). This indicates a conferring of spiritual power, according to the Holy Ghost, and we can see a connexion with the imposition of hands in Acts 6. 6, and the desire that they should be "full of the Holy Ghost" (6. 3).

(19)   SECTION 8: SAINT STEPHEN
                    (Acts 6. 8–7. 59)

A. SIGNIFICANCE

Stephen seems to have begun preaching to the Greek-speaking Jews in Jerusalem: probably he was a Hellenistic Jew himself. All the Apostolic work that we have read of so far was the work of the Aramaic-speaking Apostles, and apart from Pentecost, most of their preaching seems to have been to the local Aramaic-speaking Jews.

Stephen's preaching is therefore the first work recorded which was carried out by a delegate of the Apostles.

His great speech is a résumé of the history of God's revelation to the Chosen People of Israel in the Old Testament, and an explanation of its fulfilment in the Person of Jesus Christ.

Further, he is the "Protomartyr" of the Church, that is, the first of the Christian community to die for the Faith. St John the Baptist had indeed been killed for the sake of

Christ, but that was before Christ's own revelation was complete. St Stephen was the first to die for the Risen Christ.

Finally, we must notice the introduction of the young man, Saul, in Acts 7. 57, "consenting to the death" of Stephen (7. 59). This was the future Paul, the Apostle of the Gentiles, who is dramatically introduced here among the persecutors.

B. STORY

Stephen, filled with the Holy Ghost after his ordination as Deacon, "did great wonders and signs among the people" (Acts 6. 8). And he went to dispute with some of the Greek-speaking Jews, otherwise called the Hellenists, "and they were not able to resist the wisdom and spirit that spoke". Being therefore unable to overcome him in argument, they organised a commotion among the people, and got people to cry out against him with a double accusation. He was accused (i) of blaspheming against the Temple, and (ii) of changing the Law of Moses. Then they dragged him off for a trial on these charges before the Sanhedrin.

The High Priest asked him if these charges were true (7. 1)? He does not answer the question, but proceeds to his magnificent speech of defence. Presumably we only have an outline of the speech, but the general line of defence is clear enough.

Stephen must have been a very fine orator, for it is recorded his hearers listened enthralled, and how his face shone as he spoke (6. 15). Stephen's defence against these charges was really rather in the nature of an attack upon his Jewish hearers, in which he shows them that:

    i. God's revelation to Moses about the temple was to give place to a temple "not made by hands" (7. 48); and

    ii. God had given the Law to Moses during the history of revelation, and this contained the prophecy of

Christ: the Jews had constantly been unfaithful to the Law, and now they had rejected its fulfilment in Christ (7. 51–52).

The two ideas of the Temple and of Law are constantly interwoven throughout the speech: and Stephen shows that in history the Jews had been unfaithful to the revelation from God that is contained in both ideas.

Stephen reviews the history of the Old Testament in three periods:

1. *The Period of the Patriarchs* (Abraham to Jacob) (7. 2–19). God appeared to the Patriarchs before any tabernacle was made, he sanctified other places than Jerusalem with his presence: Mesopotamia (to Abraham), Egypt, Sinai (to Moses, before he received the Law): before the Law of Moses, the people of Israel was marked as the Chosen People by the rite of circumcision. So God was with the people before any tabernacle, and made the people his own before any Law: yet they were unfaithful, and (7. 9) sold their leader Joseph as a slave to Egypt.

2. *The Period of Moses and the Law* (7. 20–44). God raised up Moses as a leader, who was at once rejected and had to flee away into Madian, till he had the vision of the burning bush and returned to bring the people out of Egypt. Through Moses God gave the Law, but Moses taught the people of the great prophet who was to come. Meanwhile the people relapsed into idolatry. And Moses was instructed how to build the tabernacle in the desert.

3. *The Period of the Temple* (7. 45–50). When the people grew settled, living under the Law, the desert-tabernacle was replaced by the Temple in the time of Solomon: but who was to think that the Most High

dwelt really in houses made by hand? Did not the Prophet Isaias say: "Heaven is my throne: and the earth my footstool. What house will you build me, saith the Lord, or what is the place of my resting?" (7. 48–50, quoting Isa. 66. 1). It is the very teaching, therefore, of the Old Testament, that the temple-worship should pass, and that the Law of Moses should itself be superseded.

St Stephen concluded saying that the Jewish people had always rebelled: these modern Jews to whom he was speaking were similarly "stiff-necked", that is unbending, stubborn, disobedient, and "uncircumcised in hearts and ears", that is, unwilling to listen or obey, with their hearts and ears not clean, ready, and prepared to receive the word of God: they "always resist the Holy Ghost" (7. 51). "Which of the prophets have not your fathers persecuted?" They killed the prophets, you have killed him whom they foretold, Christ. You have received the revelation of the Old Testament, and you have refused it.

At this they could stand it no longer: they raged and cried out, stopping their ears in horror, and ran upon Stephen and stoned him. The death of stoning meant that the victim was bound and then thrown from a height. The witnesses who had given evidence against him (cf. before the speech 6. 13–14) then had to throw stones at him, and bystanders only did so if after his fall and the first stones he was not yet dead.

Stephen, falling on his knees, being about to be pushed over, cried out "Lord, lay not this sin to their charge"; just as Christ on the Cross had done (Lk. 23. 34): "Father, forgive them, for they know not what they do". And as he was dying he said, as so many Christians have said after him, and still say as they die: "Lord Jesus, receive my spirit" (7. 58).

C. DETAILS

6. 9   Various synagogues mentioned: that of the "Liber-
tines" was probably for that class in society who
had been slaves, and had received their freedom:
perhaps Jews enslaved when Judea first came
under the Romans.

7. 2   It should be noted that there are some historical
difficulties in the speech of St Stephen: in his
review of the history of the Old Testament, some
of the place-names, order of events mentioned, and
numbers do not tally with those we read in the Old
Testament. A bigger book than this, such as
Madame Cecilia's Commentary, pp. 154–158, must
be consulted for the explanations: and here it must
suffice to say that the intention of the speech is to
convey an idea vividly, which it does, rather than
to elucidate points of history; that, further, very
general terms are used; and that anyway we only
have notes of the discourse. Most of the difficulties
are explained by various reckoning of dates, and by
the fact that several texts are referred to at the same
time.

7. 45   "Brought in with Jesus": "Jesus" is the Greek
form of the name Josue or Joshua of the Old Testament, and here refers to Josue who led the people
after Moses.

7. 55   "Behold I see the heavens opened, and the Son of
man standing on the right hand of God". Stephen,
describing this vision, shows his belief in Jesus
Christ, as True God and True Man. The title
"Son of man", used often by Our Lord of himself,
to show his human nature, is only used this once in
the Acts.

(20)   SECTION 9: PERSECUTION; PREACHING
IN SAMARIA (Acts 8. 1–25)

A. SIGNIFICANCE

After the martyrdom of Stephen, which seems to have
been an outburst of anti-Christian feeling, rather than a
systematic persecution, a general persecution seems to have
suddenly broken out, organised by Saul. Saul now "made
havoc of the Church, entering in from house to house, and
dragging away men and women, committed them to prison"
(Acts 8. 3).

The result was the dispersion of all but the Apostles into
the rest of Judea and Samaria. This meant a considerable
spreading of the Faith. The preaching of Philip is specially
noticed.

The necessity of having contact with the *Apostles* is
especially to be observed. On hearing of the conversion and
baptism of people in Samaria under Philip, Peter and John,
as Apostles, were sent down to confirm them: this is one of
the first signs of episcopal authority on the part of the
Apostles.

At Samaria there lived Simon Magus, the man who wished
to buy the Apostles' supernatural power with money. The
sin of wishing to buy supernatural things has been called the
sin of "*Simony*" after him. Peter rebuked him severely for
this (8. 20–23).

B. STORY

It is not easy to decide the date of this persecution, or its
precise origin, any more than the exact date of the martyrdom of Stephen, which seems to have been its beginning. It
is clear, however, that it was not a persecution by the
Romans, but by the Jewish authorities. Further we do not
hear of anyone but Stephen being killed. Saul is "breathing

out threatenings and slaughter against the disciples of the Lord" (9. 1), and handing people over into prison. Paul speaks of this later (Acts 22. 4): "Persecuted this way (*i.e.* this sect) unto death, binding and delivering into prisons both men and women". "Persecuting unto death" may refer to Stephen, or it may mean "only short of killing them": because we must remember that the Jewish authorities had no right to put anyone to death without the Roman authority (*see* notes on Section 6); and it is not clear whether the stoning of Stephen was legal or not. There are several explanations:

   i. He was killed by the Jews at a time when there was no Procurator in Jerusalem: *i.e.* after the recall of Pilate in A.D. 36, and before the appointment of his successor.

   ii. The Romans had given permission for him to be killed, or at least not stopped it (as in the case of Our Lord); although this permission is not recorded.

   iii. They killed him illegally. This is probably the most likely as it seems to have happened quite suddenly as a result of the fury of the hearers of Stephen.

So the persecution will have been one of prison and torment and trial before the Jewish council.

So the Christians of Jerusalem scattered into the surrounding country, and Philip the Deacon was preaching in Samaria. The Christian message must have already spread a little outside Jerusalem, for apart from the Pentecost-pilgrims, we have already read (5. 16) of people coming "out of the neighbouring cities" to bring their friends who were ill to be cured by Peter. But Philip's message was new in Samaria. The Samaritans were a people of partly Jewish blood, who observed in part the Jewish religion. Centuries before, they had had Assyrian settlers brought

over to live among them, when the main population was
carried off by the invader (IV Kings 17. 24). Hence they
were much despised by the pure-blooded Jews of Judea.
Our Lord himself had passed through the country of Samaria
and had stayed two days at Sichar (Jn. 4. 5, 40) where he had
spoken with the Samaritan woman. Many there had "believed in him because of his own word" (Jn. 4. 41). So the
new preaching of Philip must have fulfilled and completed
these first words of Our Lord.

In Samaria therefore many people were baptised, and
then Peter and John were sent from Jerusalem to confirm
them : "They laid their hands upon them, and they received
the Holy Ghost" (Acts 8. 17). This necessity of the Apostolic
tradition is very important.

Now at the same time there was this man Simon the
Magician, called "Magus", which means "Magician". By
all sorts of magic and sorcery, probably consulting the devil,
he had performed all sorts of wonders. There was much of
this sort of thing in the pagan world at the time : and we find
Paul encountering another such magician at Paphos in
Cyprus (Elymas in Acts 13. 6), also a Jew and working
among the Jews. Elymas is there spoken of as a "false
prophet", and Simon Magus was looked upon with particular horror by the Early Church, for trying to pervert
those people who had the revelation that could lead them to
Christ. It has even been thought that Simon Magus had
been persuading the Samaritans that he himself was the
fulfilment of their hope for the Messias. Anyway many
people had followed him.

But at the preaching of Philip, many of them were converted to believe in Christ, and Simon Magus himself
among them. But when Peter and John came to bring them
the Holy Ghost, Simon Magus wanted to buy from them
that power. From this some have deduced that his conversion was only pretended, and it is said that many heresies

were started by him afterwards. But anyway he seems in some way to have repented at the time. Peter's rebuke was severe (Acts 8. 20): "Keep thy money to thyself . . . thy heart is not right in the sight of God. Do penance . . . and pray to God, if perhaps this thought of thy heart may be forgiven thee". We cannot be quite certain whether Simon Magus' rather pitiful remark indicated real penance or not (8. 24): "Pray you for me to the Lord, that none of these things may come upon me".

Simony is a sin which at the present time is not, thank God, much in evidence in the Church. But in the history of the Church there have been many examples of men trading in the sacred offices of the Church, the priesthood, bishoprics, and so forth. The Popes had to issue many decrees against it in medieval times. But the remarkably sanctified lives of the Popes and Bishops and so many of the clergy in the modern Church have greatly helped her to be rid of the abuse and sin of Simony.

Peter and John, after the confirmation of the Samaritans, returned to Jerusalem, preaching on the way back.

C. DETAILS

v. 2   "took orders for Stephen's funeral": *i.e.* assisted in burying.

v. 5   "Philip": the Deacon, for the Apostles remained at Jerusalem (v. 1, 14). In 21. 8 he is called Philip the Evangelist.

v. 10   "This man is the power of God, which is called great": these were all words current in pagan religion at the time, and show how he was regarded as a sort of religious leader, and not merely a worker of magic.

v. 14   The last mention of St John in the Acts.

(21) SECTION 10: PHILIP AND THE ETHIOPIAN
(Acts 8. 26–40)

A. SIGNIFICANCE

The chief importance of this incident related of Philip's apostolate is that here we see the private conversion to Christianity of an individual. That conversion came about, as so many have since, through reading the Bible, and wondering what exactly it means. The point was then elucidated by the preacher, Philip, and the convert saw the full reality of the Faith. He was then baptised immediately.

This convert, however, has a further special interest for us, for his home was much more distant than that of any other convert we have seen so far. Ethiopia or Abyssinia is the country surrounding the upper reaches and sources of the Nile, to the South of Egypt: and so with him the Gospel travelled far afield.

Lastly, we have in v. 37 (although many manuscripts, and probably the best ones, omit the verse) the convert's profession of Faith before his baptism. In modern baptisms, the first thing that is asked in the porch of the Church is: "What dost thou ask of the Church of God?" and the answer is: "Faith". Then, just before the actual baptism, the godfather in the name of the child expresses three times his Faith: "I do believe". Immediately on this profession of Faith, the priest says: "Wilt thou be baptised?" and he says: "I will". And in this story of the Ethiopian we have the same profession of Faith, followed straight away by the baptism.

B. STORY

Philip was guided by an angel to the desert-road from Jerusalem to Gaza, which is on the way to Egypt and so to Ethiopia or Abyssinia. On this road he met a gorgeous car-

riage going towards Egypt, and sitting inside was a gentle-
man from Ethiopia. The Ethiopians are a handsome race,
with very black skin, and this man was a highly-placed
officer at the court. Now in the East, a king or noble sometimes had very many wives, and the officer placed in charge
of the palace of the king's wives sometimes had to undergo
an operation which prevented him from being able to marry
or have children, so that there would be no danger of his
taking any of the king's wives as a wife for himself. These
officers were called eunuchs, but this title was also sometimes used for any high official at the court. This Ethiopian
was then a eunuch at the palace of the Queen of Ethiopia,
and had charge of all her treasure (8. 27). He seems to have
been a "Proselyte" or convert to Judaism, and had just made
a pilgrimage to Jerusalem to worship at the Temple.

As he returned in his carriage he was reading the Book of
Isaias in the Old Testament, and was studying the famous
chapter 53. This chapter is one of the great "Servant"
passages in Isaias, which speak of Our Lord as the "Servant
of the Lord", and foretell his suffering and his rejection by
Israel. St Jerome, speaking of this passage, says very beauti-
fully that we should call Isaias an Evangelist rather than a
prophet: so exact is his foretelling of the Passion of Our
Saviour. Many texts from this great Messianic chapter are
well known to us:

v. 3 "Despised, and the most abject of men,
A man of sorrows, and acquainted with infirmity.

And his look was as it were hidden and despised,
Whereupon we esteemed him not.

v. 4 Surely he hath borne our infirmities
And carried our sorrows:
And we have thought him as it were a leper,
And as one struck by God and afflicted.

v. 5 But he was wounded for our iniquities,
He was bruised for our sins:
The chastisement of our peace was upon him,
And by his bruises we are healed.

v. 6   All we like sheep have gone astray,
Every one hath turned aside into his own way:
And the Lord hath laid on him the iniquity of us all.

v. 7   He was offered because it was his own will,
            And he opened not his mouth:
He shall be led as a sheep to the slaughter,
And he shall be dumb as a lamb before his shearer,
            And he shall not open his mouth."

When we realise that this is prophecy and not history, it is
not surprising that this chapter 53 of Isaias is regarded as
one of the great treasures of the Bible. The Ethiopian had
just reached v. 7, and was obviously reading aloud, when
Philip reached him, and asked him if he understood what the
passage meant? The Ethiopian said he did not understand
if it referred to the prophet himself or to someone else
(8. 34): whereat Philip, being invited into the carriage began
to explain how it referred to Christ, and had been fulfilled.
He then must have explained to him how one had to be
baptised to become a Christian, for presently, the Ethiopian
exclaimed as they passed a stream: "See here is water, what
doth hinder me from being baptised?"

So the Ethiopian professed his Faith in Jesus Christ, and
they both went down into the water, and Philip baptised
him. The custom of baptism "by immersion", or by
bathing the whole body in the water remained in the Church
for many centuries, though the modern practice of pouring
water upon the head can be traced back to the second century after Christ. Immediately after the baptism, "the Spirit
of the Lord took away Philip" (8. 39): the power of God
mysteriously made him to vanish, and to be found at
Azotus, a neighbouring city on the coast whence he made
his way preaching through the coast-towns northwards.

C. DETAILS

v. 27   "Candace": the name of the Ethiopian Queen:
          apparently a name borne by all the queens of
          Ethiopia, like Pharaoh by the kings of Egypt.

v. 27   Probably the Ethiopian had come across the Jewish
        religion in Egypt, where there were a number of
        Jewish colonies. They were Greek-speaking, and,
        although his native tongue will have been Ethiopic,
        he probably read the Scriptures in Greek.

v. 33   (Quoting Isa. 53. 8): a difficult verse. It is quoted
        here from the LXX (Greek) version. The original
        Hebrew of Isaias may be thus translated : "Through
        oppression and judgement he was taken away : who
        will speak of his generation (*i.e.* those who lived
        with him)? For it is cut off from the land of the
        living".

v. 37   This verse is not found in the chief Greek Manu-
        scripts, and so is omitted in the Westminster
        Version. Still, there is ancient authority for its
        inclusion.

(22)   SECTION 11 : THE CONVERSION OF
                ST. PAUL (Acts 9. 1–22)
        (*Cf.* in Speeches of St Paul, Acts 22. 6–11 ; 26. 12–18)

A. SIGNIFICANCE

The conversion of St Paul marks a turning point in the
history of the Church, for it was through Paul that the
Church spread through the world to the Gentile peoples
outside Judaism. His conversion is celebrated as a special
Feast on January 25th, and in the collect for that day we say :
"O God, who didst teach the whole world by the preaching
of blessed Paul the Apostle, grant we beseech thee, that we,
who today celebrate his conversion, may advance towards
thee by his example".

The conversion of St Paul was of a wholly miraculous
nature, and was effected by God for his own special purposes through a vision of Christ granted to Paul. It was this

vision of Christ that in St Paul's own eyes qualified him to be counted as an Apostle (1 Cor. 9. 1): "Am I not an Apostle? Have I not seen Christ Jesus our Lord?" And again (1 Cor. 15. 8–9): "And last of all, he was seen also by me, as by one born out of due time. For I am the least of the Apostles, who am not worthy to be called an Apostle, because I persecuted the Church of God".

Further, St Paul himself says that he received all his knowledge of the Christian Faith in a miraculous way (Gal. 1. 11–12): "For I give you to understand, brethren, that the gospel which was preached by me is not according to man. For neither did I receive it of man, nor did I learn it; but by the revelation of Jesus Christ". It is very probable that he received this revelation from Christ in the vision he had at his conversion. It is to be noted that for three days after the vision his eyes were blind to things of this earth.

After recovering his sight, he began straight away to preach the Gospel of Jesus Christ (Acts 9. 20). The people in general were astonished: the Jews were furious and proposed to kill him (9. 23): and the Christians were afraid, and could not believe at first that he had been converted (9. 26). It was Barnabas who finally brought him to the Apostles, and then "he was with them . . . dealing confidently" (9. 28).

B. STORY

The full story of the conversion of St Paul is given three times in the Acts, once by St Luke as historian, and twice by St Paul in speeches reported by St Luke: one in a speech to the people at Jerusalem (22. 6–11), and the other before King Agrippa at Caesarea (26. 12–18). In Madame Cecilia's Commentary these three versions are admirably arranged in parallel columns. This goes to show how closely the three correspond.

From the three accounts in Acts, therefore, the story is

simple to reconstruct: Saul was still full of hatred, organising the persecution of the Christians, and got the
authority of the High Priest to imprison Christians that he
could (9. 1–2). For this purpose he was going to Damascus
(a journey of about 150 miles from Jerusalem), and was
already near that city about noon (22. 6), when suddenly a
bright light surrounded them, brighter than the noonday
sun (26. 13), and all the party fell to the ground, dazzled by
the light. The probability is, according to Fr Vosté, that
they had been travelling on horseback. The light was the
appearance of Christ's risen Body: so dazzling that Saul was
blinded and the others remained as if stunned. Meanwhile
they heard a sound, but Saul caught the words, a voice
speaking "in the Hebrew tongue" (26. 14), which probably
means Aramaic, saying "Saul, Saul, why persecutest thou
me?" שאול שאול למא תרדפני in Aramaic (Sha-ul, Sha-ul,
lema tardepheni?). Christ speaks of his disciples as of himself (as, indeed he had explained in the Gospel (Mt. 25. 40):
"Amen I say to you, as long as you did it to one of these my
least brethren, you did it to me"); and St Paul never forgot
this, and it was he who was to become the great preacher of
the doctrine of Christ's "mystical body", the body of the
Christians. But Saul does not yet understand: "Who art
thou, Lord?" מי אנת מריא (Me att, Marya?); and the
voice answers: "I am Jesus, whom thou persecutest"
אנא ישוע דתרדפוהי (Ena Yeshua dethardephui). All the three
accounts are exactly corresponding in these words (9. 4–5;
22. 7–8; 26. 14–15). But we read of Christ also saying: "It
is hard for thee to kick against the goad" or the pricks, that
is a prickly instrument used for driving cattle. The meaning
is that Christ has a divine power: and it is no good trying to
resist it. In 26. 16–18 St Paul tells us also how Our Lord
gave him a commission to go and teach the nations: "for to
this end have I appeared to thee".

Saul now opens his eyes and finds that he is blind, and

8

so they lead him by the hand into Damascus: apparently now they are on foot for the sake of their blind companion. He is taken to his lodgings, at the house of one Judas, and stays there fasting and praying. And he had a vision of a man called Ananias coming to restore his sight. Meanwhile God speaks to Ananias, a Christian of Damascus, and sends him to Saul. Ananias at first is afraid, but is reassured by God, who speaks of Paul as the "vessel of election" ("vas electionis"), a phrase that we use of him in the liturgy. Ananias comes to Saul and lays his hands upon him, and his sight is restored. "And at the same hour I looked upon him" (22.13), seeing the man in the flesh whom he had seen in the vision. Ananias tells him he should be baptised at once, and baptises him (9. 10–18).

Immediately Saul began to preach Jesus Christ in the synagogues, and all the people were greatly astonished. He preached straight away, without any further study, for the fulness of revelation had been made to him at his conversion. "And he was with the disciples that were at Damascus, for some days" (9. 19).

Thus began the great Apostolate of Paul. The history of his persecution by the Jews and his visit to Jerusalem (9. 23–30) will be studied later, as there is probably a considerable lapse of time between this and his conversion: St Luke says it was (9. 23) "when many days had passed". This probably means the time when he "went into Arabia, and again returned to Damascus" (Gal. 1. 17), before visiting Jerusalem.

C. DETAILS

v. 3 "nigh to Damascus": tradition has varied in fixing the site of the vision. The most likely is a spot ten minutes' walk from the city gate.

v 5 "It is hard for thee to kick against the goad": in 26. 14 these words are said by St Paul to have been spoken by Christ immediately after the words "Saul, Saul, why persecutest thou me?" In Acts 9, according to most texts they are not found at all, and the Westminster Version omits them in this verse. Probably they should appear as in the order of chapter 26. The Vulgate alone has them in 9. 5.

v. 7   "stood amazed": 26. 14 says that they all fell on the ground, but the companions of Paul probably got up before he did.

"heard a voice": 22. 9 says: "they heard not the voice of him that spoke with me". The "voice" in chapter 9 probably means a "sound", without distinguishable words.

v. 18   "there fell from his eyes as it were scales": a medical term, referring perhaps to some incrustation that followed the inflammation due to blindness.

Note.—This point, after the Conversion of St Paul, might be a convenient place to pause for the Christmas vacation. The material so far has been arranged for about 22 classes, an average length for the Michaelmas Term. This point would also make a suitable starting place for the Lent Term, beginning with the Interlude that follows.

(23)   INTERLUDE ON THE IDEA OF THE CHOSEN PEOPLE

THE CHOSEN PEOPLE

St Paul was to become the "Apostle of the Gentiles": for God had said to Ananias (Acts 9. 15): "This man is to me a vessel of election, to carry my name before the Gentiles". To the first Jewish Christians, however, it was a real problem to understand that God might bring the Christian revelation direct to those who had not even received the Jewish revelation. They "contended with" Peter when he returned from Cornelius, the first Gentile convert who had not been through Judaism (11. 2). They knew that God had chosen his people, Israel, for his revelation, and at first they could not see that any revelation could come otherwise. It is important to grasp that the choosing of the Jewish people had no other purpose than the choosing of a group of men who should receive the knowledge of God and his salvation from God himself. There are certain things (as we have explained already, in the Introduction, and Historical Background) that man cannot find out by natural means, but needs that God in a supernatural way should reveal them to him. The two fundamental facts of the Hebrew revelation are two such things: first the idea of the nature of God, the one true God, creator and Lord of all the earth; and second the idea of the Redeemer that was to come, to redeem the earth from sin by which it had fallen away from God. There have always been people in the world chosen to receive God's revelation: for centuries the people of Israel was thus chosen, and alone in the world remained the faithful bearer of the message of God: "the faithful city" of Isa. 1. 21, 26. Alone in the world Israel awaited the Redeemer, and knew they could recognise him when he came: the Jewish clergy had a straight answer to Herod's inquiry "where Christ should be born" (Mt. 2. 4). And it was among the Jews that he was first recognised: all Christ's first followers were Jews, and all those who first received the Gospel from the Apostles were Jews: they were all people prepared by the Hebrew revelation. It is the great tragedy of the Jews that the multitude of them failed to recognise him. Fifty years after the time of Christ there were probably already more Gentile Christians than Jewish Christians: there certainly are now. For it is the Christian people that are now the Chosen People: the people chosen for the Christian revelation. We, Christians, now the Chosen People, have indeed sprung from the ancient Chosen People of Israel: we still call Abraham our spiritual father in the Mass when we speak of "sacrificium Patriarchae nostri Abrahae", but the faithful people, the Jews "have blasphemed the Holy One of Israel, they are gone away backwards" (Isa. 1. 4).

THE SAFEGUARDS OF REVELATION

i. *Circumcision.* Long before God gave to the people of Israel the Law of Moses, he gave them the "covenant of the Circumcision". God commanded to Abraham (Gen. 17. 10–13) that this should be a sign of his people, and that thus they should be marked off from the other people of the world who "knew not the Lord" (Judges 2. 10). Circumcision is a small surgical operation by which the outer skin is removed from a man's sex-organ: its real purpose is hygienic, for it ensures greater cleanliness and protects him from possible infection, which is important for people living in the desert. God wished to use this to protect the health of his own people, and at the same time it was to be a physical mark in their very bodies. Thus membership of the Chosen People was indicated in this way: and it became a sign of the "covenant" or agreement between God and the People to whom he gave the revelation of himself and the Saviour that was to come. So the Jews became very jealous of this rite, and the uncircumcised person was regarded as someone quite foreign and loathsome, someone who did not belong to God in the way that the Chosen People did, someone who refused God's revelation. Hence St Peter's hesitation about being invited to the house of Cornelius, a Gentile Roman and so of course not circumcised: "You know how abominable it is for a man that is a Jew, to keep company or to come unto one of another nation" (Acts 10. 28); and the horror of the Jews at Jerusalem afterwards, who said to him: "Why didst thou go in to men uncircumcised, and didst eat with them?" (Acts 11. 3). Circumcision then came to be regarded as the great mark of distinction between the Jew, who accepted God's revelation in the Old Testament, and the Gentile, who was anyone else outside the Jewish people, mostly pagans and idolaters. St Paul speaks frequently in these terms of his Apostolate among the non-Jews, as for instance when he says (Gal. 2. 7): "To me was committed the gospel of the uncircumcised, as to Peter was that of the circumcision" (*i.e.* the Jews).

ii. *The Law and the Scriptures.* Membership of the People of God was marked by the rite of circumcision; but the life of that people was preserved both physically and spiritually by the observance of the Law. In order that God's revelation might remain intact within the people, it was necessary that the People of Israel should remain united and pure and that the stock should remain sound and unmixed. In the Law of Moses therefore there are many things that relate to *hygiene*: their life in camp when they were in the desert, their food (certain things were to be avoided as "unclean"), their marriage (they were not to become inbred, nor to marry degenerate pagan people), and so forth, as well as the law of circumcision. But also apart from the physical health of the people, many things are ordered that produce *moral* well-being: for Israel to be a worthy channel of revelation, they must have a high sense of justice, of family-duty ("Honour thy father and thy mother", for instance (Exod. 20. 12)), and of ordinary civilised relations between men (such as "Thou shalt not steal"), and so on. In the Law, therefore, there are many legal and social rules that preserved the moral life of the people. But in the Old Testament we also find much that is of a *political* nature, especially in the books of the Prophets: for Israel's "foreign policy" or her relations with other nations had to be such as to preserve her own rights and independence. Lastly her *spiritual* relation with God had to be regulated and preserved perfect: so in the Law we have many enactments about prayer and worship: so that Israel might remain in contact with the God who had revealed himself to her.

iii. *The Priesthood.* The Jewish priesthood, closely connected with the worship in the Temple, all legislated for in the Law, was the great safeguard of the Jewish *religion.* The Jewish priesthood was hierarchical, that is, it had a hereditary system of authority and government, and the priests were a class apart. Our Lord did not condemn this system: but he superseded it. He only condemned certain members of the priestly class who rejected him. And the priestly system, the existence of a hierarchy of clergy, was a thing that was taken over in the Church. So just as the continuous, organised Jewish priesthood kept the purity of the revelation in Israel, so still the organised, continuous Christian priesthood has preserved intact the Christian revelation through the history of the Church.

CONVERTS

From what has been said of the "exclusiveness" of the Chosen People, it will at once be apparent that a convert to Judaism presented a special problem. He had to be somehow incorporated into the Jewish *people*: he had to receive in his body the mark of membership: he had to observe the many hygienic and ceremonial laws. Hence arose the problem which troubled the Early Church: once the Gospel was being preached to the Gentiles outside Judaism, were they to be first incorporated into the Jewish people, to receive the Jewish revelation before they could receive that of Christ? The answer was No. The revelation to the Chosen People was a preparation for Christ: now that Christ had come, there need be no more such preparation, and it was St Paul who insisted that Christ could be preached equally to the Jew and the Gentile: and that Gentiles need never become Jews before becoming Christians: from their paganism they could join the Christian Church, the New Chosen People, the "Israel of God" (Gal. 6. 16).

(24)   SECTION 12: PETER AND CORNELIUS
(Acts 9. 32–11. 18)

A. SIGNIFICANCE

Peter made a short missionary tour of the coast country
north-west of Jerusalem: and a few events are recorded. At
Lydda, an inland town about ten miles from the coast, a man
named Eneas is cured: at Joppe, on the coast, Tabitha, a
pious Christian lady, is raised from the dead—and this is the
first occasion on which a disciple of Our Lord raised anyone
from the dead.

But the most significant event on this tour is the conversion
of the Gentile Cornelius, a Roman officer, who was inspired
by God to send for Peter. Peter indeed hesitated to go and
visit a Gentile, but was reassured by God in the vision
(10. 11–16) of the linen sheet containing both "clean and
unclean" animals, of which Peter is bidden to partake. He
thus understands that "God is not a respecter of persons"
(10. 34), and that the Gentiles are to be admitted to the
Christian revelation as well as the Jews. The understanding
of this principle is a very important fact in the story of the
spread of the Gospel.

But Peter had to defend his action of "receiving into the
Church" (as we say in modern times) a Gentile before the
Jewish Christians, for "the faithful of the circumcision, who
came with Peter, were astonished, for that the grace of the
Holy Ghost was poured out upon the Gentiles also" (10. 45).

B. STORY

Peter made a tour of the coast-land during the period
when "the Church had peace throughout all Judea and
Galilee and Samaria" (9. 31), probably visiting the parts
where Philip the Deacon had already preached (8. 40, he
preached along the coast from Azotus to Caesarea), and con-

THE HOUSE OF SIMON, THE TANNER, AT JAFFA, AS IT LOOKS TO-DAY

(*Acts* 10)

firming people, as he had done at Samaria, again following on the track of Philip (8. 14–15: "Now when the Apostles who were in Jerusalem, had heard that Samaria had received the word of God; they sent to them Peter and John. Who when they were come, prayed for them, that they might receive the Holy Ghost").

While visiting the Christians at Lydda, "he found there a certain man named Eneas, who had kept his bed for eight years, who was ill of the palsy", which meant that he was paralysed and could not move. "And Peter said to him: 'Eneas, the Lord Jesus Christ healeth thee: arise and make thy bed.' And immediately he arose" (9. 33–34).

Peter was then fetched to Joppe, where he was brought straight to the upper room where they had laid out the body of the pious Christian woman Tabitha, who had just died. Peter (as Our Lord had done when raising Jairus' daughter, Mk. 5. 40) made everyone leave, and he knelt down and prayed, and "turning to the body he said: 'Tabitha, arise'. And she opened her eyes; and seeing Peter, she sat up" (9. 40). Note that when Our Blessed Lord raised from the dead, he did it by his own divine power and immediately: "Young man, I say to thee, arise" (at Naim, Lk. 7. 14); "And taking the damsel by the hand, he saith to her: 'Talitha cumi'" (Jairus' daughter, Mk. 5. 41); on the third occasion (Lazarus), he took the opportunity of giving thanks to the Father before crying: "Lazarus, come forth" (Jn. 11. 43). Peter needs to pray first, and similarly the prayer and ritual of Eliseus in the Old Testament (iv Kings 4. 33–35) was most elaborate.

Now while Peter was at Joppe, staying with Simon the tanner, he was one day praying about midday on the flat roof, waiting for lunch (Acts 10. 9–10), when he had the vision of the sheet let down from heaven with all kinds of animals in it, those permitted by the Law of Moses for food ("clean"), and those forbidden ("unclean"). On being told by a voice "Arise, Peter, kill and eat", being a good Jew, he refused to touch anything "unclean", whereat the voice said: "That which God hath cleansed do not thou call common" (or unclean) (10. 11–16).

At the same time messengers arrived from Cornelius, looking for Peter. Cornelius was a Roman centurion, of the "Cohors Italica" stationed at Caesarea. A cohort was one-tenth of a legion, and numbered 400–600 men. Each legion had certain cohorts composed of Roman citizens who were Italians by birth: and such cohorts were sometimes called "cohors italica". Cornelius was therefore an Italian, and so a Roman pagan, but one who had been attracted to the religion of the Jews, although he had not become a "prose-lyte" or convert to Jewish religious practices. But he worshipped the True God and was very well disposed towards the Jews, like the centurion in the Gospel, who asked Our Lord to cure his servant and then said: "Domine, non sum dignus ut intres sub tectum meum", and of whom the Jews said: "He loveth our nation" (Lk. 7. 2–6). Peter, hearing the message of Cornelius, how he had been told by an angel to send for him, realised that the meaning of the vision he had had, referred to the acceptance of the Gentiles. So the next day he went with the messengers to Caesarea, about thirty miles from Joppe (Acts 10. 23).

Peter at once explained to Cornelius his hesitation about visiting a Gentile, but also how God had reassured him in a vision. Cornelius then told of his vision of an angel, and said: "Now therefore we are all present in thy sight, to hear all things whatsoever are commanded thee by the Lord" (10. 33). Peter then gave them a summary of the Gospel story, and told them of Jesus of Nazareth, his death and resurrection, and how "by his name all receive remission of sins, who believe in him" (10. 43). While Peter was speaking, the Holy Ghost came upon them, and they were "speaking with tongues, and magnifying God" (10. 44–46). "Speaking with tongues" is quite obviously here a gift of the Holy Ghost, given for the purpose of a special praising of God. St Peter thereupon "commanded them to be baptised" (10. 48).

When Peter returned to Jerusalem, he found that some of the Jewish Christians there had misgivings about the admission of these Gentiles to the Christian revelation. Peter simply told them the entire story of his vision and the desire of Cornelius, and how the Holy Ghost had come down upon Cornelius and his family and friends. "If then", he concluded, "God gave them the same grace, as to us also who believed in the Lord Jesus Christ: who was I, that could withstand God?" (11. 17). The Christians at Jerusalem immediately agreed, saying "God then hath also to the Gentiles given repentance unto life" (11. 18), *i.e.* has given them eternal life by remission of sin through the revelation of Christ.

C. DETAILS

9. 32   "the saints": the holy ones, *i.e.* the Christians.

9. 36   "Joppe": the modern harbour of Jaffa, port of Jerusalem, about thirty-five miles from the capital.

9. 36   "Tabitha, which by interpretation is called Dorcas" the name means "gazelle" (regarded as a graceful animal), and the first form is Aramaic and the second is Greek. The same name quite often appears in two languages: for instance, the names Amy and Philomena both mean "loved one" from the Latin (through French) and the Greek respectively; similarly Irene and Frieda, meaning "Peace" from the Greek and German; or Pearl and Margaret, for the latter means pearl in Greek.

10. 11   "a certain vessel": σκεῦος, an instrument or utensil, probably used like the Hebrew כלי (keli) for a "thing" unspecified: but the Westminster Version translates "sail" as in 27. 17 on the ship.

(25)   SECTION 13: PROGRESS AT ANTIOCH
                 (Acts 11. 19–30)

A. SIGNIFICANCE

In this section we have an indication of the beginning of a
real wide spreading of the Faith. We are now in a period
probably ten years from Pentecost, approaching the year
A.D. 41 when the kingdom of Judea was restored under King
Herod Agrippa I. At the dispersion of the Christians from
Jerusalem at the time of the death of Stephen, we saw that
they went about preaching in Judea and Samaria (8. 1),
Philip had been south to Azotus (8. 40), and as far north as
Damascus there were already Christians at the time of the
conversion of St Paul. Some time after his conversion,
St Paul had been sent to his native city of Tarsus (9. 30),
where presumably he had preached. But the Jewish-Christians of Jerusalem had penetrated as far as "Phenice", that
is the sea-coast of the Roman Province of Syria, round Tyre
and Sidon, and farther north to the great city of Antioch in
Syria, and also to the island of Cyprus (11. 20).

But all these had addressed themselves only to the Jews.
Certain Christians from Cyprus and Cyrene (North Africa)
had begun to speak to the Greeks, *i.e.* the Gentiles: and
here again was the problem for the Jews: could the revelation of Christ be preached to the Gentiles without their
becoming Jews first?

It is very important to notice that Jerusalem was consulted: the Church is one, holy, catholic (including all), but
also *apostolic*. Barnabas was sent as an Apostle from Jerusalem, and he "when he was come, and had seen the grace of
God, rejoiced: and he exhorted them with all purpose of
heart to continue in the Lord" (Acts 11. 22–23).

The Church at Antioch was therefore greatly increased,
and here they were first called "Christians".

Note the unity with the Christians at Jerusalem, who were all Jews: the Antiochians, both Jews and Gentiles, were anxious to help the brethren of Jerusalem in the provision of food for the expected famine, but this service of charity was to be carried out through the Apostles, Barnabas and Saul.

B. STORY

The history of this passage has for the most part been told in studying its significance, for it is an account of big movements, rather than isolated events.

The dispersed Jerusalem Christians had been preaching in Syria to the Jews: Cypriote and African disciples had preached to the Greek Gentiles. This last matter was regulated from Jerusalem by the sending of Barnabas. He will already have heard, at Jerusalem, the decision regarding Cornelius, when Peter had defended his bringing the word of God to the Gentile. So now the Greek population at Antioch was also freely to receive the revelation of Christ.

Now when the crowds of Christians increased, Barnabas went to Tarsus to fetch Saul. It is very interesting that Saul is already regarded as an Apostle: he had been previously introduced to the Apostles at Jerusalem by Barnabas (Acts 9. 26–28; Gal. 1. 18), and accepted by them. And Saul helped Barnabas with the work at Antioch for a whole year (Acts 11. 26).

At this time "there came *Prophets* from Jerusalem to Antioch" (11. 27). Prophecy is to be one of the results of the "pouring out of the Spirit upon all flesh", spoken of at Pentecost (Peter's sermon, Acts 2. 17, quoting Joel 2. 28), the Holy Ghost gave a special grace to certain people to be able to foretell the future. There are a number of references in the Apostolic writings to these Prophets and they seem to have had an accepted place among the early Christians. In Acts 13. 1 they are numbered among the Christian community at Antioch, and St Paul writing to the Corinthian Christians speaks of them as a privileged class after the Apostles: "first Apostles, secondly Prophets" (1 Cor. 12. 28), and explains that their work is one of offering consolation and encouragement (as we already noticed about the name of Barnabas in Acts 4. 36): "He that prophesieth, speaketh to men unto edification and exhortation and comfort" (1. Cor. 14. 3). It will have been necessary at the beginning of the life of the Church, when this life was, humanly speaking, unavoidably precarious, that the members of the Church should have some warning from God of future calamity or danger. God had promised that the gates of death "should not prevail" against his Church (Mt. 16. 18), and he gave the warning to the Christians through these prophets who had been given the grace to be able to see into the future. God, living in eternity, sees past, present, and future in the everlasting present of his eternity, the "standing Now of eternity" (as opposed to the "flowing Now of our passing time"), as Boethius said, and so he can impart some of his knowledge to men, and allow them as it were a glimpse into his knowledge which includes at a glance the whole of time, past, present, and future. This is the privilege which he grants to the Prophets, and this man Agabus (Acts 11. 28) was such a one.

Agabus was therefore able to warn the Christians of a famine that would come, so that they could lay in stores of food, lest all the Christian community should be wiped out through hunger. Thus the Christians of the more prosperous Syria were able to send relief to Judea which was to be troubled with shortage of provisions.

C. DETAILS

v. 20   "Greeks": the context would seem to require that this refer to the Gentile Greeks, and not to the Greek-speaking Jews. But in the manuscripts of the Greek text, some have τοὺς Ἑλληνιστάς but more have τοὺς Ἕλληνας, and of these the first is used of Greek-speaking Jews (sometimes called "Grecians" or "Hellenists"), and the second of Gentile Greeks (and translated "Greeks" as opposed to "Grecians"). Here is it probably best to follow the reading that means Gentile Greeks.

v. 22   Barnabas was probably sent in order to confirm the new converts.

v. 25   It is not certain how Barnabas came to be the friend of Paul: probably he knew him before either became a Christian, and so it was he who welcomed him when other Christians suspected him (9. 26–27), and invited him to come and work with him at Antioch. As Barnabas was a Cyprian born (4. 36), he may well have studied at Tarsus, and there got to know St Paul.

v. 28   There is evidence of several famines in the Roman Empire about this time. This famine "which came to pass under Claudius" was therefore when Herod Agrippa was king in Judea, and so was "at the same time" (12. 1) as the persecution ordered by that king, who had been put on the throne by the Emperor Claudius (A.D. 41–54). Herod's reign was A.D. 41–44.

(26)   SECTION 14: THE PERSECUTION OF HEROD (Acts 12)

A. SIGNIFICANCE

This is the third time that the Church was persecuted in the Acts. The first time was after the cure of the lame man when Peter and John were arrested (Acts 4: in our book, section 4), and they were released because the Jewish authorities feared the people. The second time was when all the

Apostles were put in prison because they had not ceased preaching the gospel of Christ (Acts 5 : section 6 in this book), and they were freed by an angel, caught again, tried before the Sanhedrin, released through the advice of Gamaliel and scourged before being let go.

But this time it was not the Jewish religious authorities, but the vassal-king of the Romans, Herod. Now the Herods were not of proper Jewish blood : they were of Edomite stock, and therefore Palestinian, but they had assimilated themselves to the Jews, and this Herod Agrippa was noted for his piety and observance of Jewish religious law and ceremonial. The royal house of Herod had been ruling in Palestine since 40 B.C., Herod the Great, the grandfather of this Herod Agrippa I, at first being Governor of Galilee, and then vassal-king of Judea under the Romans. As we saw in the Historical Background under 1. *d.* (Roman Rule in Palestine), the sons of Herod were not considered by the Romans suitable to continue the succession, and Judea was turned into a province with Procurators. When, however, Claudius succeeded as Emperor in 41, he restored the house of Herod in Judea, and this Herod Agrippa became the vassal-king of Judea in that year. There was therefore at that moment a change of government, and with it came a confusion of the rights of justice and power in Judea. The house of Herod had always attempted to gain the favour of the Jews, and now the new king knew that a persecution of the Christians would gain him favour among the Jews. It is probable that in such a vassal-kingdom the consent of any Roman authority was not needed for the local king to put someone to death, as it had been necessary in the time of the Procurators. It had only been with difficulty that the Jews had succeeded in getting the Roman consent to a condemnation to death by their own religious authorities. Now Herod Agrippa was free to act as he pleased, to gain Jewish favour. Thus the death of James was an event of a new kind in

9

Christian history: it was the civil ruler who put him to death, unlike the case of Stephen when it was a Sanhedrin punishment of doubtful legality. Herod, "seeing that it pleased the Jews" (12. 2), put Peter in prison as well.

Peter once more escaped through the assistance of an angel, and after calling at one of the Christian households, left Jerusalem, and "*went into another place*" (12. 17). This is a mysterious remark, and one cannot be certain what is meant. There is, however, an important tradition that St Peter went to Rome early in the reign of Claudius, therefore after 41. Further it is obvious that having escaped from prison, he would remain outside Judea at least until the death of Herod Agrippa in 44. The next we hear of him is the Council of Jerusalem in 49. So it is very probable that he did visit Rome during this period, and that "another place" in this verse indicates Rome.

Apart from Peter's reappearance at the Council of Jerusalem (Acts 15), this is the last that we hear of him in the Acts. Tradition tells us that first he was Bishop at Antioch, and then settled in Rome, but we cannot be certain of the dates. He may have visited Rome after his liberation in about 42 (according to the tradition about "in the reign of Claudius"), and then settled at Antioch after a missionary tour: he most probably visited the Christians in Asia Minor at some period, according to the place-names at the head of his Epistle (1 Peter 1. 1), which are probably his converts, and also Corinth, according to St Paul's remark about people there being baptised by him: "Every one of you saith: I indeed am of Paul . . . I of Cephas . . . etc." (1 Cor. 1. 12). He certainly visited Antioch at some period: "When Cephas was come to Antioch" (Gal. 2. 11). In the liturgy we keep two feasts to remember the two bishoprics that tradition tells us he held one after the other: Antioch and Rome: "St Peter's Chair at Antioch" (February 22), and "St Peter's Chair at Rome" (January 18).

B. Story

After his accession as king, Herod Agrippa to please the Jews ordered the Apostle James to be killed. This was James the Great, the brother of John the Evangelist and son of Zebedee. James and John had been partners with Simon Peter as fishermen on the Lake of Galilee, and had all been called by Our Blessed Lord at the same time: after calling Simon and Andrew and saying to them, "Come after me and I will make you to become fishers of men" (Mk. 1. 17), he went on "from thence a little farther, and he saw James the son of Zebedee, and John his brother, who were also mending their nets in the ship: and forthwith he called them" (Mk. 1. 19–20). So this James, among the first to be called, was the first of the Apostles to die: and he is the only one whose death is recorded in the New Testament. Tradition tells us how his remains were carried to Compostella in Spain, which was afterwards called by his name "Santiago de Compostella", and which became one of the great places of pilgrimage in Europe. He is the principal patron of Spain, and his feast on July 25 marks the day when his relics were brought to that country. He has been called "the Great" to distinguish him from James, whom the Gospel (Mk. 15. 40) calls "the Less", who was Bishop of Jerusalem, and who appears at the Council there (Acts 15. 13), and who was the author of the "Epistle of James" in the New Testament, and who was called the "brother (*i.e.* cousin) of the Lord".

Herod Agrippa "seeing that it pleased the Jews, proceeded to take up Peter also" (Acts 12. 3). "Peter therefore was kept in prison. But prayer was made without ceasing by the church unto God for him" (12. 5). This prayer for the leader of the Church is very notable, and is the beginning of the Church's constant anxiety for the welfare of the common father, and the special prayers Collect, Secret, and Postcommunion that are often offered for the Pope, are well known. The Secret thus prays for his protection: "Be pleased, we beseech thee O Lord, with the gifts we have offered, and guide with a careful protection thy servant (Pius), whom thou hast wished to be over thy Church as its shepherd".

And that prayer of the Church was heard and answered by a miracle: Peter, asleep in the prison, chained to a soldier on either side was woken up by an angel, and told to get ready to go. Quite bewildered ("And he knew not that it was true which was done by the Angel: but thought he saw a vision", 12. 9), he obeyed, put on his things, his chains fell off, the doors opened of themselves, and Peter walked out following the Angel in silence. Suddenly he found himself alone in a street he knew. And he stood and "considered" (12. 12), that is, tried to think what to do next.

He decided to call at the house of Mary, the mother of John Mark, a young friend who afterwards became his companion in Rome, as he shows in his Epistle from Rome (1 Peter 5. 13): ". . . saluteth you, and so doth my son Mark", and who wrote the Gospel of St Mark. He probably expected to find some of the brethren there, and indeed that night they were gathered together there for prayer. He must have been there often, for when he knocked at the door, and Rhode (that is "Rose") the maid, came to answer the door, she recognised his voice at once. She was so excited that she forgot to open the door, but ran off into the house to tell the others that it was Peter (12. 14). At first they would not believe her, but while they were talking, Peter went on knocking outside, no doubt anxious for shelter from possible guards looking for him. When they let him in, he signed with his hand that they should stop excited talking, lest too much notice should be attracted to this night-gathering, and told them the story, adding: "Tell these things to James and to the brethren" (12. 17). The position of James, singled out, is important. This of course was James the Less, Bishop of Jerusalem. But Peter would not stay: it was hardly safe, and he seems to have left Jerusalem that very night, and gone "into another place". As we have just explained, this place may have been Rome.

The next six verses are an account of the end of Herod Agrippa in the year 44. Herod looked for Peter, and not finding him, had the prison warders executed. Herod with all his splendour gained the admiration of the people, but his pride was punished by a sudden and miserable death (12. 23).

C. DETAILS

v. 4 "Four files of soldiers": four "quaterniones" or sets of four soldiers, who kept watch a set at a time. Two were chained to the prisoner and two watched outside the cell.

v. 8 "Gird thyself", etc. Sleeping in his clothes, he loosed his belt, took off his sandals and his cloak. These he would adjust, and be ready to go at once.

v. 10 "First and second ward": first guards just outside the cell, and the second guards probably at the entrance of the prison.

v. 20 Friction between Herod and the cities of Tyre and Sidon. We are not told the cause, but learn that these two seaports on the Phenician coast wanted friendly relations with Herod, because they depended on the hinterland, which was under Herod, for their agricultural supplies ("they were nourished by him"). Perhaps the trouble was a falling-off in their prosperity owing to Herod's great development of the new city of Caesarea as a seaport.

(27–28) INTERLUDE ON THE PERSON OF ST PAUL

HIS PERSON

It is clear that St Paul was a remarkable person in almost every way: his natural gifts seem to have marked him out from the beginning, the circumstances of his birth and education gave him a special position, and the gifts and power that he received from God made him into the greatest Apostle of Christ that ever was.

His birth in the cosmopolitan city of Tarsus at once gave him a wide outlook. The culture of the city was Greek and the opportunities of education considerable. The Jews there would have been Greek-speaking, and it is evident that St Paul was very familiar with the Old Testament in the Greek version then current among the Jews. But, in addition to this Greek background, St Paul was brought up as a Pharisee, "the most sure sect of our religion", as he himself said (Acts 26. 5), and spent some time studying at Jerusalem "brought up in this city, at the feet of Gamaliel, taught according to the truth of the law of the fathers, zealous for the law" (22. 3), where he acquired the Rabbinic method and thought, as a learned Pharisee should.

Already as a young man he seems to have been a leader: it was he who got the authority of the High Priest to round up the Christians, and went about "breathing out threatenings and slaughter against the disciples of the Lord" (9. 1–2; 22. 4–5; 26. 12), so much so that he had a reputation of terror among the Christians, and was known among the Jews for his bitterness against them (9. 21). At the time of the martyrdom of Stephen, when he was making "havoc of the church" (8. 3), he was still a νεανίας, a young man (7. 57). After his conversion we still can notice these qualities of leadership: "Immediately he preached Jesus in the synagogues" (9. 20), and it was his vigorous nature that spread the Gospel so far and wide to the Gentiles. After receiving the miraculous revelation from Christ, he did not hesitate to claim the leadership of an Apostle (1 Cor. 9. 1): "Am I not an Apostle? Have I not seen Christ Jesus our Lord?" And in the same Epistle (1 Cor. 11. 1) he does not doubt his authority and leadership under Christ: "Be ye followers of me, as I also of Christ". And all through his life we notice a constant zeal for the things of God: as a young Pharisee he was "zealous for the law" (Acts 22. 3), and as a Christian Apostle his eagerness and energy in preaching Christ appears in every speech we read reported in the Acts and in all his Epistles. In the greater number of Masses that are celebrated the "Epistle" is taken from the writings of St Paul, and his words are the constant companions of every Christian since he wrote them. We have already remarked how his conversion marks a turning point in the history of the Church, for it was through St Paul that the Gospel began to be spread through the world, and he looked upon this as his especial work (Gal. 2. 7): "To me was committed the gospel of the uncircumcised".

St Paul himself tells us that he was an "Hebrew of the Hebrews", that is, a pure-blooded Jew, and "of the tribe of Benjamin" (Phil. 3. 5), which showed his genealogy to be good. But, coming from Tarsus, he was in contact with the Greek-speaking world, and he was also a Roman citizen. He claimed his rights as a Roman citizen, when under arrest at Jerusalem and about to be scourged. Apparently the right of appeal from the judgment of the local governor was the chief value of Roman citizenship, and St Paul exercised this right before Festus, the governor of Judea, when he said (Acts 25. 11-12): "I appeal to Caesar"; at which Festus said, "Hast thou appealed to Caesar? To Caesar shalt thou go". And this was the cause of his journey to Rome of which we read in the last chapters of the Acts. But apparently it was forbidden to scourge a Roman citizen: the centurion at Jerusalem, finding Paul bound for scourging said (Acts 22. 26): "What art thou about to do? For this man is a Roman citizen". It was then, on being asked if this were so, that Paul made the proud reply: "I was born so" (Acts 22. 28). This meant that his father was already a Roman citizen, but we do not know how he came to have this privilege, for at this time in the East citizenship was only spread by individual grants. It has been supposed that St Paul's father had rendered some service to the Empire as a prominent and educated citizen of Tarsus.

St Paul's Roman citizenship is sometimes given as the reason for his second Latin name of Paul, his Hebrew name being Saul. The Jews still now give a Hebrew name at Circumcision ("his name in Israel"), often still distinct from the civil name. And he began to use his Roman name more generally when he began preaching among the Gentiles. Others hold, however, that Paul was a name which either he received from God (like Abraham) at his conversion, or which he took when he began to travel about the Empire. St Luke always calls him Saul in the Acts until the First Missionary Journey (13. 9), and from thence afterwards always calls him Paul, after explaining in that text "Saul, otherwise Paul".

All the above remarks about the person of St Paul refer chiefly to the very great natural gifts of the Apostle, his birth, education, and character; but what is even more important is to realise his supernatural gifts, the divine intervention that completely changed the course of his life and turned all his vast energies into the channel of the Christian Apostolate. It is important to see Paul above all as a great Christian, united to Christ with a burning love: he himself wrote (Gal. 2. 20): "I live, now not I; but Christ liveth in me". The real Christian lives for Christ, and all his daily work is in that way turned into service of Christ: work not done for Christ is work lost: "I count all things to be but loss, for the excellent knowledge of Jesus Christ my Lord" (Phil. 3. 8). And St Paul fully understood that all his work of preaching was really the work of God, merely using Paul's natural gifts (1 Cor. 2. 4–5): "My speech and preaching was not in the persuasive words of human wisdom, but in shewing of the spirit and power: that your faith might

not stand on the wisdom of men, but on the power of God".
And all the time in his teaching he had this one great
desire: to impart to his followers this same zeal and love for
Christ (Eph. 3. 8): "To me . . . is given this grace, to preach
among the Gentiles the unsearchable riches of Christ . . .
(v. 17–18) that Christ may dwell by faith in your hearts: that
being rooted and founded in charity (*i.e.* love of God), you
may be able to comprehend, with all the saints, what is the
breadth, and length, and height, and depth".

Here we should add a note about St Paul's personal appearance. From the New Testament itself we learn that he
was obviously a powerful orator, although he himself quotes
his adversaries as saying (II Cor. 10. 10): "His bodily
presence is weak, and his speech contemptible". Early
Christian tradition tells us that he was small and bald, and
in early times (in the Catacombs and elsewhere) there was a
regular representation of him with thin, worn features, a
beard, and bald head. He himself tells us that he was not
strong, when he speaks of his "infirmities", and probably
the "sting of my flesh" of which he writes (II Cor. 12. 7)
is a reference to ill-health. But it is also clear from the
amount of travelling that he did, and the frequent torments
such as scourging and stoning that he underwent, that he
must have had a very strong constitution.

His Life

From various places in the New Testament we find the
main elements in the life of the Apostle of the Gentiles, and
several of the passages we have already seen in our exegesis.
So here we shall give an outline of the life of St Paul, with
the chief passages from which we gather the information.

A. *Before his conversion.* Born at Tarsus, at about the
same time or shortly after Our Lord: round the year 32
(Martyrdom of St Stephen) he was still a νεανίας (Acts 7.
57), so probably not much over thirty, and writing to

Philemon from prison, probably in Rome and therefore between A.D. 58 and 60, he writes (Philem. 9): "Paul, an old man, and now a prisoner also of Jesus Christ", which suggests that he was about sixty. So St Paul's age probably corresponds roughly with the years A.D.

As a young man he studied at Jerusalem "at the feet of Gamaliel" (Acts 22. 3), and took part in the persecution of the Christians, being present and "consenting" to the stoning of Stephen (7. 57–59). It has been maintained that at this time he was actually a member of the Sanhedrin, because when speaking of his persecution of Christians during his youth, he said (26. 10): "When they were put to death, κατήνεγκα ψῆφον, I brought my vote" (ψῆφος means a "pebble" but, especially a pebble used in casting votes). In the midst of these efforts against the Christians, Saul was miraculously converted to Christ.

B. *After his conversion.* (Acts 9. 19–30): "And he was with the disciples, that were at Damascus for some days. And immediately he preached Jesus in the synagogues, that he is the Son of God". St Luke in the Acts then goes on to say (v. 23): "And when many days were passed . . ." But it is St Paul himself who tells us (Gal. 1. 17–18) that the "many days" were about three years, when he writes: "Neither went I to Jerusalem to the Apostles who were before me; but I went into Arabia, and again I returned to Damascus. Then after three years, I went to Jerusalem to see Peter, and I tarried with him fifteen days". St Luke does not mention St Paul's retirement during these three years, but takes us straight on to the visit to Jerusalem, telling us how the Jews of Damascus tried to catch Paul and kill him, and how the disciples "taking him in the night, conveyed him away by the wall, letting him down in a basket" (Acts 9, 23–25).

Some days therefore after his conversion he went into Arabia, but of this journey we know nothing more what-

[Photo E.N.A.

A GENERAL VIEW OF THE MODERN TOWN OF TARSUS—THE BIRTHPLACE OF ST PAUL—WHICH STANDS
ON THE SITE OF CILICIA'S ANCIENT CAPITAL

ever: we do not even know what precisely is meant by
"Arabia", as it may refer to any part of the territory that lay
desert-wards or eastwards from Damascus and Palestine,
and was inhabited by Arab tribes. It is presumed that St
Paul retired from the busy city to the quiet desert country
for peace and solitude; it has even been suggested that
during this period he visited Our Lady. There is no historical
evidence for this whatever, but it is indeed probable. The
visit to Arabia has then to be fitted in between Acts 9. 22
(Paul's first preaching in Damascus) and v. 23 (which
begins the account of the Jews' plotting, and St Paul's
escape).

Three years therefore after his conversion St Paul arrives
in Jerusalem "to see Peter" (Gal. 1. 18): "and he essayed to
join himself to the disciples, and they were all afraid of him,
not believing that he was a disciple. But Barnabas took him
and brought him to the Apostles, and told them how he had
seen the Lord" (Acts 9. 26–27). We have already noted (in
section 13) the friendship between Paul and Barnabas, and
how Barnabas stood by Paul and did him the real friendly
act of introducing him to the Apostles.

After Paul's "fifteen days" (Gal. 1. 18) with Peter in
Jerusalem, he went by Caesarea to his native city of Tarsus
in Cilicia (Acts 9. 30, and Gal. 1. 21), where he stayed until
Barnabas came and fetched him to help at Antioch. "And
they conversed there in the church a whole year" (Acts 11.
26). Paul had probably been at Tarsus for several years
before being called to Antioch to help Barnabas.

C. *His missionary work.* It was while Paul was at Antioch
helping Barnabas that "the Holy Ghost said unto them:
'Separate me Saul and Barnabas, for the work whereunto I
have taken them'" (Acts 13. 2). Thus began the first of the
three great missionary journeys of St Paul of which we read
in the Acts: chapters 13–14 for the first, and then, after the
Council at Jerusalem and a visit to Antioch, "after some

days, Paul said to Barnabas: 'Let us return and visit our brethren in all the cities wherein we have preached the word of the Lord, to see how they do'" (Acts 15. 36): chapters 15–18 are devoted to the second journey, which occupied about three years. The third journey began "after he had spent some time" again at Antioch (18. 23), and is recounted in chapters 18–21. (We shall follow the events of these journeys in more detail in the exegetical sections that are to come.) The third journey ended at Jerusalem, and barely a week after his arrival, the Jews, making a riot against him, had him arrested.

D. *Period of imprisonment.* From this point, when the Roman tribune, to rescue him from the mob, "coming near took him, and commanded him to be bound with two chains" (Acts 21. 33), to the end of the Acts, St Paul was a prisoner, kept in custody by the Romans while his offence against the Jews (who were under the protection of the Romans, and for whom the Romans administered justice) was being proved. At first he was kept at Jerusalem, but then (Acts 23. 23) moved to Caesarea. It was while at Caesarea and once more on trial, that Paul made his appeal to Caesar, claiming on the strength of his Roman citizenship, the right to be judged by the Emperor. He had been in prison at Caesarea for two years, and now ("when two years were ended", 24. 27) was sent by ship to Rome.

His imprisonment in Rome seems to have been gentler: "And when we were come to Rome, Paul was suffered to dwell by himself with a soldier that kept him" (28. 16), "and he remained two whole years in his own hired lodging: and he received all that came in unto him" (28. 30). At this point St Luke's account in the Acts breaks off.

E. *After his release.* The whole of the early Christian tradition tells us that after these two years of imprisonment in Rome St Paul was acquitted and released. And there are hints in the later Epistles that he is free: in *1 Timothy* and

Titus he no longer writes as a prisoner, but speaks of schemes for travel, such as "Hoping that I shall come to thee shortly" (1 Tim. 3. 14), or "Make haste to come unto me to Nicopolis. For there I have determined to winter" (Tit. 3. 12). And we know from his (much earlier) letter to the Romans, that he hoped to visit Spain: "When I shall begin to take my journey into Spain . . ." (Rom. 15. 23); and early tradition has held that he did make this journey after his release in Rome. But apart from the journey to Spain, he seems to have travelled about the East and visited several places which he refers to in these later Epistles.

Nevertheless he did not enjoy this regained liberty for more than a few years at the most: tradition again tells us of his further arrest and imprisonment.

F. *His second imprisonment and death.* We know very little beyond the mere fact of his further arrest and eventual martyrdom in Rome about the year A.D. 67. We shall examine these traditions in more detail in a later Interlude. II Timothy is generally regarded as the last Epistle we have from his pen, and as having been written during this second imprisonment in Rome: "I labour even unto bands, as an evil-doer: but the word of God is not bound" (II Tim. 2. 9). In this letter he gives his last words of advice to the young Timothy, while he himself waits patiently for the end which he feels cannot be far off. From here are taken the famous words of the Epistle at the Mass of a Doctor: "Be thou vigilant, labour in all things, do the work of an Evangelist, fulfil thy ministry. Be sober. For I am even now ready to be sacrificed: and the time of my dissolution is at hand. I have fought a good fight, I have finished my course, I have kept the faith" (II Tim. 4. 5–7).

His Epistles we shall study in relation to his life in a later Interlude: the first ones he wrote during his second missionary journey, and continued to write to the various people to whom he had preached right up to the end of his life. As we follow the life of St Paul, we shall try also to note something of his correspondence at the different periods.

SUMMARY. (Years A.D. correspond approximately with his age)

A. Born at Tarsus
   Studied at Jerusalem
   Was present at the stoning of Stephen   (about A.D. 32)
B. His conversion   (33)
   He stays in Damascus for some days
   He visits Arabia
   He returns to Damascus   (about A.D. 37)
   He escapes to Jerusalem
   He retires to Tarsus
   He is called to Antioch by Barnabas   (about A.D. 46)
C. His Missionary journeys   (between about A.D. 47 and 54)
   Council of Jerusalem after First Journey   (49)
D. Arrest at Jerusalem, and imprisonment at Caesarea
                                                   (55–57)
   Imprisonment in Rome   (58–60)
E. Period of liberty, with journey perhaps to Spain
F. Final arrest and imprisonment in Rome
   Martyrdom   (about A.D. 67)

(29)   SECTION 15: ST PAUL'S FIRST
          MISSIONARY JOURNEY (Acts 13. 1–14. 4)

A. SIGNIFICANCE

In this and the succeeding section we see the beginning of St Paul's apostolate. He wrote to the Christians in Rome (chiefly Jews): "I am not ashamed of the Gospel. For it is the power of God unto salvation to everyone that believeth, *to the Jew first and to the Greek*" (Rom. 1. 16). In this section we see Paul and Barnabas speaking first to the Jews,

especially at Antioch in Pisidia (Asia Minor, not Antioch in
Syria whence they started), for the Jews were the Chosen
People, and had, as it were, the first right to the revelation of
Christ. He then spoke to "the strangers who served God"
(Acts 13. 43), that is Proselytes or converts from paganism,
or else Gentiles who were favourably inclined to the
Jewish religion and worshipped the True God without
being fully incorporated into the Jewish People, such as
Cornelius: "a religious man, fearing God . . . and always
praying to God" (Acts 10. 2, cf. section 12). Next week,
however, he spoke to "the whole city almost" (13. 44),
which meant of course a crowd mainly of Gentiles, and this
caused some ill-feeling among the Jews, who began to speak
against Paul and Barnabas, "contradicting those things that
were said by Paul, blaspheming" (13. 45). Whereat Paul and
Barnabas explained clearly to the Jews their principle with
regard to the Gentiles, and "said boldly: 'To you it behoved
us first to speak the word of God; but because you reject it,
and judge yourselves unworthy of eternal life, behold we
turn to the Gentiles. For so the Lord hath commanded
us (quoting Isa. 49. 6): "I have set thee to be the light of
the gentiles; that thou mayest be for salvation unto the utmost part of the earth"'" (Acts 13. 46–47). And thus many
of those Gentiles became Christians.

The following section, dealing with the happenings at
Lystra, shows the immediate reaction (in favour of the
Apostles) among the pagans. It was only afterwards, at the
instigation of Jewish opponents, that they were thrown out
of the city.

B. STORY

While the Christians at Antioch, who now included Paul,
were praying, the Holy Ghost said to them: "Separate me
Saul and Barnabas, for the work whereunto I have taken
them" (13. 2), and the other Christians fasted and prayed

[Photo by W. F. Mansell]

THE CONVERSION OF ST PAUL, AFTER A PAINTING BY MURILLO

(*Acts* 9)

and imposed their hands upon them. Some have seen in this a consecration of them as Bishops, like the imposition of hands at the ordination to the Diaconate (6. 6). But Paul certainly already had the authority of an Apostle, and Barnabas seems also to have been looked upon as such; it is more likely to have been just a way of calling down God's blessing on the work they were about to do.

So Paul and Barnabas set off, and reached Cyprus, where they preached in the Jewish synagogues. The Roman Governor of Cyprus, called a "Proconsul", which was the correct title of the Governor of a "Senatorial Province" (cf. Historical Background, 1. b.), heard of their preaching and sent for them. A certain Jew, however, who practised magic, "a false prophet", tried "to turn away the proconsul from the faith" (13. 8). Paul tells him that God will blind him for a time for doing this, and this indeed happens, and of course the Proconsul's faith was made still stronger. In this story we have all the elements of what so often happened: the revelation of Christ is preached to the Jews, and the Gentiles are then also permitted to hear it; this causes jealousy on the part of the Jews who then try to wreck ("sabotage") the work of the Apostles by turning people against them. In the case of this Proconsul, Sergius Paulus, the victory lay with the Apostles.

Paul and Barnabas then sailed across to Asia Minor and came to Antioch in Pisidia. Here they were invited to address the people in the synagogue: "Ye men brethren, if you have any word of exhortation to make to the people, speak" (Acts 13. 15). "Then Paul rising up, and with his hand bespeaking silence" (v. 16), preached to them. He took a similar line to that taken by Stephen in his great speech (Acts 7), and going over the history of the Old Testament, showed how Israel's hope for the Saviour of Israel, to be born into their own people, was fulfilled in Christ: but "they that inhabited Jerusalem, and the rulers thereof, not knowing him, nor the voices of the prophets, which are read every sabbath, judging him, have fulfilled them" (13. 27), that is, the fact of his death is itself a fulfilment of the prophecies of the Old Testament. But his Resurrection was also a fulfilment of prophecy, and there are many "who to this present are his witnesses" (13. 31). And Paul then concluded thus: "Be it known therefore to you, men brethren, that through him forgiveness of sin is preached to you" (13. 38).

This then was the Apostles' message, the preaching of Christ, which the people wished to hear again the next Sabbath. Next week, however, as we saw, many Gentiles came to hear this preaching, and the Jews, jealous of the Apostles' success began to turn the multitudes against them, and "stirred up religious and honourable women, and chief men of the city, and raised persecution against Paul and Barnabas; and cast them out of their coasts" (13. 50). It was an ingenious plan first to stir up the women, and thus turn the chief men against them.

From Antioch they passed on to Iconium, where again after successful preaching, "unbelieving Jews stirred up and incensed the minds of the Gentiles against the brethren" (14. 2). And they fled to Lystra.

C. Details

13. 1   Barnabas among the doctors and prophets at Antioch. In section 13 we studied the position of the "prophets" in the early Church. Doctors of course means teachers. Barnabas is named first as the delegate of the mother-church at Jerusalem.

"Manahen who was foster-brother of Herod": that is, he either had received milk from the same nurse, or else been his playmate as a child.

13. 5   "John also in the ministry": this is John Mark, who returned to Jerusalem when they went on to

Antioch, and who was cousin to Barnabas as we read in Col. 4. 10. It was at his mother's house that Peter sheltered after his escape (Acts 12. 12), so perhaps this was Barnabas' sister.

13. 8 "Elymas the magician (for so his name is interpreted)" probably an Arabic name.

13. 9 "Saul, otherwise Paul": St Luke's first use of his name Paul.

SECTION 16: HAPPENINGS AT LYSTRA
(Acts 14. 6–27)

A. SIGNIFICANCE

The interest of this section is the purely pagan reaction to Paul and Barnabas: they cried out: "The gods are come down to us, in the likeness of men". The whole thing was brought to a rapid end by Jews coming from Antioch and Iconium and "persuading the multitude, and stoning Paul" (14. 18).

B. STORY

It began with a miracle, very similar to that of Peter and John (Acts 3. 1–7), the cure of a lame man who had never been able to walk. But whereas at Jerusalem the Jewish on-lookers had listened to the Christian message, and "many of them who had heard the word, believed" (4. 1), here amongst the pagans, the immediate reaction was to take them for gods, come down in the likeness of men; and they called Barnabas Jupiter or Zeus, and Paul Mercury or Hermes "because he was the chief speaker" (14. 11), elo-quence being a gift of Hermes, the messenger of Zeus the chief deity of the Greek pagans. Then the pagan priest of Zeus-outside-the-city arrived to offer sacrifice to the god who had appeared on earth. There was apparently a temple outside the walls of the town dedicated to Zeus, which therefore bore this name, just as in Rome the Basilica dedicated to St Paul is known as "St Paul's outside the walls". This priest had brought oxen and garlands (decorating the oxen) for a sacrifice. But Barnabas and Paul, rending their clothes as a sign in the Jewish manner of their horror, "leaped out among the people crying, and saying: 'Ye men, why do ye these things? We also are mortals, men like unto you, preaching to you to be converted from these vain things, to the living God, who made the heaven, and the earth, and the sea, and all things that are in them . . . filling our hearts with food and gladness'" (14. 13–14, 16).

Here was the direct preaching to the pagan Gentiles, explaining to them something of the One True God, who was to be worshipped in the place of "these vain things" that were the imaginary gods of the Greeks, by which they tried to express their idea of what was divine and supernatural. Nevertheless, "they scarce restrained the people from sacrificing to them" (14. 17).

At this point there arrived some Jews from Antioch and Iconium where the Jewish influence had already driven out the Apostles, and "persuading the multitude, and stoning Paul, drew him out of the city, thinking him to be dead" (14. 18). From the text we understand that it was the Jews themselves who attacked Paul, and we do not know how much they really influenced the Gentile crowd, although a crowd in the state of excitement that is shown by the sudden desire for a public sacrifice may easily have been swayed one way and then the other, for the Apostles and then against them.

The Christians of Lystra went out, presumably to bury him, but he recovered and got up, and the next day got away to Derbe with Barnabas. They then returned to Antioch in Syria, whence they had started, after passing back through the cities they had visited on the way out, and they "related what great things God had done with them, and how he had opened the door of faith to the Gentiles" (14. 26).

C. DETAILS

v. 10 "In the Lycaonian tongue": a dialect of which very little is known: probably a corrupted Greek with many foreign words in it. Presumably the Apostles did not understand, or they would have protested before the sacrifice was prepared. They would have spoken in Greek themselves, which was understood by everyone.

v. 22 As they passed back through the cities, they "ordained to them priests" "χειροτονήσαντες πρεσβυτέρους", i.e. they appointed elders: appointed, literally, by voting with the raised hand, or possibly, by laying on of hands. These small groups of Christians had by now to have their own priests. Later in the first century the word πρεσβύτεροι, presbyters, was regularly used for Christian priests.

(30)   SECTION 17: THE COUNCIL OF
                JERUSALEM (Acts 15. 1–35)

A. SIGNIFICANCE

Until the Missionary journey which we have just been studying, the only case of a Gentile asking for admission into the Church had been that of Cornelius, who had himself sent for Peter, and already worshipped the true God. The problem of whether Cornelius was rightfully admitted into the Church although he was not a Jew, had been raised at the time: the Jewish Christians had protested: "Why didst thou go in to men uncircumcised?" (11. 3), and St Peter had defended his action. But now, after the journey of St Paul, on which he had received many entirely pagan converts, the question was raised afresh, and some Jewish Christians had gone down to Antioch from Jerusalem, and "taught the brethren: That except you be circumcised after the manner of Moses, you cannot be saved" (15. 1). This meant that if Gentiles were going to become Christians, they must needs first be circumcised and thus become members of the Jewish people. On this matter "Paul and Barnabas had no small contest with them" (15. 2), and indeed Paul had but recently said in the synagogue at Antioch in Pisidia, on his missionary journey, in that speech that made so much impression in the city (13. 38–39): "Be it known therefore to you, men brethren, that through him (Jesus) forgiveness of sin is preached to you: and from all the things, from which you could not be justified by the law of Moses, in him everyone that believeth is justified". St Paul had therefore already clearly stated that Christ justified men, that is brought them to everlasting life, while the law of Moses of itself could not. St Peter had declared earlier still, while defending himself before the Sanhedrin: "Neither is there salvation in any other" (4. 12). It was therefore decided to hold a meeting to discuss the point, and come to a decision. This gathering has been known as the "Council of Jerusalem", as indeed it was the first Council of the Church. As a result of the Council a decree was published, which made the issue quite clear to all Christians, and the decree favoured the view of Peter, Paul, and Barnabas, with a proviso added at the request of James, the Bishop of Jerusalem about foods forbidden by the Law of Moses. The way that the Council arrived at their decisions is the object of our study in this section. This decree was the first decision taken officially by the Church, and then published for the guidance of the faithful, and it is important to note the lead taken by St Peter in the discussion.

B. STORY

It was agreed at Antioch, after the dissension about the necessity of circumcision (that is, incorporation into the Jewish people) for Christians, that "Paul and Barnabas, and certain others of the other side, should go up to the apostles and priests to Jerusalem, about this question" (15. 2). This is presumably the visit of St Paul to Jerusalem which he refers to in his Epistle to the Galatians: "Then after four-teen years, I went up again to Jerusalem with Barnabas, taking Titus also with me" (Gal. 2. 1). These fourteen years appear in our chronology of the life of St Paul (in the Inter-lude above), as roughly between his visit to Jerusalem after escaping from Damascus on his return from Arabia about A.D. 37, and the year 49, after the first missionary journey, taking parts of a year as a year. It is to be noted that he took with him the young Titus, who was a Gentile Greek con-vert, and therefore uncircumcised. He brought him ap-parently as a living example of the fruit of his work among the Gentiles. On their way to Jerusalem they called on various Christian communities, and their story of the beginnings of the conversion of the Gentiles "caused great joy to all the brethren" (Acts 15. 3).

The party who held that before a Gentile could become a Christian he must first become a Jew, were themselves Christian converts from Pharisaism ("Some of the sect of the Pharisees that believed" (15. 5)), and are often referred to as the "Judaizers", or those who would "make people into Jews", following St Paul's phrase: "πῶς τὰ ἔθνη ἀναγκάζεις Ἰουδαΐζειν;": "Why do you compel the Gentiles to 'judaize'?" (Gal. 2. 14).

The discussion at the Council went on these lines:—

JUDAIZERS: Gentiles must be circumcised, and com-manded to observe the law of Moses (Acts 15. 5).

PETER: By my mouth Gentiles have heard the Gospel, and believed (a reference to Cornelius): and God made no difference between them and us (Jewish converts), for he sent them equally the Holy Ghost. Let us not therefore put on the Gentiles the yoke of the Law of

Moses, which we ourselves find difficult to bear. Both we and they are saved by the grace of Christ (v. 7-11).

PAUL and BARNABAS tell of the conversions they made among the Gentiles on their recent journey (v. 12).

JAMES: Let us not therefore disturb the Gentile converts: but let us just ask them not to touch food that has been offered in a pagan temple, or food that is unclean to the Jews, and not to follow the widespread vicious practice of the pagans in disrespecting marriage by "free love" or fornication: for all these things are an abomination to the Jewish brethren (v. 13-21).

As the trouble had begun in Antioch, Paul and Barnabas were commissioned to go to Antioch, together with Judas and Silas, and there to make known these decisions. To assist them, the Apostles and the priests or ancients drew up a letter addressed: "*To the Brethren of the Gentiles that are at Antioch and in Syria and Cilicia*" (v. 23). In this letter they explained that by the authority of the Holy Ghost and their own authority as Apostles of Christ ("It hath seemed good to the Holy Ghost and to us" v. 28), no further burden (as Circumcision) would be laid upon them, except for the prohibitions suggested by St James. The letter was very gladly received by the the Gentile Christians at Antioch, who were now no longer worried by the Judaizers' idea that they must first submit to the Law of Moses before they could submit to Christ.

But here we must add a note. If we accept the order of events in the Epistle to the Galatians, and take them as referring to the Council of Jerusalem and the time immediately following, it appears that the Decree addressed to the Gentiles in Antioch did not put an end to the trouble. St Peter seems to have visited Antioch, and mixed freely with the Gentile Christians, according to the arrangements of the Council. But when a group of Jewish Christians came from

Jerusalem, still observing all the strictness of the Mosaic Law (for the Decree of the Council had not touched them), Peter drew back from the company of the Gentiles, for fear of shocking the Jewish Christians. Now although Peter had first made contact with the Gentiles (in the case of Cornelius), and had supported Paul at the Council against the Judaizers, yet here for the sake of these Jews, he pretended to behave entirely as a Jew would. St Paul tells us that "to his dissimulation (that is, pretence) the rest of the Jews consented" (Gal. 2. 12). So Paul says: "I withstood him to the face, because he was to be blamed" (Gal. 2. 11). St Paul seems to have won his point, showing that if the Gentiles need not live as Jews, so neither need the Jewish Christians do so, "knowing that man is not justified by the works of the Law, but by the faith of Jesus Christ" (Gal. 2. 16). And from this time we hear no more of the difficulty with the Judaizers, and St Paul himself, saying how he brought Titus the Greek with him to Jerusalem, adds: "But neither Titus, who was with me, being a Gentile, was compelled to be circumcised" (Gal. 2. 3).

C. DETAILS

v. 2   "Apostles and priests": Priests is again "presbyters" or elders or "ancients" (as it is translated in Acts 11. 30), as in the last section in 14. 22. These presbyters had a rank already in the Church, but were probably not yet distinct from the Bishops.

v. 7   Peter reappears in the Acts for this Council. If in 12. 17, when he "went into another place", he went to Rome, he must have returned for this meeting, and presumably visited Antioch on the way back to Rome.

v. 12   "And all the multitude held their peace" after Peter had spoken, but when he had risen to speak it was "when there had been much disputing" (v. 7).

v. 13 James, the Less, who has always been counted as the first Bishop of Jerusalem, and when he appears in the Acts, it is always with a special connexion with Jerusalem, and in a position of authority there. In 12. 17 Peter wants him to know of his movements, and singles him out: "Tell these things to James and to the brethren". Here he takes a leading part in the discussion. In 21. 18 Paul visits him in particular at Jerusalem. He is the author of the Epistle of James.

v. 23 Silas, who afterwards became the companion of St Paul, and is mentioned several times as his companion by St Paul in his Epistles, but under his Latin name of Silvanus. (This is another example of a Hebrew and Latin name both in use by the same person.)

Note i.—The position and authority of Peter at this Council will be discussed in the Interlude that follows, on the Councils. His relation and unity with Paul will be studied later in a further Interlude.

Note ii.—We have here supposed that the Epistle to the Galatians is referring to the Council, and to a dispute at Antioch after it. Some authors hold, however, that this Epistle was written earlier than the Council, and that both Paul's visit to Jerusalem recounted there, and the dispute at Antioch with Peter took place before the Council of Jerusalem.

(31)   INTERLUDE ON COUNCILS OF THE CHURCH

WHAT IS A COUNCIL?

After our study of the Council of Jerusalem, which was the first gathering at which a decree of the Church was published, it would be useful to understand something of the great Councils of the Church, which have been held at intervals ever since to decide points of importance to the Church, and to see how much they have in common with this first Council of the Church in New Testament times.

First of all we must understand that the Church has the right, and the authority from God to teach the faithful in matters of faith and morals: in other words, in order to be Christians we must think like Christians, that is, we must believe certain things about God and about Christ (*Christian Faith*), and also we must behave like Christians, that is, we must follow the teaching of Christ in our conduct and our relations with others (this is *Christian Morality*).

Now the Church is a divine institution, but is composed of human members, and these human members need study and discussion to find out what exactly are the elements of Christian Faith and Christian Morality. This study and discussion in the Church is guided by those whom Christ put over the Church, and these at the beginning were the Apostles, with Peter at their head, and afterwards were their successors, the Bishops, with the Pope at their head. It is important to understand that the teaching authority of the Church lies with the Bishops, with the Bishop of Rome at their head. That is why every Bishop is at once called "Dr So-and-so", because "Doctor" just means Teacher. This continuity of the teaching authority of the Apostles among the Bishops, with their authority thus coming from Christ himself, was already an accepted notion at the end of the first century and early in the second: St Clement (third successor of St Peter) already wrote (Letter to Corinthians 44. 2) of the Apostles that they "appointed Bishops, so that when they should pass away, other approved men should take on their duties": and St Ignatius of Antioch: "It is necessary that whatever you do, you must do nothing without the Bishop, but you must be subject to the Priesthood as to the Apostles of Jesus Christ" (Letter to the Trallians 2. 2), and: "The Bishops appointed to the regions of the earth, are by the will of Jesus Christ" (Letter to Ephesians 3. 2). St Ignatius, writing a few years later than St Clement, wrote shortly before the year A.D. 107.

The body of Bishops in the Church, the successors of the Apostles, is known as the *Hierarchy*, and at intervals in the history of the Church they have met in order to decide what exactly is the revealed teaching of Christ, and what therefore they, as the teaching authority in the Church, must put forward as the true standards of Christian Faith and Morality. Such meetings are called *Councils*. A Council of the Church can therefore be described as a "Legitimate gathering of the Hierarchy, in order to judge and decide affairs of the Church", that is, chiefly matters of Christian Faith and Morals.

If it is a Council in which the whole Hierarchy of the Church is to take part, it is then called an Œcumenical Council (οἰκουμένη means the "inhabited world", from οἰκέω "to inhabit", from οἶκος "a house"); and nowadays can only be called together by the head of the whole Hierarchy, which is the Bishop of Rome or the Pope.[1] A Provincial Council or "Synod" is a local gathering of Bishops, called by the chief Bishop in the district.

ITS AUTHORITY

From what has been said of the Hierarchy as the teaching authority in the Church, it is clear that a Decree of an Œcumenical Council is really and truly the voice of the Church, and therefore contains the teaching of Christ, and binds all the faithful to obedience. Christ himself, after telling the Apostles to go and teach all nations, said (Mt. 28. 20): "Behold I am with you all days, even to the consummation of the world", clearly implying that he would be with them as teachers. Also when he gave the promise of the Holy Spirit, he said (Jn. 16. 13): "When he, the Spirit of Truth,

---

[1] Nowadays: *i.e.* according to Modern Church Law (canon 222). In history, however, we find the early Œcumenical Councils called by the Roman Emperors, but with the consent or at least the acquiescence of the Pope, and his confirmation of the decrees.

is come, he will teach you all truth" (*cf*. earlier Interlude on the Person of the Holy Ghost). Modern Church Law puts it concisely: "Christ the Lord entrusted the 'Deposit of Faith' to the Church, so that she, with the constant help of the Holy Spirit, should guard the revealed doctrine as a sacred trust, and faithfully expound it" (Codex of Canon Law, canon 1322, § 1). With regard to the manner in which the Church puts forward these doctrines, the Church Law further says: "To make such solemn decree belongs either to an Œcumenical Council or to the Roman Pontiff (the Pope) when he speaks 'ex cathedra'" (*i.e.* when he speaks precisely *as* Head of the Hierarchy) (canon 1323, § 2).

Since, therefore, an Œcumenical Council, being a gathering of the whole of the Hierarchy, represents the whole Church, and its decrees therefore represent the teaching of the Church, it is obvious that these decrees are infallible (*i.e.* can contain no error), and have complete authority on earth and claim an entire obedience from the faithful, in an equal manner with the "ex cathedra" pronouncements of the Pope.

The Pope's Part

The Pope's part in such a gathering of the teaching authority of the Church, is that of the Chief Bishop, or head of the Hierarchy. Since it belongs to the head to call the gathering, no such Council called nowadays without his approval can possibly be valid. (This also applies to Local Councils of Bishops, which must obviously have the approval of the Head of the Hierarchy). Further, it is necessary that the decrees of an Œcumenical Council be not only approved by the Pope, but that they be published only by his authority (canon 227). Thus an Œcumenical Council, because it is the voice of the teaching authority of the Church, is in itself infallible, but it also needs the confirmation of the Head of the Hierarchy, who has himself taken part in the Council (and must take part, at least through his delegates: canon 222).

The Council of Jerusalem

This Council cannot be considered Œcumenical, for not only was the Hierarchy (at that time the Apostles) not present complete, but the matter only concerned a particular situation: that of Gentiles who were being persuaded to become Jews by the Judaizers. But it has all the elements of a local Council: it was a gathering of the Hierarchy at Jerusalem, and Peter, who had previously gone "into another place" (Acts 12. 17), came in order to be present as Head of the Hierarchy. Further after the "much disputing" was over, it was Peter who formulated the point that was to be decided. After James, as the local Bishop, had added another point, the decree was drawn up, and published by the body of the Apostles (which included Peter, the Head). That this decision of the Hierarchy was put forward with authority as the teaching of God, is shown by the phrase: "It hath seemed good to the Holy Ghost and to us" (15. 28).

Other Councils

In the history of the Church there have been so far no less than twenty Œcumenical Councils, at which the whole Hierarchy of the Church has been represented. The first one was at Nicaea (in Asia Minor) in the year 325, after the Christian Religion had been freed in the Roman Empire by the Emperor Constantine, who himself attended the Council. The "Nicene Creed" was drawn up at this Council. The 19th Œcumenical Council was the longest and drew up the greatest number of decrees, and this was the great Council of Trent, at the time of the Reformation (1545–1563). The last Œcumenical Council, known as the Vatican Council, opened in 1869, but within a year had to be interrupted, and although the important decree about the Infallibility of the Pope was passed, this Council is still unfinished.

(32)   SECTION 18: SECOND MISSIONARY
         JOURNEY; HAPPENINGS AT PHILIPPI
                  (Acts 15. 36–17. 14)

A. SIGNIFICANCE

This missionary tour began as a journey for the purpose
of re-visiting the places that Paul had preached in on the
previous tour, but when they reached Troas (on the western
coast of Asia Minor, facing Greece), Paul had a dream in
which a Macedonian appeared and said: "Pass over into
Macedonia, and help us" (16. 9). Paul realised that this was
the will of God, and went, and thus *the Gospel passed over
into Europe.*

At Philippi in Macedonia, Paul and his companion Silas
were put into prison, but the prison was opened by an
earthquake, and the situation became awkward for the
governor, when, for the first time, they claimed their Roman
citizenship.

After further preaching in Macedonia, the Apostles went
on to Athens, the centre of the Gentile-Greek world, and
preached there. His preaching at Athens will be the subject
of the next section.

We must also note as an important feature of the present
part of his journey the first of the "WE-passages". The
author of the Acts, relating the voyage from Troas to
Philippi (16. 10–17), writes: "we sought to go into Macedonia . . . . we came . . . to Philippi, we were in this city
some days", showing that for this section of the journey the
author accompanied Paul and Silas. There are three such
passages in the Acts, where St Luke uses "We". The
others are later on, on a return journey from Philippi
to Troas, and again on St Paul's journey to Rome as a
prisoner.

[Photo E.N.A.

THE GATE OF ST PAUL, IN TARSUS

11

The "WE-passages"—

   (1) Chapter 16. 10–17, Troas to Philippi (here).

   (2) Chapter 20. 5–21. 18, Philippi to Troas.

   (3) Chapters 27–28, Caesarea to Rome.

   (See also further notes in the Interlude on the Person of St Luke)

B. STORY

The story here moves rapidly. Paul and Barnabas, at Antioch after the Council of Jerusalem, decide to "return and visit our brethren in all the cities wherein we have preached" (15. 36). On their last journey Paul and Barnabas had taken Mark with them, but he had accompanied them only to Cyprus (13. 13). Barnabas wanted Mark to come again, but Paul wanted someone who would be prepared to travel farther, and so Barnabas and Mark made a short journey to Cyprus, and Paul chose another companion in the person of Silas, also called Silvanus, who became his colleague for long afterwards.

Paul and Silas therefore left *Antioch* and toured through the cities where Paul had preached before, publishing the decrees "that were decreed by the apostles and ancients who were at Jerusalem" (16. 4). At this time is introduced a disciple from Asia Minor named Timothy, son of a Jewish mother and Gentile father, from Lystra. He became a very close friend of St Paul, was later made Bishop of Ephesus at the command of St Paul (1 Tim. 1. 3: "I desired thee to remain at Ephesus when I went into Macedonia, that thou mightest charge some not to teach otherwise"), and to whom St Paul addressed two personal letters, with careful directions as to how he was to govern. On this journey Paul would have Timothy "to go along with him" (16. 3), and he applied the principle of the Council of Jerusalem that the Law of Moses did not bind the Gentiles,

but did continue to bind the Jews, or at least the Jews even
if they kept it themselves might not impose it on the Gentiles. So because Timothy was of Jewish blood, Paul insisted on his being circumcised "because of the Jews who
were in those places". On the contrary he tells us that Titus,
who was a Gentile, was not circumcised) Gal. 2. 3).

When they reached *Troas*, where St Luke joined them,
Paul had this dream of a Macedonian "standing and be-
seeching him" (16. 9), and immediately they left for Macedonia, "being assured that God had called us to preach the
Gospel to them" (16. 10). So they reached *Philippi*, where
they stayed in the house of a new convert lady named Lydia.
Before long, however, they were brought to the magistrates,
and denounced as Jewish disturbers of the peace. The men
who had them arrested were the masters of a slave-girl,
whom they used to use to make money because of her
capacities in magic, "a pythonical spirit", and out of whom
this spirit had been cast by Paul. The loss of revenue to her
masters gave them a case against Paul.

A riot was then caused in the city, and Paul and Silas
were thrown into prison. At midnight, while Paul and Silas
were praying, suddenly there was an earthquake and the
prison-doors were opened. The gaoler was terrified, but
Paul cried out that he had not run away. The gaoler, who had
been about to kill himself, because of the supposed escape
of the prisoners, came up to Paul and was instructed in the
Christian Faith. "Masters, what must I do, that I may be
saved?" he asked (16. 30): "Believe in the Lord Jesus",
they replied, and presently the gaoler was baptised with all
his family at home.

The magistrates then wished to let Paul and Silas go
quietly but they pointed out the serious mistake that had
been made: "They have beaten us publicly, uncondemned,
men that are Romans, and have cast us into prison: and now
do they thrust us out privately? Not so, but let them come

and let us out themselves" (16. 37–38). This was the first claim of a Christian to be a Roman citizen and therefore immune from such treatment. The magistrates did not know before that these men were Roman citizens, and now were very much afraid, for the authorities of Rome had sometimes given severe punishment to governors who had in this way violated the rights of a Roman citizen. There was an instance of the punishment of the whole free state of the Island of Rhodes, for the execution of Roman citizens. The magistrates therefore came in person to Paul and Silas, and "besought them" (16. 39), imploring them to hush up the affair.

Paul and Silas then agreed to leave the city quietly, and moved on to *Thessalonica*, where they preached in the synagogue. The situation that followed was very similar to that which had arisen earlier at Antioch, on the first journey (section 15): many Jews believed, many Gentiles friendly to Judaism or already converts or proselytes, and many pagans ("of the Gentiles a great multitude", 17. 4). But here again the Jews "moved with envy" (17. 5), organised a riot and accused the Apostles of disturbing the peace, and of "saying that there is another king, Jesus" (17. 7). They had been staying at Thessalonica with a friend named Jason, who apparently went bail for them on this occasion, *i.e.* paid a sum to the magistrate for their release: "Having taken satisfaction of Jason . . . they let them go" (17. 9).

They therefore escaped to the city of *Berea*, about fifty miles away, where they were very well received. "These were more noble than those in Thessalonica, who received the word with all eagerness, daily searching the scriptures, whether these things were so" (17. 11). Thessalonian Jews followed them however, and the brethren there immediately sent Paul away to Athens, although Silas and Timothy (who had been accompanying them) remained at Berea.

C. DETAILS

16. 20 "magistrates": στρατηγοί, the two officers in charge of the Roman colony at Philippi.

16. 35 "serjeants": ῥαβδοῦχοι or rod-bearers, lictors who carried before the magistrates the bundles of rods "fasces", which were the symbol of their authority. These municipal magistrates were entitled to two lictors.

17. 5 Who was this Jason with whom they had been staying at Thessalonica? We do not know. It was a name common both among Greeks and Hellenistic Jews. Some writers think he is the same as the kinsman of St Paul of this name mentioned in Rom. 16. 21.

(33)   SECTION 19: ST PAUL AT ATHENS
              (Acts 17. 15-34)

A. SIGNIFICANCE

The importance of St Paul's visit to Athens is his contact with what was undoubtedly the intellectual capital of the Greek-speaking world. All the new ideas that went about the ancient world appeared some time at Athens and were examined by the Athenians who still retained their inborn love of philosophy and speculation in thought. With St Paul came the Christian idea, and it was examined by the Athenians like any other philosophy of life.

So far we have seen St Paul speaking either to Jews, or to groups of Gentiles in the Provinces, attracted through contact with Jews. Only once so far have we read of close meeting with real pagan religion (when at Lystra they were taken for gods: section 16). Here he met with Greek pagans who worshipped all the Greek gods, but also with Greek philosophers who were trying to work out a religion that was according to man's reason, that would bring happiness to man, and that was actually independent of the ordinary pagan Greek system of many gods. St Paul, a man of great culture and education, knew his Greek literature, and knew how to approach the Athenians: his manner of presenting the Gospel here is quite different from his usual style. This visit is the history of the first meeting of Christianity with the world of the Greek philosophers.

B. STORY

Paul was brought by Christian friends to Athens from Berea, while Timothy and Silas stayed behind. He then sent them a message "that they should come to him with all speed" (Acts 17. 15), but apparently they did not catch him up until he had already moved on from Athens to Corinth (18. 5 at Corinth, "When Silas and Timothy were come from Macedonia").

According to his custom, Paul first went to the Jewish community, which included "those that served God", *i.e.* Gentiles who practised the Jewish religion, and he "disputed therefore in the synagogue".

At Athens it had long been the practice for various speakers, especially philosophers, to speak publicly in the market-place or ἀγορά and explain their doctrines. It was the delight of the Athenians to pass through the market-place and listen, and their curiosity and constant desire to hear something new was proverbial. Even St Luke remarks on this (Acts 17. 21): "Now all the Athenians, and strangers that were there, employed themselves in nothing else but either in telling or in hearing some new thing". On one side of this market-place was a portico or arcade, στοά, where people could meet and discuss. One special group of philosophers used always to meet here, and hence were called the "Stoics"; they looked to Zeno the philosopher as their founder, who had lived in the early third century B.C. The school of the Stoics was still flourishing at the time of St Paul, and the only other notable school of philosophy in Athens at the time was that of the Epicureans, called after their founder Epicurus who lived at about the same time as Zeno. Both these parties are mentioned in the Acts (17. 18): "And certain philosophers of the Epicureans and the Stoics disputed with him". The other great Athenian schools of philosophy, the Peripatetics, followers of Aristotle, and the Academicians, followers of Plato, were of smaller importance at the time of St Paul.

Both the Stoics and the Epicureans were trying to discover the secret of human happiness. Both agreed that this was to be found in the practice of Virtue (ἡ ἀρετή), but for the Epicureans on the one hand this meant the full enjoyment of the things of this world, that is, the feelings and desires of our nature were deliberately to be followed, and thus peace of mind was to be attained. In modern English we therefore say of a man who is much interested in matters of eating and drinking that he is an "epicure". For the Stoics, on the other hand, Virtue meant the complete detachment from all things of this world, by which such peace of mind was to be attained that one remained entirely indifferent to anything that happened, whether it should bring one pain or pleasure. Hence in modern English we say of a man who bears pain and trouble without a murmur that he is a "stoic". Neither of these schools believed that man had an after-life, because the highest ideal for both was the attainment of happiness in this world: so when St Paul spoke to them of the Resurrection, "some indeed mocked" (17. 32), but others were interested in something so new.

Now St. Paul, after talking with the Jews in the synagogue, went, like any other philosopher, and spoke "in the market-place every day with them that were there" (17. 17). Of the fashionable philosophers at the time, the Stoics and Epicureans, some, arguing with him, just considered him a "prater" (thus does the Westminster Version translate σπερμολόγος, which is apparently Athenian slang, properly of a bird that gathers seed, used of an empty speaker, a "word-sower"); while others considered him to be "a setter forth of new gods", or strange gods unfamiliar to Athens (17. 18). Such was their reaction in the market-place to St. Paul's preaching about Jesus and the Resurrection.

"And taking him they brought him to the Areopagus" (17. 19). The Areopagus, ὁ Ἄρειος πάγος, the hill of Ares, the god of war, whom the Romans called Mars, was one of the four hills of Athens which flanked the market-place (the others being the Acropolis, the Pnyx and the Museum). The Areopagus was the meeting-place of those who formed the highest court of justice in Athens, who were called Areopagites, and who apparently also had much control in the administration of the city. Probably this body had only a few members, and these had to be of noble birth and to be over sixty years old.

It is not clear from the text who took St Paul to the Areopagus, or why; but it is evident that they wanted more details about the doctrine he had been preaching in the market-place. Some writers think that St Paul was cited before the very tribunal of the Areopagus itself; but it is more probable that these elders of the city (whose interest it was to safeguard religion as well as law and order in the city), wanted more precise information on this new thing that was being preached to the citizens, and invited Paul to come and explain. "May we know what this new doctrine is which thou speakest of? For thou bringest in certain new things to our ears. We would know therefore what these things mean" (17. 19–20).

So St Paul addresses the gathering on the Areopagus, either just the Areopagites, or also those they may have invited. He begins in the usual style of the orators: "Ye men of Athens" (17. 22). He knows that he has been accused of introducing new gods: but he proceeds to show that not only is this not so, but on the contrary, the One True God whom he is preaching they have been worshipping in Athens without knowing it: the God who is "Lord of heaven and earth" (17. 24), and this God they should seek, and this God is now declaring himself through St Paul's preaching, that men may do penance, because this God will one day judge the world by "the Man whom he hath appointed" (17. 31), that is, Our Lord Jesus Christ, whom, however, he does not mention by name, but only says that God "raised him up from the dead". This is the doctrine he was preaching, the doctrine of the One True God, and "the Man whom he hath appointed" and also raised from the dead.

St Paul well knew how to say all this to an Athenian audience: "I behold you", he began, "in all respects not a little religious. For as I was passing along and noticing the objects of your worship, I found also an altar bearing the inscription *ΑΓΝΩΣΤΩ ΘΕΩ*, TO THE UNKNOWN GOD" (17. 22–23, in the Westminster Version). You are religious, because you have been worshipping the True God without knowing it. But this God is "not far from any one of us: *for in him we live and move and have our being*: as also some of your poets have said: *for we are his very offspring*" (17. 27–28, in the Westminster Version). Both quotations are from Greek poets, the first from Epimenides (a Cretan who lived around 600 B.C.) in his *Minos* (a poem lost to us in the original Greek), and the second from Aratus (a Cilician who lived around 270 B.C.) in his *Phaenomena*. We must therefore "not suppose the divinity to be like unto gold or silver, or stone" (17. 29). But now the time of ignorance is at an end, and mankind is called to penance and the recognition of the True God, because he will come to judge the world "by the Man whom he hath appointed", giving faith to all, by raising him up from the dead" (17. 31).

The reaction of his hearers was that some laughed, but

others said: "We will hear thee again concerning this matter" (17. 32); and so St Paul left them, but a few men accepted his doctrine and believed, and one of the Areopagites is specially mentioned: Dionysius or Denis: and he is said to have become the first Bishop of the Christians at Athens, and to have died a martyr.

C. DETAILS

v. 28 Epimenides is again quoted by St Paul in the famous passage in the Epistle to Titus, who had been appointed Bishop of Crete, when he writes (Tit. I. 12), "One of them . . . said: *The Cretans are always liars, evil beasts, slothful bellies*".

v. 33 Denis the Areopagite was later wrongly identified with St Denis who was the first Bishop of Paris about A.D. 250 and a martyr, and is one of the Patrons of France. He is also not the same as the author of the famous mystical works, *De caelesti hierarchia* and others (from which we get much of our theology of the Angels), written under his name in the fifth century. This author is now usually referred to as the "Pseudo-Dionysius".

(34) SECTION 20: ST PAUL AT CORINTH: RETURN TO ANTIOCH
(Acts 18. 1–22; Epistles to the Thessalonians)

A. SIGNIFICANCE

St Paul's visit to Athens stands out as an exceptional sort of ministry in St Paul's general work: it was an approach to the Greek philosophical mind that was found at Athens. Now he moves on to Corinth, again a Greek city, but as cosmopolitan or mixed in population as most of the great cities of the Empire at the time, and Paul's apostolate returns to the same kind as he had been engaged on before, as "he reasoned in the synagogue every sabbath, bringing in the name of the Lord Jesus, and he persuaded the Jews and the Greeks" (18. 4).

For the first time on his missionary journeys he made here at Corinth a long stay, and stayed for one and a half years. During this period he founded here a really settled Christian community chiefly among the Jews, and the Church of Corinth became soon one of the most important centres of Christian life in the whole Church. St Paul's prolonged stay in the city enabled them to develop a regular Christian life here, and the first document that we have from a Pope after St Peter is Pope St Clement's Letter to the Corinthians, in which he speaks of the honourable reputation of the Christians of Corinth in early times: "Who that hath sojourned among you hath not experienced the firmness of your faith, and its fruitfulness in all good works; admired the temper and moderation of your piety in Christ; proclaimed the magnificent spirit of your hospitality; and thought you happy in your perfect and certain knowledge of the Gospel?" (Epistle to Corinthians, chapter 1 in Dr Brownlow's translation). Such was the opinion in the Church around the year A.D. 96 of the Christians of Corinth, the Church which St Paul founded and fostered during the visit we are studying.

But it was also at this time that St Paul began writing to the other communities which he had founded before, and while he was here for that year and a half, he wrote two Letters to the community at Thessalonica, where he had been preaching before his visit to Athens (Acts 17. 1–10: section 18 of this book), and where he had made a number of converts both among the Jews and the Gentiles. In these Letters he speaks of his care and worry over them: "making remembrance of you in our prayers without ceasing" (1 Thess. 1. 2), he encourages them in the Christian Faith and Christian virtues: "We pray and beseech you in the Lord Jesus, that as you have received of us (*i.e.* as we taught you), how you ought to walk (*i.e.* behave as Christians), and to please God, so also you would walk" (1 Thess. 4. 1); "For this is the will of God, your sanctification" (4. 3); and "yourselves have learned of God to love one another; for indeed you do it towards all the brethren in all Macedonia: but we entreat you, brethren, that you abound the more" (4. 9–10). These two *Epistles to the Thessalonians*, when they are read at the same time as this period of the life of St Paul is studied, throw much light on the work and manner of St Paul: his care of his converts after he has left them, and his anxiety to solve the difficulties which arose among them after his departure. It should be noted that I and II Thessalonians are probably the first of the many Epistles that St Paul wrote to the various communities where he had preached (unless, as some hold, the Epistle to the Galatians is much earlier: *cf.* Note ii after section 17).

B. STORY

Corinth was an important trade centre, lying on the narrow isthmus which connects the northern mainland of Greece with the southern peninsula of Morea, and had two ports, the one Cenchrea on the side facing the Ægean Sea (eastwards), and the other, Lechaeum at the head of the Gulf of Corinth towards the Adriatic (westwards). Corinth was one of the biggest cities of the ancient world, and in the first century A.D. was said to count 460,000 slaves alone in its population: it was also noted in antiquity for the vice and wickedness practised there.

When St Paul arrived in Corinth he went to stay with "a certain Jew, named Aquila, born in Pontus (in Asia Minor), lately come from Italy, with Priscilla his wife" (Acts 18. 2), they had been expelled from Rome by the edict of the Emperor Claudius banishing all Jews: probably they were already Christians, and so would welcome the Apostle Paul when he came to Corinth to preach Christianity in that city. They were tent-makers by trade, and their travels to Rome, Corinth and (presently, v. 26) to Ephesus, and finally back to Rome (they are mentioned in St Paul's later Epistle to the Romans 16. 3), were probably for business purposes, since the large number of military kept under arms by the Roman Empire would have made this trade an important one. St Paul, according to the Rabbinic custom by which good Jews of every class could practise a trade, also had a trade, and it happened to be the same one of tent-making, so they worked together. In 1 Thess. 2. 9 and 11 Thess. 3. 8, St Paul speaks of his thus working for his living: "lest we should be chargeable to any of you".

St Paul in Corinth was joined by Silas and Timothy whom he had left at Berea when he went to Athens. He sent Timothy to visit the Christians in Thessalonica, either while he was here at Corinth, or while he was still at Athens. When therefore "Silas and Timothy were come from Macedonia" (Acts 18. 5) to Corinth, St Paul got the news from Thessalonica, and immediately wrote a letter to them, in which he says (1 Thess. 3. 6): "But now when Timothy came to us from you, and related to us your faith and charity, etc.". Both this and the second Epistle to the Thessalonians are written in the name of Paul and these two companions of his, beginning thus: "Paul and Sylvanus and Timothy: to the Church of the Thessalonians". (Note that St Paul uses the Roman form of Silas' name: Silvanus.)

During his long stay at Corinth, St Paul, apart from his tent-making and writing to the Thessalonians, was very active: he "was earnest in preaching, testifying to the Jews that Jesus is the Christ" (Acts 18. 5). But once more he was rejected by the Jews for his doctrine about Christ, and even brought before Gallio the Roman proconsul, who, however, refused to hear their case, saying (18. 15): "If they be questions of word and names, and of your law, look you to it: I will not be judge of such things", for "Gallio cared for none of those things" (18. 17). And once again Paul turned to the Gentiles, saying to the Jews: "Your blood be upon your own heads: I am clean: from henceforth I will go unto the gentiles" (18. 6). And after that he stayed with a certain Titus Justus, a Gentile convert, who lived next door to the synagogue. The interest of this is the fact that it was the house of this Gentile that became the Christian centre in Corinth, quite distinct from the synagogue. Probably St Paul no longer attended synagogue-services next door, but he did keep up his Jewish contacts, for the "ruler of the synagogue believed in the Lord" (18. 8). "And many of the Corinthians hearing believed, and were baptised" (18. 8), and God strengthened Paul in a dream and commanded him to go on with his preaching: "For I have much people in this city".

Finally St Paul left Corinth and sailed for Antioch in Syria, by way of Ephesus. But Paul, who was so anxious that no Jewish burdens should be laid on Gentile Christians, was zealous for Jewish practices for Jews such as himself, and towards the end of his stay at Corinth he made a vow in the Jewish manner. This meant abstention from all wine and grapes for the period of the vow, and the hair might not be cut. The rules for these vows are in the Old Testament (Num. 6. 1–21), and at the end of the "time of consecration" or the "days of separation", the head was shaved, and a sacrifice had to be offered in the temple. Paul ended his vow just before sailing, and had his head shaved at Cenchrea, the eastern port of Corinth (18. 18). He completed the vow when he visited Jerusalem from Antioch, as we read in 18. 22: "He went up, and saluted the church". This phrase can only refer to "going up" to the capital, Jerusalem, where the mother-church was still "the church" par excellence: so much so, that the Rheims Version has inserted the words "to Jerusalem". And so he "came down to Antioch" (18. 22), concluding his second great journey.

C. DETAILS

18. 2 the Edict of Claudius banishing Jews is mentioned by the Roman historian Suetonius, who also says that the reason was tumults caused by one "Chrestus" (Life of Claudius 25). This is generally believed to be a garbled reference to the presence of Christians among the Jews in Rome, and the riots may well have been anti-Christian. If there was already at this time a Christian community in Rome (perhaps converts of St Peter on his first visit? *Cf.* Acts 12. 17, and section 14 of this book), it would explain the supposition that Aquila and Priscilla were already Christians.

18. 8 "Crispus the ruler of the synagogue believed": St Paul himself baptised him, as he tells us in I Cor. 1. 14: "I baptised none of you, but Crispus and Caius".

(35) SECTION 21: THIRD MISSIONARY JOURNEY: HAPPENINGS AT EPHESUS
(Acts 18. 23–28; 19; 1 Corinthians)

A. SIGNIFICANCE

This third journey, like the previous one, involved a long stay in one place. Just as last time he made Corinth his base, and stayed there one and a half years, founding and organising the Christian community there, and staying long enough to guide its growth; so this time he stayed over two years at Ephesus, and similarly laid the foundations and guided the growth of the Christian community there.

Further, last time he chose Corinth, for it was the biggest city of Greece, and her most important harbour; so now he chose Ephesus, which was the biggest city of the Roman Province of Asia, and the chief port of the west coast of Asia Minor facing Greece. Like Corinth, after the labours of St Paul, Ephesus became a very important Christian centre, and all the early tradition of the Church tells us that the Apostle John took up his residence here after the destruction of Jerusalem in A.D. 70. The history of the foundation of these Christian centres, like Corinth and Ephesus, in New Testament times, is one of the most important elements in our study of the beginnings of the Church.

Ephesus was also important as a centre of pagan religion. The "Temple of great Diana" (19. 27) was originally a place of worship of a local Asiatic goddess, turned in these Greek times into a temple of the Greek goddess Artemis (whom the Latins called Diana). The riot that arose against Paul was begun by the devotees of this goddess, and was again a contact with real paganism.

Another important element in this stay at Ephesus was meeting with the little group who indeed called themselves "disciples" (the ordinary word for Christians at the time), but who seemed to know no more of Christianity than the Baptism of John the Baptist, which was no more than a preparation of the minds of men for the coming of Christ. Paul therefore had them baptised properly: "in the name of the Lord Jesus" (19. 5).

Lastly it should be noted that it was during his stay at Ephesus that St Paul next wrote a Letter to one of the other Christian communities: the *First Epistle to the Corinthians*. From Corinth, a year or two previously, he had written to his converts at Thessalonica (last section), and now in turn he writes to the community he had lived with at Corinth. Towards the end of this Epistle (1 Cor. 16. 8) he writes to them: "I will tarry at Ephesus until Pentecost". In the two Interludes that follow we shall study some points that St Paul explains to the Christians at Corinth in this Epistle.

[Photo E.N.A.

RELICS OF THE TEMPLE OF ARTEMIS, KNOWN TO TRAVELLERS OF ALEXANDER'S TIME AS ONE OF THE SEVEN WONDERS OF THE WORLD, AND SITUATED IN EPHESUS, WHERE ST PAUL ONCE SOJOURNED

(*Acts* 19)

The Second Epistle to the Corinthians belongs to the time he spent in Macedonia after leaving Ephesus.

B. STORY

Paul had once paid a short visit to Ephesus, on his way back from Corinth on the second journey, and "when they desired him, that he would tarry a longer time, he consented not. But taking his leave and saying: 'I will return to you again, God willing', he departed from Ephesus" (18. 20–21).

Now he set off on his third journey (apparently still with Timothy, whom he later sent into Macedonia from Ephesus (19. 22), and once more visited the friends of his first journey in Galatia and Phrygia (Asia Minor), and so made his way to Ephesus, fulfilling his promise to return.

Here he found a little group of "about twelve" (19. 7), whom he asked: "Have you received the Holy Ghost since ye believed?" But they said to him: "We have not so much as heard whether there be a Holy Ghost" (19. 2), whereat it came out that they only knew about the Baptism of John the Baptist, which, as we said above, was no more than a preparation for Christianity. They were therefore "baptised in the name of the Lord Jesus. And when Paul had imposed hands on them, the Holy Ghost came upon them, and they spoke with tongues and prophesied" (19. 5–6). Here again, as in the case of Cornelius (10. 44–46: section 12), the coming of the Holy Ghost brought with it the "Gift of Tongues", evidently here nothing to do with preaching, but rather with a special manner of praising God (*cf.* special note in section 3 on Pentecost). Such special gifts of the Holy Ghost, as the gift of tongues and prophecy, are sometimes called "Charismata" (*i.e.* special favours or graces). That the Holy Ghost was also at the time giving such "charismata" to the Christians at Corinth, is plain from the whole of chapter 14 of 1 Corinthians.

Once more St Paul began, as at Corinth, by preaching

in the synagogue, and he continued to do so for three months. The Christian message, however, was not entirely new to the Jews of Ephesus: they had already been "taught diligently the things that are of Jesus" (18. 25). This was the preaching of one *Apollo*, an important person of whom, however, we do not hear very much. He was an Alexandrian Jew, an eloquent and learned man, "mighty in the Scriptures" (18. 24), but whose Christianity when he first came to Ephesus was apparently like that of those twelve men who only knew about John the Baptist's Baptism. Priscilla and Aquila, however, who accompanied Paul as far as Ephesus on the last journey, and who were not only instructed by Paul, but probably had already been Christians in Rome before meeting him at Corinth, took the opportunity and "expounded to him the way of the Lord more diligently" (18. 26). Apollo then moved on to Corinth, and "helped them much who had believed" (18. 27). St Paul, writing to the Corinthians, mentions several times the work of Apollo there, notably when he speaks of how Apollo has continued the work that Paul himself had begun there, in the famous passage (1 Cor. 3. 6): "I have planted, Apollo watered, but God gave the increase". Apollo seems to have left Corinth again later on, but Paul was anxious that he should return and go on with his work there, for he writes in the same Epistle (1 Cor. 16. 12): "Touching our brother Apollo . . . I much entreated him to come unto you . . . he will come when he shall have leisure".

But after three months' preaching in the synagogue, Paul found that once more the Jews were turning against him, and so "he separated the disciples" (19. 9), and began teaching in a school or lecture-room "of one Tyrannus" (19. 10), probably a Gentile. This is very much the same thing as happened at Corinth, when he had to break with the synagogue there (*cf.* in last section). Here the Christians were quite deliberately "separated" from the Jews.

And here again, as at Cyprus on the first journey (section 15), and at Philippi on the second journey (section 18), St Paul comes in contact with those who practised magic (19. 13–19), and this time those who gave up their magic and believed in Christ "brought together their books and burnt them" (19. 19): a thing that has quite often happened since to books of magic, in the history of the Church.

Just before Paul left Ephesus, there was a great riot in the city. It began with the silversmiths, who made a lot of money by making small silver models of the great Temple of Artemis for the devotees of the goddess, and so objected to Paul's preaching against the pagan gods. They dragged off two of Paul's companions, and everybody began shouting "Great is Diana of the Ephesians", but "the greater part knew not for what cause they were come together" (19. 32). And when they saw that a Jew was in the middle of the tumult they all began to shout their slogan "with one voice, for the space of about two hours" (19. 34). Paul wanted to go out and speak to the crowd, but his friends would not let him. Presently, however, the town-clerk came out and calmed the multitude, chiefly by telling them that the Romans may well punish the whole city "for this day's uproar" (19. 40). So the noise stopped and everyone went home.

St Paul now decided to leave Ephesus, and go on to Macedonia.

C. Details

18. 24 the name "Apollo", in the Greek is Ἀπολλώς (so the Westminster Version always calls him "Apollos"), which is not the same name as that of Apollo the Greek god, son of Zeus, the god of music and perpetual youth, which is in Greek Ἀπόλλων. Apollos is probably an abbreviation of the name Apollodorus or Apollonius, both Greek names which might have been taken by Jews.

19. 35 "The town-clerk": γραμματεύς, *i.e.* the secretary. This was the official who came between the Roman governor of the province and the municipality. He was like a mayor, but came under the Roman "magistrates" who represented the Roman Government (*cf.* 16. 20).

(36) INTERLUDE ON UNITY OF BAPTISM
(*A propos* of 1 Cor. 1. 12–15 and 12. 12–13)

THE ONE BAPTISM IS THE BAPTISM OF CHRIST

While St Paul was at Ephesus, and Apollo had been to Corinth and apparently baptised some people there, there had begun at Corinth some rivalry and divisions between those who attached themselves to Paul and those who attached themselves to Apollo. St Paul, who always wished to be kept *au courant* of how things were going in the churches he had founded, had been duly informed of these troubles (1 Cor. 1. 11): "It hath been signified unto me . . . that there are contentions among you". When therefore he wrote to the Corinthians from Ephesus, he tried to explain to them that it is their Baptism in the name of Christ that makes them united, one in the unity of Christ, and that it does not matter who happens to have been the minister of their Baptism. This unity in the Baptism of Christ is really the key to unity amongst Christians: and the Christian Baptism, given "In the name of the Father, and of the Son, and of the Holy Ghost" is therefore given in the name of Christ, and makes us Christians. The Catechism tells us that Baptism "cleanses us from original sin, makes us Christians, children of God, and members of the Church" (n. 256). We spoke at the very beginning of our study with this book (Introduction 1.), of the way in which the idea of the Church, and our membership of it, lies at the very roots of our life as Christians. We also spoke there of the way of speaking started by St Paul, in which we think of the "body of Christians", or the body or group of men who are followers of Christ, as the "Body of Christ" (which later theologians called the doctrine of the "Mystical Body of Christ"). We even gave then the reference to this Epistle to the Corinthians (1 Cor. 12. 12–13), and we now know much more about that Epistle, and the sort of people it was written to. So it is particularly interesting, in view of the quarrels at Corinth about who had baptised them, to notice how St Paul connects this idea of his about the "Body of Christ" with the idea of Baptism, when he writes (1 Cor. 12. 12–13): "For as the body is one, and hath many members; and all the members of the body, whereas they are many, yet are one body; so also is Christ. For in one Spirit *were we all baptised into one body*". We become members of that "Body of Christ" which is the Church by being "baptised into it". Later, writing to the Christians at Ephesus, while he was staying at Corinth, he speaks in a similar manner, urging that their Christian Baptism is the foundation of their unity amongst themselves (Eph. 4. 3–5): "Careful to keep the unity of the Spirit in the bond of peace: one body and one Spirit . . . one Lord, one faith, one Baptism". Hence the ridiculousness of the divisions that he hears of at Corinth, and which he tries to correct in the Epistle to the Corinthians (1 Cor. 1. 12–13): "Every one of you saith: 'I indeed am of Paul: and I am of Apollo: and I of Cephas: and I of Christ'. Is Christ divided?" They must remember their unity in the Baptism of Christ, and not worry about who baptised them (1. 13–16): "Was Paul then crucified for you? Or were you baptised in the name of Paul? I give God thanks, that I baptised none of you, but Crispus and Caius: lest any should say that you were baptised in my name. And I baptised also the household of Stephanas: besides, I know not whether I baptised any other". Whoever baptised them, they were "baptised into one body", the Body of Christ.

THE POSITION OF PETER

Some of these Corinthians, saying: "I am of Paul, I of Cephas (*i.e.* the Aramaic name of Peter)", were imagining that the converts of Peter (of whom there were probably some among them) and the converts of Paul were different kinds of Christians. St Paul here is specially anxious to get rid of this idea. The Baptism of Peter is just as much the Baptism of Christ. As Apostles their authority is equal, as he explains (in a later Epistle) (Gal. 2. 8): "He who wrought in Peter to the apostleship of the circumcision, wrought in me also among the gentiles", and just before this (Gal. 2. 7): "To me was committed the gospel of the uncircumcision, as to Peter was that of the circumcision". The unity of Peter and Paul in the Apostolate was further shown in the unity of their Baptism. They were different "ministers of Christ, and dispensers of the mysteries of God" (1 Cor. 4. 1), and all equally devoted to preaching Christ (1 Cor. 3. 22–23): "For all things are yours, whether it be Paul, or Apollo, or Cephas . . . all are yours, and you are Christ's". The one Apostolate, preaching the one Faith, the one Baptism, is the foundation (1 Cor. 3. 11): "For other foundation no man can lay, but that which is laid; which is Christ Jesus". And speaking at the beginning of this book of the foundation of the Apostolate, we quoted St Paul's words to the Ephesians, which now have the added meaning of the unity of baptism built upon the unity of the Apostolate (Eph. 2. 20): "Built upon the foundation of the apostles and prophets, Jesus Christ himself being the chief corner-stone". While studying the Council of Jerusalem (section 17, and the Interlude on the Councils) we saw the attitude to St Peter as the "Primate" or the Head of the body of Apostles, equal in authority as Apostles, but under Peter in matters of decisions and government.

THE BAPTISM OF JOHN

It was at this same time, while St Paul was at Ephesus, that the question was raised whether the Baptism of John the Baptist was sufficient to make someone a Christian. There was that little group at Ephesus who had only received the Baptism of John: and Paul immediately had them baptised "in the name of the Lord Jesus" (Acts 19. 5). He explained that John baptised with the "Baptism of penance, saying that they should believe in him who was to come after him, that is to say, in Jesus" (19. 4). John the Baptist himself had insisted that his Baptism was only a preparation (Mt. 3. 11): "I indeed baptise you in water unto penance, but he that cometh after me, is mightier than I, whose shoes I am not worthy to bear; he shall baptise you in the Holy Ghost and fire". John's Baptism was only a sign of the state of mind of those who received it, the state of mind of penance, or prayer to God for the forgiveness of sin. The Christian Baptism, by the power of the Holy Ghost, brings with itself the forgiveness of sin (and not merely the desire for it), makes men members of the Body of Christ, and opens to them eternal life with God. Our Lord himself said to Nicodemus (Jn. 3. 5): "Unless a man be born again of water and the Holy Ghost, he cannot enter into the Kingdom of God". But the Baptism of John worked none of these things, but only taught those who received it to think aright: it therefore did not in itself have an effect on these men, as a Sacrament does, by giving them divine Grace, but only helped them to the idea of penance. Further it had not that essential quality of a Sacrament, which is its institution by Christ, for Christ had not yet come. St John the Baptist's Baptism was therefore a preparation for Christianity, but was not itself sufficient to make people Christians. The men at Ephesus were therefore immediately baptised with the Baptism of Christ.

(37) INTERLUDE ON LITURGICAL UNITY AND *KOINΩNIA*. (*A propos* of 1 Cor. 10. 16–17)

RÉSUMÉ ON UNITY

This is the third Interlude that we are devoting to the idea of Unity. The first one (before section 4), was on the Unity of the Church in general, and based upon the remark in Acts 2. 42, that after Pentecost the disciples were persevering (1) in the teaching of the Apostles, (2) and communion (κοινωνία), (3) the breaking of bread, (4) and prayers. At the time we discovered how there are two meanings to the word κοινωνία or 'communion' (a "having in common"), the one representing having a government in common, or being one body of men, and this we called juridical unity; and other referring to worship in common, especially in Eucharistic worship ("the breaking of bread") by partaking of one bread, and this we called *liturgical unity*. The phrase "going to Communion" is in this latter liturgical sense, and the phrase "being in Communion with someone" is in the former juridical sense, *i.e.* being under the same government. And at the same time we pointed out how liturgical unity normally follows on juridical unity, since we receive the Sacraments from those who are under the same authority, *i.e.* are one with us juridically (under the same "jus" or law).

In that first Interlude on Unity we noted how this juridical unity is based on a single authority, the authority of the Apostles, and how therefore Acts 2. 42 makes the first "Mark of Unity" to be "the teaching of the Apostles".

In the Interlude before this one (on Unity of Baptism) we explained how it is the Baptism of Christ that makes us partakers of this juridical unity, that makes us members of the Church, the Body of Christ: as St Paul puts it (1 Cor. 12. 13): "All baptised into one Body".

Now here in this Interlude we are studying the liturgical unity, the "third Mark of Unity" of Acts 2. 42: the "breaking of bread" or the Eucharist, to which St Paul appeals in I Cor. 10. 16–17 as a further bond of unity among the Corinthians.

LITURGICAL UNITY IN THE EUCHARIST

St Paul has spoken elsewhere of the body of Christians as "One Body", meaning the Body of Christ in his sense of the Church. Here he goes further, saying (1 Cor. 10. 17): "We, being many, are *one bread*, one body, all that partake of one bread", and just before this, he says (10. 16): "And the bread, which we break, is it not the partaking of the body of the Lord?" Thus St Paul uses not only the word Body both in the "juridical" sense of the body of Christians, but also in the "liturgical" sense of the Body of Christ in the Blessed Sacrament of the Eucharist, which makes us "one bread, one body": and at the same time he uses the word κοινωνία also in both senses, either in the juridical sense of sharing the one government or teaching, as in a later Epistle (Phil. 1. 5): "Your communication (κοινωνία) in the gospel of Christ from the first day until now"; or in the liturgical and Eucharistic sense, as here (1 Cor. 10. 16): "The chalice of benediction, which we bless, is it not the communion (κοινωνία) of the blood of Christ? And the bread, which we break, is it not the partaking (κοινωνία again) of the body of the Lord?" (From these passages we can see how variously the word is translated in the Rheims Version: the Westminster Version translates "fellowship" throughout.)

St Paul, therefore, through his use of the word κοινωνία for the sharing of the Eucharist, has linked together the ideas of the Unity of the Church with the Unity of the Eucharist, and in I Corinthians points to the Eucharist as the great bond of unity between Christians. And just as the juridical unity is reduceable through the teaching of the Apostles to the unity of Christ, so also the liturgical unity of Communion depends upon the unity of the one Body of Christ which we all receive: when we receive Holy Communion we become *one body* because we partake of *one bread*, that is the Body of Christ. In the early days of the Church, so much was the Blessed Sacrament regarded as the bond of unity between Christians that the Sacred Species were usually taken home to the sick who could not come to Mass, so that none should fail to take part in this Sacrament of unity, which united Christians among themselves because it united each of them to Christ. For it was the general practice in the Early Church for everyone to go to Holy Communion when he went to Mass. This practice had fallen off in the history of the Church, but in modern times, with a greater realisation of the true meaning and deep value of liturgical prayer, the practice of frequent and daily Communion has returned: and it is becoming more and more normal nowadays for people to go to Holy Communion when they go to Mass. It was Pope Pius X who decreed in 1905 that "Frequent and daily Communion is open to everyone of the faithful who is in a state of grace and has a right and holy intention". Frequent Communion was not at all general at that time. So now in the modern Church the way is again open to the power of this the greatest of the Sacraments, the Eucharist, to be a bond of unity among Christians.

EUCHARISTIC RITUAL IN NEW TESTAMENT TIMES

In Apostolic times the celebration of the Eucharist was referred to as the "breaking of bread", and there are not many references. Two passages in the Acts we have already noticed (in the Interlude on Unity, and in section 5); then there is this passage in I Corinthians, and one more in Acts.

    i. Acts 2. 42: after Pentecost, perseverance in the break-
       ing of bread.

   ii. Acts 2. 46: "breaking bread from house to house".

  iii. 1 Cor. 10. 16 (quoted above).

  iv. 1 Cor. 11. 20–29: correction of behaviour at the
       Eucharistic celebrations at Corinth.

   v. Acts 20. 7–12: the celebration at Troas.

From these texts (especially 1 Cor. 11. 20–29), as well as
evidence of practice in the second century, we gather that
the Christians met for a common meal in the evening, which
was later known to the early Christians as the ἀγάπη (*i.e.*
brotherly love). For it has always been among men an
accepted sign of friendship to eat together, like the modern
invitations to a meal. During this meal a priest would consecrate the bread and the wine with the words of Our Lord,
and all would partake of the Body and Blood of Our Lord.
St Paul in 1 Cor. 11. 24–25 gives the words of Our Lord
which we can also read in the Gospels, which were used at
Corinth for the Consecration, and are still used at every
Mass. There are slight differences of wording in the phrases
given by Matthew, Mark, and Luke, and by Paul in 1 Corinthians; but the Church has fixed the exact words that a
priest is to use at Mass (although the sense in each of the
accounts is the same). The words as appointed to be said
in the Latin Mass are these: "Hoc est enim Corpus meum"
("For this is my Body"), and "Hic est enim calix Sanguinis
mei, novi et aeterni Testamenti, mysterium fidei: qui pro
vobis et pro multis effundetur in remissionem peccatorum"
("For this is the chalice of my Blood, of the new and
eternal Testament, a mystery of Faith: which shall be shed
for you and for many, to the remission of sins"). These
words, which are the very centre of the Mass, can therefore
be traced back, almost entirely unaltered, right to the
Apostles and so to Our Blessed Lord himself. But the

[*Photo E.N.A.*]

THE SCENE OF ST PAUL'S ESCAPE AT DAMASCUS, SHOWING THE REMAINS OF ST PAUL'S TOWER WITH THE TRADITIONAL WINDOW FROM WHICH THE APOSTLE WAS LET DOWN IN A BASKET BY HIS FOLLOWERS

(*Acts* 9)

practice of celebrating the Eucharist at the evening meal had fallen completely into disuse by the fourth century, and the Eucharistic meeting, the Mass, became quite separate. Even in the time of St Paul this banquet had been an occasion of abuse (1 Cor. 11. 20): "When you come therefore together into one place, it is not now to eat the Lord's supper", some people even got drunk. "In this I praise you not" (11. 22). It was such corrections that St Paul wrote to the Corinthians.

But lastly we should note that it was the evening meal that led to the Sunday celebration of the Eucharist. The first Jewish Christians would attend the synagogue service of the closing of the Sabbath on Saturday evening, and then after nightfall go on to the Christian meeting. At such a meeting ("on the first day of the week", the day beginning at the previous sunset according to Jewish reckoning), Paul "continued his speech till midnight" (Acts 20. 7), and the "breaking bread" took place after midnight, that is on the Sunday itself in the early hours.

(38)   SECTIONS 22: END OF THE THIRD MISSIONARY JOURNEY
(Acts 20; 21. 1–26; Epistles: II Corinthians, Galatians, Romans)

A. SIGNIFICANCE

This is a period of much travelling of Paul: we shall summarise the journey in the next paragraph. After Ephesus, Paul re-visits Macedonia and Corinth, and then turns to Jerusalem. Returning eastwards from Corinth, he knows that this is his last missionary journey: at Miletus he addresses the priests of Ephesus, and it is an address of farewell (Acts 20. 22–24): "I go to Jerusalem: not knowing the things which shall befall me there: save that the Holy Ghost in every city witnesseth to me, saying: that bands and afflictions wait for me at Jerusalem. But I fear none of these things". In this speech, which shows the whole atmosphere of this last journey, he shows himself the real Christian Apostle. He speaks of his own work of preaching, how he has kept back nothing that might be profitable to them, how he has not feared the conspiracies of the Jews, how he cares for nothing but the "ministry of the word which I received from the Lord Jesus, to testify the gospel of the grace of God" (20. 24). He tells them that they shall see him no more, but that he has done everything while he was with them, not only to be no burden to them ("such things as were needful for me and them that are with me, these hands have furnished" (20. 34), an allusion to his trade), but that he has set them a Christian example of how to support the weak, and how "to remember the word of the Lord Jesus, how he said: 'It is a more blessed thing to give, rather than to receive'" (20. 35).

This speech, which ends on this note of Christ's own teaching is exceedingly beautiful and touching. The Apostle is ready to crown his work for Christ by dying for him, as he said to the brethren at Caesarea (21. 13): "I am ready not only to be bound, but to die also in Jerusalem, for the name of the Lord Jesus".

But no sooner had he arrived in Jerusalem than false charges were made against him, that he taught apostasy from the religion of the Jews. It was these charges that led to his arrest a few days later. Yet Paul's willingness to counteract their accusations, by strict Jewish observance of the Law in making a vow, should specially be noticed. He had similarly made a vow at the end of the second journey (section 20).

Lastly we should observe that this section contains the second "WE-passage" (20. 5–21. 18), in which the narrator, St Luke, is present from Philippi to Jerusalem. (*See* note in section 18.)

B. STORY

The history of this journey after Ephesus occupies exactly a year: from Ephesus St Paul wrote (I Cor. 16. 8): "I will tarry at Ephesus until Pentecost", and then after visiting Macedonia, and staying three months in Greece, he started off back to Palestine, hoping "to keep the day of Pentecost at Jerusalem" (Acts 20. 16). It would probably be simplest to make a summary of the stages of travel during this year.

1. *Ephesus to Macedonia* (probably Thessalonica). St Paul lingered in Macedonia, awaiting an answer to his first letter, for he feared that perhaps his corrections in that letter had been too stern (II Cor. 2. 1): "I determined this within myself, not to come to you again in sorrow". But Titus brought him good news from Corinth, "relating to us your desire, your mourning, your zeal for me, so that I rejoiced the more" (II Cor. 7. 7), so he wrote to them his *Second Epistle to the Corinthians*, to tell them of the work of God in Macedonia, to tell them that he is coming to see them, and that he hopes for some contribution from them for the fund he is starting for the Christians in Jerusalem. He speaks to them with great affection, and writes to them more advice on the Christian life.

2. *Macedonia to Corinth*. The visit he promises in II Cor. 13. 1. From here, during his three months' stay (Acts 20. 3), he wrote the *Epistle to the Romans*, *i.e.* to the Jewish-Christians in Rome, and main theme of this letter is the solution of the problems that face the Jewish convert in the matter of his Judaism. Probably (unless one holds that it was written before the Council of Jerusalem: *see* section 17) the *Epistle to the Galatians* was written at the same time, and deals with the same problems, with some account of St Paul's own difficulties.

3. *Corinth through Macedonia (Philippi) to Troas*. St Paul travelled this way, instead of straight across the sea from

Corinth, because of a plot of the Jews that was discovered in time (20. 3), he was joined by St Luke at Philippi (20. 6 : "We sailed from Philippi"), and reached Troas (on the coast of Asia Minor). Here we have the account of the Sunday Eucharist that was mentioned in the last Interlude, during which an accident occurred to a youth named Eutychus, who was sitting on the window, and fell asleep ("as Paul was long preaching" 20. 9: he went on till midnight, 20. 7), and fell out of the window and was killed. Paul immediately went downstairs, and "laid himself upon him; and embracing him, said : 'Be not troubled, for his soul is in him' . . . And they brought the youth alive, and were not a little comforted" (20. 10–12). This is the only time that we read of St Paul raising the dead to life, and the medical witness of St Luke (who was present) is particularly valuable on this occasion.

4. *Troas to Miletus.* Immediately after the Mass at Troas, the party (which included Timothy and Luke) sailed away and eventually arrived at Miletus. This is another port on the coast of Asia Minor, about thirty miles south of Ephesus. He deliberately missed visiting Ephesus, so as not to waste time, but he invited the priests of Ephesus to come and see him at Miletus, where he made them the address about which we spoke under "A". In this address, not only does he bid them farewell, but also, now that he will no longer be able to watch over them, he warns them about the future (Acts 20. 29–31): "I know that after my departure ravening wolves will enter in among you . . . and of your own selves shall arise men speaking perverse things . . . therefore watch": he can foresee the calamity of heresy arising in the Church. But apart from human watchfulness, there is only one way of safeguarding the Faith: trust in God: "And now I commend you to God" (20. 32); and here again St Paul shows his attitude of the true Christian, who knows that he must have confidence in God, and that "unless the Lord

13

keep the city, he watcheth in vain that keepeth it" (Ps. 126. (Heb. 127.) 1).

5. *Miletus to Jerusalem by Caesarea.* At Caesarea the party were met by Agabus, the prophet, whom we met in 11. 28 (about thirteen years previous to this: section 13, when Prophecy was discussed), and who then prophesied a famine, and this time foretells the arrest of Paul in Jerusalem. Again St Paul proclaims his readiness to suffer for Christ. When they arrived at Jerusalem, the party went the very next day to visit St James, the Bishop of Jerusalem. It is important to notice the honour with which St James, as the local Bishop, was treated at Jerusalem: St Paul's first visit was to him. (*Cf.* note on 15. 13 in section 17, the Council of Jerusalem). The priests of Jerusalem, who with James received Paul, told him what the Jews at Jerusalem were saying about Paul, that he was turning Jews away from the Law of Moses. This, of course, was false, as Paul's idea was that Jewish Christians should keep the Law, but that Gentile Christians should not have the Jewish Law imposed on them. So the priests recommended that Paul, as a Jew himself, should show how much he valued the Law for Jews by joining four Jewish Christians who had a vow, and by going through the full ritual for the end of a vow, performed publicly in the temple. (For this vow, *cf.* section 20, when Paul took a similar vow on his second journey). Paul took their advice, "and the next day being purified with them, entered into the temple, giving notice of the accomplishment of the 'days of purification'" (Acts 21. 26). It was on the occasion of these ritual visits to the temple that certain Jews stirred up a riot against him, which finished with his arrest (*see* next section).

C. DETAILS

20. 8–9 Remarks about the number of lamps in the room, and the length of Paul's preaching are typical of an eye-witness.

20. 17 and 21. 18: "the ancients": the presbyters or priests,
as in 11. 30, several times in 15, 16. 4, and here
21. 18 (of the priests of Jerusalem, who worked
with the Apostles); also 14. 22 (of priests ordained
in the various churches of Asia Minor) (*see* note in
section 16, and on 15. 2 in section 17); and here
20. 17 (of the priests of Ephesus). These are all
the passages in Acts referring to πρεσβύτεροι.

20. 28 "Bishops": it is not certain whether at this time this
indicated a rank different from the presbyters.

20. 35 "The word of the Lord Jesus": one of the words of
Jesus not recorded in the Gospels.[1] There must
have been many such, which were well known to
the early Christians, though this is the only one
quoted in Scripture.

21. 8 "Philip the Evangelist, who was one of the seven",
i.e. deacons, now living at Caesarea. He was last
heard of in chapter 8, after preaching to the Ethiopian (about thirteen years before), making his way
up the coast from Azotus "till he came to
Caesarea" (Acts 8. 40).

Note.—It might be found convenient to pause about here for Easter, at
the conclusion of St Paul's Missionary labours, having concluded
the Michaelmas term with his Conversion. The material since then has
been arranged in about 16 classes. But even though the date of Easter
might recommend this halt to be made earlier or later, it may be
found useful anyway to begin the Summer Term with the following Interlude on St Luke.

(39)   INTERLUDE ON THE PERSON
         OF ST LUKE, AND HIS TWO BOOKS

THE PERSON OF ST LUKE

Tradition has been quite constant about St Luke being
the author of the two books which we know as "The Gospel
of St Luke" and "The Acts of the Apostles". It is obvious

---

[1] Therefore known as the ἄγραφον (unwritten).

from the prologues to these two books that they are merely two successive volumes of the same work, written in the same manner and for the same purpose. But the name of the author never appears in either, any more than it does in most books apart from the title-page, and since the modern usage of thus labelling books with the name of the author was not general in antiquity, it is not surprising that the name of Luke does not appear. From the earliest days it was generally known that Luke was the author: probably the earliest witness was St Ireneus who wrote his great work "Adverses haereses" about the year A.D. 185, where he says (III 1. 1): "And Luke, the follower of Paul, recorded in a book the gospel that was preached by him", and speaking of the journeys of St Paul and in particular the "WE-passages", he says (III 14. 1): "Since Luke was present at all these things, he wrote them up most carefully". And in the document written about the same time, known as the Muratorian Fragment, we read: "In the third place, the book of the Gospel according to Luke: this Luke, a doctor, after the ascension of Christ, when Paul had taken him as an escort,[1] wrote under his own name what he had heard, although he never saw him (*i.e.* Christ) in the flesh, and therefore wrote whatever he was able to find out: and so began with the birth of John (the Baptist)".

So we have in the earliest traditions references to St Luke as the author of the Gospel and the Acts, and the identification of him with the Luke whom St Paul in his Epistles mentions as his "fellow-labourer" in Rome (Philem. 24), and as "Luke, the most dear physician" in an Epistle written at the same time from Rome (Col. 4. 14). He was also St Paul's companion in his last imprisonment in Rome (II Tim. 4. 11): "Only Luke is with me". (These are the three references that St Paul makes to Luke, and the only mentions of him by name in the New Testament.)

---

[1] If this is the meaning of IURIS STUDIOSUM, as Lagrange explains.

From these references, and the "WE-passages" in the Acts (16. 10–17; 20. 5–21. 18; 27. 1–28. 16; *cf.* notes in sections 18 and 22), we gather that St Luke was a physician, and companion of St Paul on part of his second journey, on the return section of his third journey, on his journey to Rome under arrest and during both his imprisonments in Rome (the first, Acts 28, Colossians, Philemon; the second, II Timothy). The tradition that he was a Gentile is perhaps confirmed by his being mentioned in Col. 4. 14 apart from a group who are called "of the circumcision" (4. 11). And here should be mentioned the theory that he was perhaps the brother of Titus, mentioned several times by St Paul in his Epistles.

Later tradition tells us, and gives it as an accepted fact, that Luke was a doctor from Antioch in Syria (a Greek-speaking city), and a Gentile, but it is not certain whether or not he ever practised the Jewish religion before embracing Christianity; but anyway his writings show much acquaintance with Jewish observance, and he would have studied these carefully for the purpose of writing his history. (The historian Eusebius, who died in A.D. 340, has preserved these traditions for us, in his "Historia Ecclesiastica" II 22. 6.)

Still later is the tradition that he was a painter: there are many Madonnas or pictures of Our Lady that are attributed to him, notably the one known as "Our Lady of Perpetual Succour". The traditions about these paintings are never recorded before the fourth century, but although there is nothing earlier than this to prove them, there is no reason for disbelieving them: and, as Lagrange said: "Why attribute the paintings to this physician, if he was not known to be a painter?"

Most writers have called attention to the gentleness or St Luke in his writings, and to the attention he pays to the part played by women in his history, especially the part of Mary who was "blessed among women", and indeed the story of the Annunciation is recorded only by St Luke.

About St Luke's life after the death of St Paul (A.D. 67), our information is very vague. He is said to have preached in Greece and in Gaul and died a martyr, and all accounts state that his relics were removed to Constantinople, though usually no notice is taken of the claim of the city of Padua in Northern Italy to possess his bones in the Church of St Justina, in the north transept, where an inscription records their transport from Constantinople.

HIS TWO BOOKS

But it is chiefly as an historian that we know St Luke: he was indeed a doctor, and he probably was a painter, but his greatest importance lies in the fact that he was a very good historian.

We have already noticed that the two prologues to the Third Gospel and to the Acts of the Apostles, show that these two books are only two volumes of a single work. And in the prologue to the Gospel the author tells us his object in writing, and his method. He tells us that he has set about his task purely as an historian, so that the reader may be able to verify the truth of the facts of his faith. The first volume ("the former treatise"), he says at the opening of the second volume, was an account "of all the things which Jesus began to do and teach" (Acts 1. 1), and the second volume takes on the history of Christianity from the time of Jesus, and is the centre of our study this year.

In the prologue then to the whole work, he outlines what he will do. We will quote it entirely here, in the Westminster Version, which is easier to understand and brings out more clearly the meaning of the Greek: "Inasmuch as many have attempted to put together an account of the things that have been fulfilled amongst us, even as the original eyewitnesses and ministers of the word delivered them to us, it hath seemed good to me also, who have followed up all things carefully from the beginning, to write for thee an orderly account thereof, Excellent Theophilus, in order that thou mayest realise the certainty of the words wherein thou wast instructed" (Lk. 1. 1–4).[1]

From this prologue we understand that Luke was not an eyewitness, but that he investigated everything from the beginning so as to write an "orderly account" of the whole history. The very beginning of the Christian Revelation was with John the Baptist. St Luke therefore began here, with an account of his parents (Lk. 1. 5). It is to St Luke that we owe the story of the "Gospel of the Infancy", and all the details of the birth of Our Lord. These facts could have come from no other source but Our Blessed Lady herself. (In fact the whole account of Christ's childhood is from St Luke, apart from St Matthew's short history of his birth from the Virgin Mary, and his account of the flight into Egypt after the visit of the Magi, not mentioned by St Luke.) St Luke therefore follows up Our Lady right into the second volume, when he says (Acts 1. 14) that the Apostles after the Ascension "were persevering with one mind in prayer with the women, and Mary the mother of Jesus". St Luke's acquaintance with Our Lady is therefore an almost necessary supposition, apart from the tradition that he painted her portrait; and indeed most of what we know of her comes to us through him.

The accuracy of St Luke's facts, especially in the second part of his work, the Acts, in which so much complex history is told, and so many people are mentioned (110 in all), is well proved by profane history as well as the rest of the New Testament.

The book of the Acts was presumably written in Rome

---

[1] In the Rheims version: ". . . *they* have delivered them unto us, who from the beginning were eyewitnesses. . . ." The "*who*" refers to "they", not to "us", as is clear in the Greek text.

during the two years of St Paul's first imprisonment, when St Luke was with him, as they are together there when the story breaks off. His Gospel must therefore have been either written at the same time, or somewhere else beforehand.

(40) SECTION 23: ST PAUL'S ARREST AND IMPRISONMENT UNTIL HIS APPEAL TO CAESAR
(Acts 21. 27–25. 12)

A. SIGNIFICANCE

The various stages in the two years of St Paul's imprisonment at Jerusalem and Caesarea are vividly related in these chapters of the Acts. St Luke must either have been present, or at least in close contact with the march of events (he had arrived at Jerusalem with Paul, and at the end of this time sailed with him to Rome).

What stands out especially is the eagerness of the Sadducean priestly party at Jerusalem to defeat Paul at all costs. But they had to have him condemned by the Roman authority: and this the Romans continually refused to give. Yet the Romans would not release him. Although they were giving him military protection from the mob yet the Roman Governors, out of weakness and a desire to get the favour of the people they were trying to govern, were constantly proposing further trials "to know more diligently for what cause he was accused by the Jews" (for instance 22. 30). After no less than four such trials in the hearing of Roman officials, when the Jews were prosecuting, "objecting many and grievous causes which they could not prove" (as St Luke puts it, not without humour, in 25. 7), St Paul, exasperated, and knowing well that the final word must come from the Romans, appeals to Caesar (25. 11), that is, he exercises his right as a Roman citizen to have his case heard by the Emperor, and so to be rid of the party squabbles in Palestine. There stand out in contrast the jealous efforts of the Jews against Paul, and the Roman desire both to let their subject people have their say, but nevertheless not to allow their Roman justice to be misused.

B. STORY

It was while St Paul was finishing the ritual of the vow mentioned at the end of the previous section, that the Jews in Jerusalem who had been speaking against him (as the Christian priests of Jerusalem had warned him: Acts 21. 21), stirred up the people with the same false charges, namely that he had preached against the Jewish people, the Law of Moses, and the Temple, and not only turned Jews away from their faith, but had introduced Gentiles into the Temple itself. The accusations were false, based on a misunderstanding of Paul's teaching that Jewish Law should not be imposed on Gentiles. It was therefore even against his principles to bring a Gentile into the Temple, and a supposition on their part from seeing him with a Gentile convert Trophimus, in Jerusalem. However, these Jews laid hands on him and there was a general riot.

The Roman authorities responsible for order in the province therefore stepped in, and rescued Paul from the crowd. They wanted details of his identity, thinking he was a certain Egyptian who had recently led a rebellious movement among the people: so they do not expect him to be able to speak the usual language, Greek, but find that he does so readily, and states his real identity rather proudly (21. 39): "*I am a Jew of Tarsus, a citizen of no mean city*": far from being an Egyptian brigand.

And as he stands with the soldiers on the steps of the castle, he asks leave to address the people, and begins his *First Defence*, speaking (to the astonishment of both the Romans and the crowd) in Aramaic, the language of the country.

In this speech he tells the story of his life and conversion, and emphasises his zeal for the Law. But when he speaks of his commission to go and preach to the Gentiles, all the tumult starts again.

The Roman officer, presumably not understanding the Aramaic, and thinking that this will never lead to an explanation of his offence, "commanded him to be brought into the castle, and that he should be scourged and tortured" (22. 24). This means of getting a confession of guilt at the beginning of a trial was forbidden by Roman Law: Augustus had decreed "Non esse a tormentis incipiendum"; but often this was interpreted of the treatment of Roman citizens, and considered not to bind in the case of slaves and strangers. So the soldiers bound Paul with straps, to scourge him. But Paul turned to the centurion, and asked him (22. 25): "*Is it lawful for you to scourge a man that is a Roman, and uncondemned?*" St Paul knew his Roman Law. We have already seen that a Roman officer who infringed the rights of a citizen was liable to heavy punishment (Acts 16. 37, at Philippi, section 18): so the Tribune (the officer in charge) hastened to release him, asking him if it were true that he was a Roman citizen, adding that he himself had obtained his citizenship "with a great sum", to which Paul proudly replied (22. 28): "*But I was born so*".

But the Tribune wanted to find out more about this case, and on the next day "commanded the priests to come together, and all the council: and bringing forth Paul, he set him before them" (22. 30). So St Paul began his *Second Defence*, before the Sanhedrin, protesting that he had lived as a good Jew. He had barely started when the High Priest ordered a servant to hit him on the mouth for saying such a thing. Paul, in a moment of anger, cried out (23. 3): "God shall strike thee, thou whited wall. For sittest thou to judge me according to the law, and contrary to the law commandest me to be struck?" (23. 4-5): "And they that stood by said: 'Dost thou revile the High Priest of God?' And Paul said: 'I knew not, brethren, that he is the High Priest. For it is written: "Thou shalt not speak evil of the prince of thy people"'", quoting Exod. 22. 28. Perhaps from where he stood he could not see where the High Priest was, or had not seen who had given the order for him to be struck. But Paul began again, declaring that he was a devout Pharisee, and believed in the Resurrection. He knew that this would divide his audience, as a great part of the Sanhedrin were Sadducees (*cf.* study of these sects in section 6, when Peter is brought before the Council). Again a riot broke out, and again Paul was rescued by Roman soldiers. That night Christ appeared to Paul telling him to be constant "for as thou hast testified of me in Jerusalem, so must thou bear witness to me also at Rome" (23. 11).

The next day the Sadducean Jews, having once more failed to get Paul condemned, made a plot to kill him. But fortunately Paul's nephew (his sister's son), who was living in Jerusalem, heard of this, and went and warned the Tribune, who immediately made arrangements to save the life of Paul by having him transferred under strong escort (no less than 470 soldiers) to another prison at Caesarea. Caesarea, about eighty miles north-west of Jerusalem, had been chosen by the Romans as their capital, and as the residence of the governor of the Province of Judea. St Luke gives us the full text of a typical Roman letter from the Tribune at Jerusalem to the Governor of Caesarea (23. 26–30), describing the prisoner as one accused by the Jews "concerning questions of their law, but having nothing laid to his charge worthy of death or bands" (23. 29).

Once Paul had arrived at Caesarea, the Governor, Felix, decided to hear the case again; and after five days a deputation came down from Jerusalem, including the High Priest and a specially employed Roman barrister named Tertullus to present the case against Paul. Tertullus began with a few words of flattery to the Governor, and made his accusation under three heads (24. 5) : sedition ; being the "author of the sedition of the sect of the Nazarenes" (note that this is the first time that the followers of Jesus of Nazareth are called by this name) ; and profanation of the Temple. Paul then makes his *Third Defence*, showing that he had never stirred up the people, that his adherence to the sect of the Nazarenes was the fulfilment of the Law and the Prophets, and that his presence in the Temple was the ritual conclusion of his vow.

Once more the trial ends without a condemnation, and Felix proposes to hear the case again in the presence of the Tribune from Jerusalem, ordering meanwhile Paul to be kept a prisoner, but with a certain freedom and at liberty to receive visits from his friends. Probably Luke would have been among such visitors. This lighter imprisonment went on for two years (24. 27), during which time Felix spoke with Paul often (hoping for a bribe from him), and his Jewish wife also talked with him. But the trial never came off.

After these two years, Felix was recalled to Rome (on account of complaints against his harsh rule), and replaced by Festus, and Felix, wishing to depart in good odour with the Jews, did them the favour of leaving Paul in prison. The new Governor was at once approached by the Jews on the matter of the condemnation of Paul, and again a deputation came down from Jerusalem to prosecute. Paul makes his *Fourth Defence* on the same lines as before. But Festus would not find him guilty, and offered a further trial at Jerusalem. St Paul, however, now decides to be rid of these local trials in Judea, where the maliciousness of the Sadducean party of the High Priest was always against him, and where the local Roman Governors were all the time hedging, in order to curry favour with their subjects. St Paul knew his rights as a Roman citizen (25. 10–11): "I stand at Caesar's judgment-seat, where I ought to be judged. To the Jews I have done no injury, as thou very well knowest. . . . *I appeal to Caesar*". That was the end of his trials before local Justice. Festus passes the cause to the Supreme Court of the Emperor (25. 12): "Hast thou appealed to Caesar? To Caesar shalt thou go".

C. DETAILS

21. 27 It is not certain what part of the ritual of the vow is meant by the seven days, but it is probably a period of "purification" before actually concluding the vow.

21. 31 "A Tribune" (in Greek χιλίαρχος): a Roman officer in charge of 1000 infantry and 120 horsemen. Here he was in charge of the garrison at Jerusalem.

21. 40 Aramaic was the popular language that had replaced Hebrew in Palestine, and was akin to Hebrew, which had become a "classical language" by this time. Aramaic was spoken of as "the Hebrew tongue", much as Italian or Spanish may be called "Latin languages" now.

24. 5 "Nazarenes": this name is still used for Christians in the East in the Arabic and Syriac languages.

24. 5 "Author of the sedition of the sect of the Nazarenes": πρωτοστάτης better, "leader" τῆς αἱρέσεως of the "heresy", *i.e.* of the "peculiar doctrine", in which they differ from others (from αἱρέομαι to choose).

24. 14 "heresy": the same word translated "sect" in v. 5.

(41) SECTION 24: ST PAUL IS SENT TO ROME
(Acts 25. 13–28. 31)

A. SIGNIFICANCE

This section represents the imprisonment of St Paul after his appeal to Caesar, and is the last stage of the History of

St Luke called "The Acts of the Apostles". St Luke's story breaks off rather abruptly, leaving St Paul a prisoner in Rome, with the author obviously present in Rome with him. This section, from chapter 27 onwards, when they sail from Palestine, is the last "WE-passage" of the Acts. The presence of St Luke in Rome as companion to St Paul during this first imprisonment in Rome, for "two whole years" (28. 30), is further witnessed (as we have already observed in the Interlude on St Luke) by the references to him in two Epistles of St Paul of this period: Philem. 24, and Col. 4. 14, when Luke sends his greetings with the letters of Paul.

The story in these chapters is again full of movement, and told for the most part by an eyewitness. The story of the shipwreck, and the voyagers' final safety in Malta has become famous, and is not only graphically told, but is also remarkably accurate from the sailor's point of view.

This section and the preceding one show us St Paul no longer the active preacher, busily spreading the Gospel among Jews and Gentiles in Asia Minor and Greece, but St Paul the "prisoner of Christ Jesus" (as he writes: Philem. 1), who nevertheless has a constant concern for the new Christians (Col. 2. 1): "I would have you know, what manner of care I have for you". Although he is now a prisoner, he still looks upon himself as a minister of the Gospel (Col. 1. 29): "Wherein also I labour, striving according to his (Christ's) working which he worketh in me in power". In this same Epistle, written from Rome, he speaks of himself (Col. 1. 24): "Who now rejoice in my sufferings for you".

The Epistles that belong to this Roman imprisonment are Ephesians, Colossians, Philemon, and Philippians.

B. STORY

Shortly after Paul's appeal to Caesar, by which he rid himself of local Palestinian trials, and while he was still awaiting his transfer to Rome, for his case to be heard there, the new Governor, Festus, received a visit from King Agrippa, son of Herod Agrippa who had been for a short time king of the restored kingdom of Judea (*see* Historical Background 1. *d*; and Acts 12: section 14 in this book). The young Agrippa had only recently been granted by the Roman Emperor the title of king over the territory that lay to the north of the Roman Province of Judea. This visit was obviously a state visit of the king of the neighbouring territory to the new Governor of Judea. Agrippa was a Jew, and was naturally interested in the prisoner Paul, and wanted to hear him speak.

Agrippa therefore came with his sister Bernice to Caesarea, and Festus arranged for Paul to be brought before them. Festus made an introductory speech, in which he said that he could not himself find Paul guilty although the Jews were crying for his death; but that since Paul "himself hath appealed to Augustus, I have determined to send him" (Acts 25. 25). Still, he is at a loss what sort of letter to write to Rome about him ("For it seemeth to me unreasonable to send a prisoner, and not to signify the things laid to his charge", 25. 27), and hopes that King Agrippa may understand the situation better, and suggest what he should write.

Paul therefore makes his *Fifth Defence*, before King Agrippa. Once more he outlines his life and his conversion, and recounts his recent troubles with the Jews of Jerusalem. He then begins to preach Christ "saying no other things than those which the prophets and Moses did say should come to pass: that Christ should suffer, and that he should be the first that should rise from the dead, and should shew light to the people and to the Gentiles" (26. 22–23). At this, the Roman pagan Festus, not understanding at all, cries out (26. 24): "Paul, thou art beside thyself: much learning doth make thee mad". But Paul replies very politely (26. 25–26): "I am not mad, most excellent Festus, but I speak words of truth and soberness: for the king knoweth of these things", and turning to the King he cries: "Believest thou the prophets, O King Agrippa? I know that thou believest" (26. 27), and Agrippa answered: "In a little thou persuadest me to become a Christian" (26. 28), which was probably genuine, but of course he never followed it up. Finally, consulting with Festus, Agrippa says (26. 32): "This man might have been set at liberty, if he had not appealed to Caesar".

However, since he had appealed to Caesar, he was now shipped off to Rome, together with some other prisoners, under a Centurion named Julius, who "treating Paul courteously, permitted him to go to his friends, and to take care of himself" (27. 3). Among these friends of Paul on board was Luke. At Myra [1] they change ships, and catch one from Alexandria to Italy. It was by now the end of September ("The fast was now past", 27. 9), and "sailing now was dangerous" because of the storms. Paul, with the authority of his age (he was close on 60) and travelling experience, warns the centurion of the danger, but as the "master of the ship" was willing to go on they went. Off Crete, however, they were caught in a bad storm, and driven by the gale. It was only under the lee of the small island of Cauda, now called Gavdo or Gozzo, about twenty miles south of Crete, that they had sufficient shelter to reduce sail and to perform the awkward task (done sometimes in antiquity and right until the age of iron ships) of "undergirding" or "frapping" the ship, that is, passing ropes crosswise or athwart under the hull, to keep the timbers more firmly together. The loops were let down under the bows, and then pulled aft to their positions and made fast. At the same time they were able to get their dinghy aboard, for they

[1] A port of Lycia, on the south coast of Asia Minor: for which "Lystra" in 27. 5, according to the Vulgate text, is certainly a mistake, and the better Greek texts followed by the Westminster Version read "Myra".

feared to lose her. It is not easy to hoist a waterlogged boat on board, especially in a rough sea, and Luke took part in this job, as he says (27. 16): "We had much work to come by the boat", while the other operations are described in the third person plural.

But the storm grew worse, and they lightened the ship by throwing tackle and cargo overboard. For fourteen days they tossed, and they had nothing to eat, but Paul assured them that God would not allow them to perish. One night the sailors thought they were near land, and soundings showed shallow water, so (27. 29) "fearing lest we should fall upon rough places, they cast four anchors out of the stern, and wished for day". The ship was steadier now, and they all had some refreshment. When daylight came they saw a creek ahead, and so slipped the anchors and sailed towards the shore. The bows presently ran aground, but the stern began to be broken up by the waves. It was proposed to kill the prisoners lest thy should escape, but the centurion refused to do this, and commanded those who could swim to swim ashore, and the others to get ashore on floating spars and boards. "And so it came to pass, that every soul got safe to land" (27. 44).

They then discovered that they had landed at the island of Malta. The Maltese were good to them, and lit a fire. Paul was helping to gather sticks, and as he put some sticks on the fire a viper jumped out and fastened on to his hand, at which the Maltese thought this must be vengeance on this prisoner, but when he just shook it off into the fire again they said he must be a god. The party, or probably the Roman citizens among them, were then entertained by the local Roman Governor named Publius, whose invalid father was cured by St Paul. Tradition has it that this Publius became a Christian and succeeded Dionysius the Areopagite (*cf.* section 19) as Bishop of Athens, and eventually died a martyr. He is one of the Patron Saints of the island of Malta.

14

After three months they caught a ship that was going from Alexandria to Italy by way of Malta. They called at Syracuse in Sicily and at Reggio di Calabria (Rhegium), and finally arrived at Pozzuoli (Puteoli in Latin) in the Bay of Naples. This was a regular port for travellers to Rome, 140 miles away: "And so we went to Rome" (28. 14). While they stayed seven days at Pozzuoli the news of their arrival reached the Christians in Rome, of whom a group came out along the Via Appia to Appii Forum, about forty miles south of Rome, to meet them. This point was the northern edge of the Pontine Marshes (now a drained and fertile land), through which the Via Appia was bordered by a canal for use in times of flood. Another party met Paul at the Three Taverns, about thirty-three miles out of Rome on the Via Appia.

When they reached Rome, Paul was allowed to "dwell by himself with a soldier that kept him" (28. 16), and "he remained two whole years in his own hired lodging: and he received all that came to him" (28. 30). From St Paul's own letter to the Philippians, written from this lodging, we can gather something of St Paul's finances, and thus how he was able to rent a house in Rome, for he thanks the Christians of Philippi for their gifts to him, and remarks that he has accepted such assistance from them only, adding (Phil. 4. 18): "I have all, and abound: I am filled, having received from Epaphroditus the things you sent".

Of all the people who came to see him, among the first were the chief people of the Jews in Rome ("after the third day", Acts 28. 17) to whom St Paul made his *Sixth Defence* recorded in the History of his imprisonment. In this short address he explained that he had in no way injured the Jewish people, but on the contrary "for the hope of Israel I am bound with this chain" (28. 20). These Jews of Rome listened to him willingly, and arranged another meeting, when "there came very many to him unto his lodging, to whom he expounded testifying the kingdom of God, and persuading them concerning Jesus, out of the law of Moses and the prophets, from morning until evening" (28. 23). As these Jews departed, some convinced and others not, he said (28. 28): "Be it known therefore to you that this salvation of God is sent to the Gentiles, and they will hear it". And he was "preaching the kingdom of God, and teaching the things which concern the Lord Jesus Christ with all confidence, without prohibition" (28. 31): these are the last words of the *Acts of the Apostles*.

C. DETAILS

27. 11 "The pilot": κυβερνήτης: the man who steers, the navigator.

27. 35 "Taking bread, he gave thanks to God": this probably does *not* refer to the Eucharist celebrated on board, but to a blessing before an ordinary meal; although some writers take it for the Eucharist.

27. 39 "A certain creek": still known in Malta as "St Paul's Bay", and easily identifiable from St Luke's descriptions.

28. 1 "Barbarians": *i.e.* not Greek- or Latin-speaking. The Maltese spoke a Phenician dialect, and their civilisation is probably one of the oldest in the Mediterranean.

28. 7 "The chief man of the island" (πρῶτος τῆς νήσου), a title used in Malta and among the Phenicians to denote a high rank, and probably taken over by the Romans for their own officials there.

(42)   INTERLUDE ON THE FOUNDATION OF THE CHURCH OF ROME BY SS PETER AND PAUL

Pope St Leo († 461), preaching in Rome on the Feast of SS Peter and Paul (June 29), said: "Today's festival, apart

from the honour which it deserves throughout the whole
world, should be observed in this City of ours with a rejoicing altogether special and our own. . . . For these are
the men, O Rome, through whom the Gospel of Christ
enlightened thee". And in the Collect for the same Feast (as
we noticed in the Introduction on the Apostolate), Saints
Peter and Paul are spoken of in relation to the Church as
"those through whom she received the beginnings of her
Faith" ("per quos religionis sumpsit exordium"). The
Vesper hymn includes the well-known stanza:

> O Roma felix, quae duorum Principum
> Es consecrata glorioso sanguine:
> Horum cruore purpurata ceteras
> Excellis una pulchritudines.

All this shows how Christian Rome looks to these two
Apostles as her founders, and honours them as her great
glory. In fact we cannot keep the Feast of St Peter without
St Paul, nor on the next day (June 30) that of St Paul without commemorating St Peter.

St Peter in Rome

We have already remarked (in section 14 on the Persecution of Herod) how St Peter, after escaping from prison by a
miracle, "went into another place" (Acts 12. 17). Eusebius,
the historian († 340), in his "Historia Ecclesiastica", II 14,
and St Jerome († 419) in his "De Viris Illustribus", chap. 1,
have preserved for us the traditions that after his escape from
Jerusalem, St Peter visited Antioch and became their first
Bishop, that after this he preached in the cities of Asia
Minor afterwards to be visited by St Paul, and in the second
year of the Emperor Claudius (about A.D. 42) came to Rome.
We have also already noticed (in section 14) how there are
traces of St Peter's visits in the address of his First Epistle
to the faithful in various provinces of Asia Minor (1 Peter
1. 1), and in St Paul's reference to those baptised by him at

Corinth (1 Cor. 1. 12). St Peter's own phrase, at the end of his Epistle, sending greetings, "The Church that is in Babylon ... saluteth you" (1 Pet. 5. 13), is understood by nearly everybody to refer to Rome. Before St Paul's arrival in Rome as a prisoner in A.D. 58 there were already Christians there, for they came out to meet him (Acts 28. 15), and the couple Aquila and Priscilla, whom St Paul met at Corinth (Acts 18. 2), were probably Christians already in Rome, and banished with the Jews by Claudius about the year 50. (*See* note on this passage in section 20.) All this fits in with the tradition that St Peter preached the Gospel in Rome early in the reign of Claudius (A.D. 41–54), and had Rome as his residence from then until his death, a period of about twenty-five years, A.D. 42–67, although he seems to have paid several visits to the East during that period. Of St Peter's martyrdom in Rome we shall treat later.

ST PAUL IN ROME

St Paul's first visit to Rome (at any rate as an Apostle) was as a prisoner in A.D. 58; but about A.D. 55, writing from Corinth towards the end of his Third Missionary Journey, he told the Christians of Rome: "I long to see you ... I have often purposed to come unto you" (Rom. 1. 11–13). As we know, that journey ended in his arrest at Jerusalem, so the visit to Rome was not to be. Yet St Paul had hesitated about coming to Rome "lest I should build upon another man's foundation" (Rom. 15. 20): for the Church of Rome was not a foundation of St Paul, as the other Churches to which he wrote were, but was "another man's foundation", and the evidence in the preceding paragraph shows that it was St Peter's. Still, he wants to visit them "because your faith is spoken of in the whole world" (Rom. 1. 8), and "so (as much as is in me) I am ready to preach the Gospel to you also that are at Rome" (Rom. 1. 15). Much of Paul's preaching was encouragement and confirmation in Christianity to those who already had the Faith (usually his own previous converts) and his preaching in Rome would be of this kind. We saw (in the last section) how he spent his two years of milder imprisonment in Rome preaching to those who came to see him, and (in the Interlude on the Person of St Paul) how after his acquittal he had a period of liberty during which he would have been freer to preach in Rome, and was also able to travel in the East. We know from the names of the people mentioned as sending greeetings at the end of the letters that St Paul wrote from his captivity in Rome (especially Colossians and Philemon), how many friends he had there, and we can guess how great his influence was among the Christians in Rome. It is this fact, and the fact that he returned to Rome for his second imprisonment and final martyrdom, that has caused him to be regarded as co-founder of the Church of Rome. He was the only other Apostle beside Peter who came to live in Rome, and who honoured that City with his martyrdom.

The Apostolate of Peter and Paul

St Paul in his First Epistle to the Corinthians, correcting those who cried out "I indeed am of Paul . . . I of Cephas (Peter) (1 Cor. 1. 12), added: "All things are yours, whether it be Paul, or Apollo or Cephas" (1 Cor. 3. 22), and in the Interlude on the Unity of Baptism we saw that the One Baptism showed the unity of the Apostolate of Peter and Paul. As Apostles they had equal authority, both were equally sent by Christ, but St Peter was the Chief of the Apostles and the Head of the Hierarchy. It was with a realisation of these facts that St Paul wrote his defence to the Galatians. In this Epistle he is at pains *to prove his own right as an Apostle*, and at the same time *to show his sub-ordination to Peter*. These two points had obviously been called into question among the Galatians. He insists first (Gal. 1. 11-12): "That the Gospel which was preached by me is not according to man, for neither did I receive it of man, nor did I learn it; but by the revelation of Jesus Christ". And then he goes on to tell how he went up to Jerusalem, to "them who seemed to be something" (Gal. 2. 6), to "James and Cephas and John, who seemed to be pillars" (Gal. 2. 9), and "conferred with them the Gospel which I preach among the Gentiles, but apart with them who seemed to be something (*i.e.* with the authorities): *lest perhaps I should run, or had run in vain*" (Gal. 2. 2). This passage cannot be understood except in the light of Paul's anxiety to have his own Apostolate recognised by the authority of the mother-church at Jerusalem, for without this submission he would have "run in vain". It was then that their different spheres of Apostolate were arranged, and they "who seemed to be pillars, gave to me and Barnabas the right hands of fellowship (κοινωνίας): that we should go unto the Gentiles, and they unto the circumcision" (Gal. 2. 9). Thus it was that in a Unity of Apostolate, Peter and Paul worked in their own spheres, Peter among the Jews, and Paul among the Gentiles: but in their history we have seen their work overlap, and Peter preaching to Gentiles and Paul to Jews. Their apostolates were indeed separate, once (at Antioch in Gal. 2) they were even in conflict, yet their unity and working together is further illustrated from St Peter's point of view in the remarkable passage in his Second Epistle, where he writes (II Pet. 3. 15–16): " . . . as also our most dear brother Paul, according to the wisdom given him, hath written to you: as also in all his Epistles, speaking in them of these things; in which are certain things hard to be understood, which the unlearned and unstable wrest, as they do also the other Scriptures, to their own destruction". This is a great tribute from Peter to Paul, even including his Epistles as Scripture, but also admitting that his style is sometimes difficult. Their manner was different, their work different, but they completed each

other; and so are regarded as the twin Patrons of the City
of Rome, because there they worked together, and made
Rome the special glory of the Church. Tradition says that
they were martyred on the same day in Rome, and the
Antiphon at II Vespers on their common Feast-day runs:
"Gloriosi Principes terrae quomodo in vita sua dilexerunt se,
ita et in morte non sunt separati" ("The glorious Princes of
the earth, just as in life they loved each other, so neither
in death were they separated").

THE "PETRINISM" AND "PAULINISM" OF SOME PROTESTANTS

There have been some Protestants who, chiefly through
being unwilling to accept the value of Tradition in the life
of the Church, or to accept the doctrine of Peter's Primacy,
have refused to admit the fact of Peter and Paul completing
each other and producing the Catholic unity, but have rather
looked upon them as rivals with completely different out-
looks and interpretations of Christ's teaching. They hold
that most of the Apostles' writings are unhistorical, and are
later attempts to cover up the gulf between Petrinism and
Paulinism. A disagreement like that at Antioch recorded in
Gal. 2 (*see* section 17) is claimed as a proof of this division,
but the Unity of the Church that followed on their common
foundation is regarded as an artificial device of later times.
There is a failure to understand the Tradition of the Church
as springing from the Apostles themselves.

(43–44)   INTERLUDE ON THE EPISTLES OF ST PAUL

A particular study of the Epistles of St Paul is the work
covered in this series by Volume VII; but in order better to
understand the beginnings of the Church in this volume we
have, while studying the life and work of St Paul, frequently
referred to his letters, which tell us not only his doctrine,

i.e. what he was teaching to people, but also much about the people he preached to, and the places he visited. As we studied a particular period of St Paul's activity we glanced at the Epistles written at the time, for in this way, when we are thinking about the people and circumstances of the moment, the meaning of the letter becomes much more real to us. Now, having already studied the chief events of St Paul's life in detail, it will be useful to have a quick glance at the whole of the Pauline writings taken together. Such a rapid survey, in order to supplement and fix our passing acquaintance in exegetical sections on the Acts and in previous Interludes, is the object of the present Interlude.

GENERAL REMARKS

There are fourteen Letters of St Paul in the Bible. Of these, ten are addressed to Christian Communities in particular places, though in the case of *Hebrews* it is not clear what place. *Hebrews* also differs from the others in this: whereas the other Letters were apparently dictated by St Paul (*cf.* Rom. 16. 22: "I, Tertius, who wrote this Epistle"), and then often signed by Paul with a PS. written by himself (*e.g.* Col. 4. 18: "The salutation of Paul with my own hand. Be mindful of my bonds (*i.e.* Remember that I am in prison). Grace be with you. Amen"). *Hebrews* was probably written entirely by someone else, conveying the thought and teaching of Paul. For these reasons it stands in our Bible by itself at the end of the series of St Paul's letters. Some letters were probably written throughout by St Paul, notably *Philemon*, for in the 19th of its 25 verses, he says: "I, Paul, have written it with my own hand".

Apart therefore from *Hebrews*, the ten Letters to the various Christian Communities are grouped together in our Bible, and are known as the "*Epistles to the Churches*". Three other Epistles are addressed to individual Bishops and, because their object is to teach these people to be good "pastors" or shepherds of their flocks, these three Letters are known as the "*Pastoral Epistles*", and are also grouped together in our Bible. *Philemon* (only one chapter of 25 verses, and the shortest "Book" in the Bible except for the Prophecy of Abdias in the Old Testament which has only 21 verses, and II and III John of 13 and 14 verses each), stands alone, being addressed to a single private individual, and not concerned with pastoral care. Last in the series comes *Hebrews*.

The 14 Epistles of St Paul stand therefore in our Bible according to their groups as follows:—

Epistles to the Churches:	1. *Romans.*
	2. *I Corinthians.*
	3. *II Corinthians.*
	4. *Galatians.*
	5. *Ephesians.*
	6. *Philippians.*
	7. *Colossians.*
	8. *I Thessalonians.*
	9. *II Thessalonians.*
Pastoral Epistles:	10. *I Timothy.*
	11. *II Timothy.*
	12. *Titus.*
The two remaining Epistles:	13. *Philemon.*
	14. *Hebrews.*

Here we should add that of these, *Ephesians*, *Philippians*, *Colossians*, and *Philemon* are often called the "*Epistles of the Captivity*" as they were written from St Paul's first imprisonment in Rome.

The Epistles in the Life of St Paul

From what we have said above, it is clear that the order in which the Epistles stand in our Bible is a group-order, and not a time-order corresponding to the stages of St Paul's life. As we have studied these various stages, we have mentioned the various Epistles, and now we will arrange the life of St Paul as a chronological table with reference to the various Epistles. It is possible to discover with a fair certainty (except in the case of *Hebrews* and perhaps *Galatians*) the period to which each Epistle belongs, both from remarks made in the Epistles, and from what we know of St Paul's activities from the *Acts*. In this table we will follow the divisions of St Paul's life that we gave in the Interlude on the Person of St Paul (after section 14). He did not write any of these letters (unless perhaps *Galatians*) before his Second Missionary Journey.

Life	Place of writing	Epistles	Section in this Book
A. Before Conversion			
B. After Conversion			
C. His Missionary work			
I. Journey			
II. Journey	from Corinth	1. *I Thessalonians*	20
		2. *II Thessalonians*	20
III. Journey	from Ephesus	3. *I Corinthians*	21
	from Macedonia	4. *II Corinthians*	22
	from Corinth	5. *Romans*	22
		6. *Galatians*	22
D. Captivity	from Rome	7. *Ephesians*	24
		8. *Colossians*	24
		9. *Philemon*	24
		10. *Philippians*	24
E. Period of Liberty	on travels?	11. *I Timothy*	
		12. *Titus*	
		13. *Hebrews* (probably)	
F. Final Imprisonment	from Rome	14. *II Timothy*	

A GLANCE AT THEIR CONTENTS AND PURPOSE

It is not for us in this year's course to examine in any detail the contents of St Paul's Epistles: but we have many times already looked at various Epistles to help us to understand the missionary work of St Paul. Several times while studying the Missionary Journeys we have outlined the theme of the Epistles written during the journeys. Here, therefore, in order to help to understand better St Paul's work in the foundation of the Church, we shall glance at the thought of the Epistles in this connexion.

Many of St Paul's letters, apart from the address and the conclusion (which often includes many greetings sent from other people), fall easily into two parts, the first dealing with matters of Christian *belief* (Christian Faith), and the second dealing with matters of Christian *conduct* (Christian Morals): these new Christians must be taught how to *think* as Christians, and also how to *behave* as Christians.

Most of these letters are written, we must remember, to people whom St Paul knew well: often, therefore, he speaks of himself, or justifies his own actions, and often he corrects or encourages his readers in a very personal way. Nearly always we can see his personal anxiety and concern about them, and his frequent prayer to God for them.

1. *I Thessalonians* (an Epistle of medium length: 5 chapters). First St Paul speaks of his previous work among them earlier on his Second Journey, and of their conversion; he then urges them to be holy and devoted to God, and to love one another, for Christ will come again on the last day.

2. *II Thessalonians* (a short Epistle: 3 chapters). He warns them against the Antichrist "the man of sin", "the son of perdition" who will come before the end of the world. He encourages them to keep the Faith which he taught them, and to avoid idleness. It is at the end of this Epistle that he signs in his own hand as a proof that it is really from him (3. 17): "The salutation of Paul with my own hand: which is the sign in every Epistle. So I write".

3. *I Corinthians* (a long Epistle: 16 chapters). He corrects various faults of the Corinthian Christians, of which he had heard while at Ephesus: notably the growth of various parties at Corinth, so he urges unity: and the Eucha-

ristic meal was being abused, so he instructs them on this (*see* Special Interludes). He answers problems they had put to him, and speaks especially of the Love of God (in the famous chapter 13). He emphasises the doctrine of the Resurrection.

4. *II Corinthians* (a long Epistle: 13 chapters). He speaks much of affairs at Corinth, and their improvement. He describes the service of God as an Apostle, and justifies his own work, telling them much about his own experience. Finally he encourages them to be of one mind and have peace.

5. *Romans* (the longest Epistle: 16 chapters). St Paul explains very fully the problem that faces the Jew converted to Christ. Belief in Christ frees the Jew from the bondage of the Law, and Jew and Gentile are equal before Christ, yet the Jew comes first, and has the advantage because "the words of God were committed to them" (3. 2). It all turns round the Christian's Faith, and the Christian must live according to the "perfect will of God" (12. 2). Once more he urges his readers "to love one another" (13. 8).

6. *Galatians* (a medium Epistle: 6 chapters). Again an explanation of the Jewish-Christian problem, but this time to people he knows, so there is much description of his own solutions. We studied this in connexion with the Council of Jerusalem, and in the last Interlude on the matter of his relations with Peter.

7. *Ephesians* (a medium Epistle: 6 chapters). Writing from prison, he speaks all through this Epistle of the Unity of Christians, united in Christ, who is "head over all the Church, which is his body" (1. 22–23). That the Christian is one with Christ is the main theme of this and the other "Epistles of the Captivity". And to be in this unity, the Christian must be "built upon the foundation of the Apostles" (2. 20). Life in Christ means "putting off the old man" (*i.e.* before they were Christians), and putting on

"the new man" (*i.e.* the Christian man), phrases which have become famous (4. 22–24).

8. *Colossians* (a short Epistle: 4 chapters). He is again concerned with his teaching of "Life in Christ", who is the head. At Baptism the "old man" is buried with Christ, and rises again as the "new man" with the risen Christ (2. 12, 3. 1). These Epistles show a great development in St Paul's own thought.

9. *Philemon* (the shortest Epistle). An Interlude: it is concerned with the private matter of a runaway slave, Onesimus, who became a Christian through St Paul in Rome, and is now recommended back to his master Philemon at Colossae. But even in this short letter St Paul mentions Christ nine times, so much is his thought always centred on him.

10. *Philippians* (a short Epistle: 4 chapters). St Paul writes from prison to thank them for their help (*cf.* note in section 24), encourages them in Christian virtue, and warns them against Judaizers, saying that all things are valueless outside Christ: "I count all things to be but loss, for the excellent knowledge of Jesus Christ my Lord" (3. 8).

11. *I Timothy* (medium: 6 chapters). A letter of advice to his young disciple, who was put in charge of the Church of Ephesus, on how he is to conduct himself as Bishop, and how he is to guide others.

12. *Titus* (short: 3 chapters). A similar letter of advice to his disciple who was made Bishop of the Christians in Crete.

13. *Hebrews* (long: 13 chapters). Written to Jewish Christians, to explain how the Christian Revelation fulfils that made to the Jews, and especially how the Priesthood of Christ is superior to that of the Jews. There is much exposition from the text of the Old Testament.

14. *II Timothy* (short: 4 chapters). St Paul's last writing, as he awaits the end: last words of advice to his beloved disciple. As for himself: "I have fought a good fight, I have finished my course, I have kept the Faith" (4. 7).

(45) INTERLUDE ON THE CATHOLIC EPISTLES

After the fourteen Epistles of St Paul there come in the Bible seven other Epistles by other Apostles. These seven Letters are known as the "Catholic Epistles", because they are addressed not to particular communities, or to particular individuals, as are the Letters of St Paul, but to Christians in general: καθ' ὅλου (from κατά according to, and ὅλος the whole). Their purpose is therefore "catholic" or universal.

The Catholic Epistles are these:—

1. *The Epistle of St James* (James the Less, Bishop of Jerusalem, not James the son of Zebedee and brother of John).
2. *The First Epistle of St Peter.*
3. *The Second Epistle of St Peter.*
4-5-6. *The First, Second, and Third Epistles of St John* (John the Evangelist).
7. *The Epistle of St Jude* (called thus by St Luke in his Gospel and the Acts, but called Thaddeus by Matthew and Mark. He was the brother of James the Less).

The Epistles of John we shall treat of in a later Interlude devoted to St John's later life, and anyway they stand rather apart from the other Catholic Epistles.

We have seen how Peter and Paul at Jerusalem agreed "that to me (Paul) was committed the Gospel of the uncircumcision, as to Peter was that of the circumcision" (Gal. 2. 7), that is that Paul's work was to be chiefly among the Gentiles, and Peter's among the Jews. The Epistles therefore of St Paul are as often concerned with the instruction of pagans as of Jews, and his discussions of Judaism (as in *Romans*) are largely occupied with the relation of Jew and Gentile in Christianity.

In the Epistles of Peter, James, and Jude, we have writings of Apostles who were primarily concerned with

Jews, and James' Letter is often considered the "most Hebraic" of all the Epistles. Although the Catholic Epistles are intended for all Christians, yet they are addressed primarily to Jewish converts and all abound in references to the Old Testament. The *Epistle of Jude* even quotes some current Jewish legendary literature: a book called "The Assumption of Moses" in v. 9, and "The Book of Enoch" in v. 14. These were popular works much read at the time, and incidents are quoted from them as illustrations. The *Epistle of James* is addressed to "The twelve tribes which are scattered abroad" (Jas. 1. 1), which means all Jewish Christians, wherever they may live. The Catholic Epistles therefore are a counterpart to the Epistles of Paul, for they relate chiefly to the Apostolate among the Jews.

St James

Tradition tells us that James, the Bishop of Jerusalem, and "brother" (*i.e.* cousin) of the Lord, was put to death by the Jews while there was no Roman Governor in Palestine, after Felix had been recalled and the new Governor Festus had not yet arrived (A.D. 57), and Paul remained a prisoner at Caesarea, only to appeal to the Emperor at his first trial under the new Governor. The last that we heard of James in the New Testament is about two years before this, just before Paul's arrest in Jerusalem, when Paul, just returned from his Third Journey visits James and receives advice from him and the priests at Jerusalem about taking a vow. (Acts 21. 18–25; section 22.) So James' Letter must have been written before many of Paul's.

His *Epistle* consists of advice to Christians, and advice of an essentially practical nature. Speculations about the relations of Jew and Gentile are absent, and doctrinal instruction is of the simplest. Many familiar passages on the life and conduct of a Christian come from here; for instance: "Blessed is the man that endureth temptation: for when he hath been proved, he shall receive the crown of life, which God hath promised to them that love him" (1. 12); "Let every man be swift to hear, but slow to speak and slow to anger" (1. 19); "If any man offend not in word, the same is a perfect man" (3. 2), and the whole of chapter 3 is concerned with sin by word, and how we must bridle our tongues, and the tongue is shown to be responsible for so much evil in the world, although it is "indeed a little member" (3. 5), and is likened to the tiny rudder, which yet can turn the huge bulk of a whole ship (3. 4). Rich and poor must be treated equally among Christians (chapter 2), and in this chapter he also explains the principle that Faith, "if it have not works, is dead in itself" (2. 17), that is, if we think like Christians and pray like Christians, we must also behave like Christians and love our neighbours, "and shew . . . by works my faith" (3. 18). It was this doctrine that good works are necessary in addition to Faith that was denied by Luther, who therefore refused to accept this Epistle, calling it an "Epistle of straw". In this Epistle also we have the important witness to the use of the Sacraments of Extreme Unction and Penance among the very followers of Our Lord: "Is any man sick among you? Let him bring in the priests of the Church, and let them pray over him anointing him with oil . . . and if he be in sins, they shall be forgiven him" (5. 14–15); and "Confess therefore your sins one to another" (5. 16) (cf. Catechism n. 304 for Extreme Unction). It has been pointed out that so much of James' practical teaching is a direct echo of Our Lord's teaching, especially in the Sermon on the Mount which, of course, James, as one of the Apostles, had heard.

St Peter

St Peter's *First Epistle*, written from Rome ("Babylon" 5. 13), is a message of consolation and encouragement to the Christians, especially those in Asia Minor, who were

15

apparently suffering trials and persecution for their Faith:
"That the trial of your Faith . . . may be found unto praise
and glory and honour at the appearing of Jesus Christ: whom
having not seen, you love: in whom also now, though you
see him not, you believe" (1. 7–8). St Peter's words might
equally well be addressed to Christians throughout history
to present times. He repeatedly holds up to them the
example of the sufferings of Christ. Like St Paul, in *Ephesians* and *Colossians*, he has words of advice for the various
classes of society, for servants, wives, and husbands, and
for the clergy (2. 18, 3. 1, 3. 7, 5. 1). He urges watchfulness
in the passage used by the Church at the beginning of
Compline: "Fratres, sobrii estote et vigilate, quia adver-
sarius vester diabolus tamquam leo rugiens circuit,
quaerens quem devoret: cui resistite fortes in fide"
("Brethren, be sober and watch, because your adversary
the devil, as a roaring lion, goeth about seeking whom he
may devour: whom resist ye, strong in faith") (5. 8–9).

St Peter's *Second Epistle*, like St Paul's *II Timothy*, is a
last word from one who is awaiting the end: he writes: "I
will endeavour, that you frequently have after my decease,
whereby you may keep a memory of these things" (1. 15),
referring to the continuation of preaching, or perhaps to the
Gospel of St Mark. He again encourages their belief: "For
we have not by following artificial fables, made known to you
the power and presence of our Lord Jesus Christ; but we
were eyewitnesses of his greatness" (1. 16). He warns his
readers against heresy (2. 1), and in 3. 15 (already referred
to) he commends the preaching of Paul, and warns them
against those who pervert it. This again might be written
to present-day Christians.

St Jude

The *Epistle of St Jude*, in a way similar to *II Peter*, warns
the faithful against heresy "to beseech you to contend

earnestly for the faith once delivered to the saints" (v. 3). It is a very short letter of twenty-five verses, and some have thought that since Jude writes *as* the brother of James, it was to encourage principally the Christians of Jerusalem after James, their Bishop, had been killed, for which reason he says: "I was under a necessity to write unto you . . . for certain men are secretly entered in . . . denying the only sovereign ruler, and our Lord Jesus Christ" (vv. 3–4).

(46) INTERLUDE ON THE MARTYRDOM OF SS PETER AND PAUL IN ROME

Tradition has preserved for us some details of the martyrdoms of the two Princes of the Apostles in Rome, and claims that they died under Nero on the same day, June 29 (when their common Feast is observed in the Church), presumably about the year A.D. 67.

St Peter

There is the old legend, told briefly in the Magnificat Antiphon at I Vespers of SS Peter and Paul, according to which Peter, in danger of being arrested by the Romans, fled out of the City along the Via Appia. The spot is still shown where he is supposed to have had a vision of Our Lord walking towards the City. He cried out "Domine, quo vadis?" ("Lord, where are you going?"), and Our Lord replied "Venio Romam iterum crucifigi" ("I am coming to Rome to be crucified again"). This reply so touched Peter, that he immediately turned back to the City and faced the danger.

St John, in his Gospel (Jn. 21. 18–19), tells us that Our Lord had already shown Peter what his death should be: "But when thou shalt be old, thou shalt stretch forth thy hands, and another shall gird thee, and lead thee whither thou wouldst not". It is important to realise that John wrote these words down long after Peter has been martyred.

Peter was then arrested, and condemned to be crucified, but protested that he was not worthy of being treated like his Master, but asked to be crucified head downwards. This probably took place near where the Basilica of St Peter now stands.

St Paul

St Paul, being a Roman citizen, was put to death by beheading outside the City. It is said that as his head fell, it bounded three times on the ground, and that at these three places springs of water welled up. These three springs are still shown at the Sanctuary called "Le tre Fontane" several miles from the City. Legend also says that his blood, as it stained the tunic of the executioner, suddenly appeared white as milk. He was buried nearby on the Via Ostiensis (Road to Ostia), near where the Basilica of St Paul's-outside-the-Walls now stands.

In the Vesper Hymn we therefore sing: "Per ensis ille, hic per crucis victor necem" ("The one had his victory by the death of the sword, the other by that of the cross").

INTERLUDE ON THE SUCCESSORS OF PETER

In the Canon of the Mass after venerating the memory of Our Lady and of the Apostles, we add also the memory "Lini, Cleti, Clementis" and then of other Bishops and Martyrs.

Ancient traditions in several cities of Italy speak of disciples of St Peter sent by him from Rome, such as Paulinus to Lucca, Apollinaris to Ravenna and Romulus to Fiesole. But he also took care to provide for the future needs of the See of Rome itself, and would seem to have ordained all three of those who successively held his position as Bishop of Rome after him. These three were *Linus*, *Cletus*, and *Clement*. Owing to this there is confusion in some of the early lists as to who succeeded Peter directly.

But tradition generally puts them in this order, the order in which their names occur in the Mass.

St Linus is believed to have assisted Peter in the management of the Church of Rome, and after his death he succeeded him. St Paul, writing from Rome during his last imprisonment, mentions him as sending greetings: "Eubulus and Pudens, and *Linus* and Claudia, and all the brethren salute thee" (II Tim. 4. 21). Pudens is said to have been a senator, and Claudia, his wife, the daughter of Caractacus the British King, brought captive to Rome. Linus was probably their friend. He was an Italian by birth, and held the See for about twelve years, so till about A.D. 79, when he was martyred. Close to the tomb of St Peter there was found in the sixteenth century a sarcophagus simply inscribed LINVS.

St Cletus was apparently a Roman by birth, and succeeded Linus, holding office for about twelve years, *i.e.* till A.D. 91. There is some confusion in the early documents as to whether "Anacletus", mentioned as one of the early successors of St Peter, is the same person or not. Anacletus was said to have been a Greek; but it is most likely that Cletus and Anacletus are only two forms of the same Greek name; and this tradition is preserved for us by the words of the Canon of the Mass, which (as we said on the first page of this book) may go back to the second century A.D., to within a short time of the life of Cletus himself. Cletus also died a martyr.

St Clement comes third on the list. Apparently he was of a good Roman family, and the well-known Church of St Clement in Rome (one of the most ancient Christian monuments, and now in charge of the Irish Dominicans) is said to have been built on the site of his family home. St Clement is chiefly noted for having been the first Pope after Peter to leave a written document in his own name: his Epistle to the Corinthians. St Ireneus (who died about the year 200) says ("Adversus Haereses", III 3): "When, then, under the same Clement, a no small dissension had arisen amongst brethren at Corinth, the Church of Rome wrote a most powerful letter to the Corinthians, with a view to restore them to peace, to repair their faith, and to announce to them the tradition which but recently it had received from the Apostles". We have already referred to this letter in connexion with Corinth (section 20), and it is generally looked upon as a most important document, being the first written example we have of a successor of St Peter asserting his authority over the other Churches. St Clement "superintended the preaching of the Divine Word nine years" (as Eusebius says: "Historia Ecclesiastica", III 34), and then, according to tradition, was banished by the Emperor (about the year 100) to the Crimea, where he eventually suffered martyrdom by having an anchor tied round his neck and being pushed from a cliff into the Black Sea. Because of this, the anchor is his symbol.

St Clement, dying about A.D. 100, brings us to the end, in this list of Popes, of the Apostolic age, that is, he was the last to have known the Apostles personally and worked with them and under them.

(47) INTERLUDE ON THE TRADITIONAL SPREAD OF THE GOSPEL THROUGH OTHER LANDS BY THE OTHER APOSTLES

It is difficult to know how much trust one can put in the traditional legends which follow. Most of them probably are originally local legends which grew up in the places in question. Many we can trace back to fourth- or fifth-century writers like Eusebius and Jerome, but a fruitful source is the

[Photo E.N.A.

A GENERAL VIEW OF CITTÀ VECCHIA, IN MALTA, SHOWING ST PAUL'S CATHEDRAL

(*Acts* 28)

great compilation of legends about the Saints by Symeon Metaphrastes, a Greek of the tenth century, who made a point of collecting his material from every possible source, and, it would appear, reproduced them faithfully.

The most obvious place where we can look them up is in the Breviary for the various Feasts, where there is usually a short account drawn from the various earlier writers. Various Lives of the Saints should give the main features; but of course the completest references will be in the "Acta Sanctorum" of the Bollandists, where the full stories are quoted under their sources. Since all these accounts are arranged according to the Calendar, we shall give in each case the Feast-Day of the Apostle.

Scripture itself of course helps us in some cases: those of Peter and Paul very fully (as we have seen all during this year of study), those of James the Great and James the Less in part, and in part that of Barnabas. We shall indicate when Scripture guides us.

In this Interlude we are of course only concerned with the activities of the Apostles after their dispersion after Pentecost, and we shall add notes on Barnabas who seemed to rank with the Apostles, and on the two Evangelists who were not Apostles, Mark and Luke. The order is that in the Gospel in Mk. 3. 16–18.

1. *Peter and Paul*. Their acts are fully recorded in *Scripture*. Peter preached first in Palestine, and then visited Antioch, and so through Asia Minor to Rome (Section 14 and Special Interlude on Peter and Paul in Rome). Paul after his conversion and visit to Arabia preached at Tarsus, Antioch, all over Asia Minor, Macedonia, and Greece on his Journeys, in Palestine and finally in Rome. (We saw this more fully in the special Interlude on the Person of St Paul.) (June 29.)

2. *James the Great*, son of Zebedee. After Pentecost he preached in Sardinia and then in Spain. (The tradition about Spain has been much discussed, but the Bollandists finally

decide to accept it.) He returned to Jerusalem for the Pasch, and as we read in *Scripture* (Acts 12. 2) he was arrested by Herod to please the Jews, and was killed by the sword. The Jews refused to bury his body, which was taken away by some Christians at night and immediately removed to Spain, to Compostella, which then became a world-famous shrine, since always known as Santiago de Compostella. He is the chief patron of Spain. He was the first of the Apostles to die. (July 25.)

3. *John* the brother of James. (*See* Special Interlude.)

4. *Andrew* preached in Scythia (the land now covered roughly by Rumania, the Ukraine, and the south of Russia), in Thrace and in Greece. He suffered martyrdom at Patras (northern part of Morea) on the "St Andrew's Cross". When he saw the Cross on which he was to suffer, he cried out: "O good Cross, which hast received comeliness from the limbs of the Lord. O much longed for, and earnestly desired . . . restore me to my Master: that through thee he may accept me, who through thee has redeemed me!" When told to sacrifice to idols, he said: "Daily to God Almighty I offer the sacrifice of the spotless Lamb upon the altar" (a very early reference to daily Mass). He was tied to the Cross with ropes, and remained alive for three days, preaching to the people. The Russian Church honours him as their founder, and he was chosen by Scotland as their patron. (November 30.)

5. *Philip* spent twenty years in Scythia (*see* Andrew), where occurred the incident of a dragon leaping from the statue of Mars he was asked to worship: whereat Philip ordered the dragon to be off into the desert. It immediately went out, and everyone was so much impressed that Philip was released. Later he went to Asia Minor, and was martyred at Hierapolis by being fixed to a Cross and then stoned. (May 1.)

6. *Bartholomew* visited Arabia, Persia, and North-Western

India, where a Christian philosopher Pantaenus found some of his converts in the second century, along with a Gospel of St Matthew in Hebrew. From here he went to Armenia, where at the wish of the pagan priests his whole skin was pulled off and he was finally beheaded. (August 24.)

7. *Matthew* preached first to the Jews in Palestine, for whom he wrote his Gospel. He then went to Ethiopia, where he converted many people including the king. But when this king died, the new king persecuted the Christians and had Matthew stabbed in the back as he was saying Mass. (September 21.)

8. *Thomas*, after founding the Church of Edessa in Syria, went to the Parthian Empire (the area round Turkistan, south-east of the Caspian Sea), and so into India, where he reached the South of India. He founded many Christian communities on the Malabar (south-west) coast of India, who still call themselves the "St Thomas Christians", and use a Syriac Liturgy. He met his death by lances on the Coromandel (south-east) coast of India, where his tomb at Meliapor is still greatly honoured. He is the patron of the Syriac Church and of the South Indian Churches. (December 21.)

9. *James the Less*. We know from *Scripture* how he presided over the Church at Jerusalem (Acts 15. 13, the Council of Jerusalem; Acts 21. 18, Paul's visit to him; Galatians 2. 9–12, Paul's discussion; *see* sections 17 and 21, and Interlude on the Catholic Epistles where there is a note on his martyrdom). Probably while St Paul was in prison at Caesarea, and the Jews were failing to get his condemnation, they arrested James in the absence of a Governor, and threw him down from a pinnacle of the Temple, and then began to stone him. But one of the priests cried out, "Stop! He is praying for us!" but a man below went and finished him off with a fuller's pole. He is the author of the Epistle of St James. (May 1.)

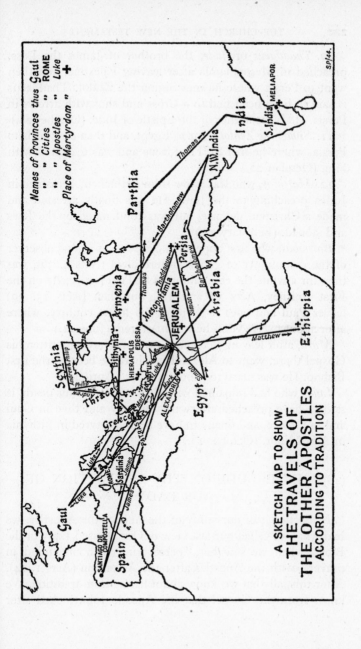

A SKETCH MAP TO SHOW
THE TRAVELS OF
THE OTHER APOSTLES
ACCORDING TO TRADITION

Names of Provinces thus Gaul
  "   " Cities   " ROME
  "   " Apostles " Luke
  "   " Place of Martyrdom ✝

10. *Thaddaeus* or *Jude*, the brother of James the Less, preached in Mesopotamia after leaving Palestine, and then went to Persia where he met Simon the Zealot. Thaddaeus is said to have been tied to a Cross and shot with arrows in Persia. He is the author of the Epistle of Jude. (October 28.)

11. *Simon the Zealot* went to Egypt, and then eastwards to Persia, where he met St Thaddaeus and was martyred with him. (October 28.)

12. *Matthias*, who was a Jew from Bethlehem, remained in Judea preaching to the Jews. He was finally arrested and made a Christian defence, but was condemned by the Jews and stoned. (February 24.)

Barnabas, who first appears in *Scripture* as a good observer of the community of goods at Jerusalem (Acts 4. 36), was then for a while the companion of St Paul (especially on the First Journey, Acts 13 and 14), but then (Acts 15. 39) leaves Paul and goes to Cyprus, his home country, where after about twelve years he was martyred. (June 11.)

Mark, after leaving Peter in Rome, and having written his Gospel there, went to Alexandria where he became the first Bishop. He was martyred about A.D. 62. (April 25.)

Luke, who had remained with Paul right until his death, is said to have preached afterwards in Italy and then in Gaul and in Greece, and finally to have been martyred in Bithynia in Asia Minor. (October 18.)

(48)   INTERLUDE ON THE ASSUMPTION OF OUR LADY

In Section 1 of our study of the Acts of the Apostles, we had what we called our last view of Our Blessed Lady in the Bible, when we saw her "persevering with one mind in prayer" with the Apostles after the Ascension (Acts 1. 14). After this, all that we know about her is from tradition. We know from the Gospel that the Apostle John looked after her after the Crucifixion: it was the dying request of Jesus on the Cross: "After that he saith to the disciple: 'Behold thy mother'. And from that hour, the disciple took her to his own" (Jn. 19. 27). But where she lived under the protection of John, or how long, we have no idea. We have guessed at St Luke's acquaintance with her (Interlude on St Luke), and we have suggested that St Paul visited her after his conversion (Interlude on St Paul). But the fact of her blessed death and her Assumption into Heaven is brought to us by the most ancient and unswerving tradition. It is therefore fitting that at the close of our study of Apostolic times, of the foundation of the Church upon the Apostles, having noticed her company with them at the very beginning of their work, their work of continuing the work of Christ on earth, we should notice her departure from them once their labours were started. She had shared with them the strengthening of the Holy Ghost at Pentecost: she knew more than anyone about Our Blessed Lord: she must certainly have been a great source of understanding of him to the Apostles, she who noticed everything about his life and "kept all these words in her heart" (Lk. 2. 51): and the Apostles, through whom "God would make known the riches of the glory of this mystery among the Gentiles" (Col. 1. 27), must certainly have gone to her to learn more about him, and we therefore frequently honour her with the title "Regina Apostolorum", "Queen of Apostles".

THE MEANING OF THE "ASSUMPTION"

Most feasts of the Saints mark the day of their death. Now death means a separation of the soul (the principle of life) from the body. The body remains upon the earth, is buried and usually turns into earth itself after some time. The soul is born into an eternal life, a life of blessedness (Heaven) or of preparation for this blessedness (Purgatory) in the case of the just, and of damnation (Hell) in case of the wicked who have hated God. This doctrine about the after-life of the soul is "of Faith", that is, we accept it by Faith as doctrine revealed by God through the Divine Authority of the Church. In the same way we believe that the souls of the just, that is, of those who die in a state of grace, free from sin, and without any punishment due to them, straight after death pass to the everlasting happiness of the vision of God in Heaven.

Of all the holy people who might have received this privilege of their souls going straight to Heaven, Our Blessed Lady, who was entirely free from all sin (as the Church teaches) was indeed the most worthy.

The day of her death, the day of her "birthday in heaven" is therefore her principal Feast-Day: August 15: and this used to be called the Feast of the "Dormitio" or "Falling asleep" of Our Lady, for on this day her body, as it were, fell asleep upon earth, and her blessed soul entered Heaven.

But all Christians believe that on the last day our bodies will be raised up by God and joined once more in a glorious way to our souls. This is what we mean when we say in the Apostles' Creed: "I believe in . . . the resurrection of the body". But it has been the constant tradition of the Church, that God, out of special honour for Mary, raised up her body from the tomb either immediately or very soon after her death upon earth. So that while the bodies of most people are allowed to corrupt in the earth, and will only be raised up on the last day, the body of Mary was never allowed to corrupt, but was almost straight away raised up and joined again to her soul in Heaven. This is called the *Privilege of the Assumption*, given alone to Mary out of honour towards her. "Assumptio" in Latin just means "a taking-up".

THE LEGEND

Although writers of the fifth and sixth century already mention the fact of the Assumption, it is not at all certain when and how it happened. There are several legends about it, and the main points of them are as follows.

When Mary was about to die, an Angel came and told her that soon she was to rejoin her son. She was living at the time in John's house at Jerusalem, but John was away at Ephesus, and the other Apostles scattered on their various missions. But every one of the Apostles found himself suddenly transported by a miracle to the door of her house, however far away he might have been. Only Thomas, who had doubted about the Resurrection of Our Lord (Jn. 20. 25), failed to arrive in time. All the other Apostles then stood round the bed of Mary, and John wept bitterly. The Virgin then breathed her last breath, and died most peacefully. At once the voices of Angels were heard in the air. The Apostles then carried her body out to the Garden of Gethsemani and put it into a tomb, and for three whole days the music of the Angels went on. On the third day Thomas arrived and was anxious to see the body of the Virgin. So they went out again to the tomb and opened it for him, and not only found the tomb empty, but noticed within a miraculous sudden growth of many flowers and a wonderful fragrance. Thomas was then allowed to see her in Heaven, and she threw down to him her girdle, which he always kept as a treasured gift.

Some writers think the Assumption happened before the Apostles scattered and St Peter went to Rome, *i.e.* about the persecution of Herod (A.D. 42), during which St James the Great was killed, though an old Syriac legend maintained that some of the Apostles were already dead, and miraculously appeared again on earth for the occasion.

THE DOCTRINE

Whatever we may choose to believe of these old legends, the fact remains certain, that the Virgin's body was taken up into Heaven by the power of God. This is shown by the

Church having instituted the Feast and celebrating it with great honour in all the world. Nevertheless it is not one of the "defined dogmas" of the Church, or the things we believe strictly "on faith". But the doctrine follows from the defined doctrines that Mary was entirely pure, and her body without corruption because she was the Mother of God: for it is a consequence of sin that our bodies corrupt, and Mary was entirely without sin. At the Vatican Council, in 1869, 200 Bishops asked that the Assumption of Our Lady be declared by the Church to be a "defined dogma", and this may still happen.

(49) INTERLUDE ON THE LATER LIFE OF ST JOHN

Of all the Apostles the last to die was John the Evangelist. He is believed to have died at a great age about the year 100, and as he was probably born about the same time as Our Lord, this would make him about 100 years old at his death. His writings: the *Apocalypse*, the *Gospel* and the three *Epistles*, were by far the latest parts of the New Testament to be written. All of them were written during his old age, when all the other Apostles and Evangelists were already dead, having all died violent deaths as Martyrs (*cf.* Recent Interlude on the Apostles), and written their books in any case some time before, sometimes as a direct help to their preaching, as St Matthew and St Mark their Gospels.

The fact then, that St John was the last of the Apostles to die, and that his were the last books of the Bible to be written, makes his later life and death mark the end of the Apostolic Age, and we pass out of New Testament times. For this reason we have left this study until the very end of the year: after this we come to the "Sub-Apostolic Age" and the domain of Church History rather than Scriptural study. Our effort in this year's study has been to understand something of the growth of the Church of God under the hands of the Apostles, especially as reflected in the writings of the New Testament, and it is to St John that we owe the finishing touches of the Apostles' work.

IN SCRIPTURE

From Scripture we get some impression of St John's life after Pentecost. We know (as we remarked in the last Interlude) from John 19. 27 that after the Crucifixion he looked after Our Lady. The last view we have of John in the *Acts* is his being sent to Samaria with Peter from Jerusalem, and laying hands on the Samaritans, "and they received the Holy Ghost"; and after meeting Simon Magus they return to Jerusalem (Acts 8. 11–25). But St Paul in Gal. 2. 9 speaks of him still at Jerusalem: "James and Cephas and John, who seemed to be pillars, gave to me and Barnabas the right hands of fellowship". But after this, Scripture tells us no more, except that at a certain time John was on the Island of Patmos, and in exile there, for he writes at the beginning of his *Apocalypse*, after the address: "I, John . . . was in the island which is called Patmos, for the word of God and for the testimony of Jesus", and he calls himself a "partner in tribulation . . . and patience" (Apoc. 1. 9), The *Gospel* and the *Epistles* give no indication of when or where they were written, and so do not help us to discover much of his activity.

IN TRADITION

John was held in great honour by the early Christians, for not only was he their last link with Our Lord, but also was the closest possible link, having been the special friend of Our Lord on earth: "the disciple whom Jesus loved", as he often wrote himself in the Gospel (Jn. 13. 23; 19. 26; 21. 7; 21. 20). Two chiefly of the ancient writers were regarded with special distinction because they had been the

16

disciples of John; Ignatius, Bishop of Antioch; Polycarp, Bishop of Smyrna; Papias, Bishop of Hierapolis (writing about A.D. 130); and Ireneus, who wrote about the year A.D. 185, were eager to collect from them details about St John. So from these sources we can get reliable information about him.

It seems certain that after leaving Jerusalem St John lived for a long time at Ephesus. Ireneus tells us that, while at Ephesus, he once met the heretic Cerinthus in the baths (Cerinthus refused to admit that Our Lord was God and taught that men's final happiness would consist in worldly and vulgar pleasures). John cried out: "Let us fly, lest even the bath-house fall down, for Cerinthus, the enemy of truth, is within!" This reminds us of John's remark in the Gospel about the ungrateful Samaritans (Lk. 9. 54): "Lord, wilt thou that we command fire to come down from heaven and consume them?" and John's advice about false teachers (II John 10): "Receive him not into the house, nor say to him 'God speed you'".

A later tradition tells us how John was then summoned to Rome by the Emperor Domitian, and near the Latin Gate of the City was condemned to be let down into a cauldron of boiling oil, but, as Tertullian (writing about the year 200), said, "suffered nothing", but on the contrary "purior et vegetior exiverit quam intraverit" ("came out better and healthier than when he went in"). This event is commemorated on the Feast of St John before the Latin Gate (May 6), also called the Feast "Sancti Joannis in Oleo". There is an ancient church dedicated to him at the spot in Rome.

After the "failure" of this martyrdom the Emperor banished John to the Island of Patmos, one of the (now Italian) islands in the Ægean Sea, where he had the wonderful vision of the life of the Church in the world and in heaven, which he wrote down for us in the Book called the

"*Apocalypse*" or Revelation. It is a book most difficult to interpret, as it speaks of things not of this world. It will be studied in a later year's work with Volume VII of this series.

When, however, the gentler Emperor Nerva succeeded Domitian in A.D. 96, he released many people who were being unjustly punished by his predecessor, and among these was St John who was able to return to Ephesus. Here he met a previous disciple of his who had become a robber, and by his tenderness he converted him. It was then that he wrote his *Gospel*, with particular emphasis upon the Divinity of Our Lord, and reporting at length the words of Our Lord about his Unity with the Father (for instance, Jn. 10. 30: "I and the Father are one"), because of the Cerinthian and other heretics in Asia Minor. In his three *Epistles* the protection of the Christians against false teachers is his constant preoccupation, and he speaks of heretics who have left the Church (1 Jn. 2. 19): "They went out from us; but they were not of us". But also in his *Gospel* as well as in his Epistles, he is continually impressing upon his readers the great Christian Doctrine of brotherly love. For instance (1 Jn. 3. 14–15): "He that loveth not, abideth in death. Whosoever hateth his brother is a murderer" (1 Jn. 4. 7): "Dearly beloved, let us love one another". These are famous passages, as also is this one (1 Jn. 4. 16): "God is charity (*i.e.* love): and he that abideth in charity, abideth in God, and God in him". This insistence upon Christian Charity or brotherly love is further shown in the tradition preserved by St Jerome that in his very old age, having to be carried to Church, and having little strength to speak, he used very often to repeat: "Filioli, diligite alterutrum" ("Little children, love one another"). At last one day his disciples asked him: "Master, why do you say the same thing to us every day?" To which he replied: "Because this is the commandment of the Lord, and if you keep this commandment it is enough", and St Jerome adds, "Dignam Joanne sententiam!" ("a remark worthy of John!")

Of John's actual death we have no details, but he did not die a martyr, although during his life he suffered an attempted martyrdom and exile for the Faith. He died and was buried at Ephesus.

Perhaps we should add a note here that although John at the beginning of his *II* and *III Epistles*, refers to himself as the "Ancient" or the "Presbyter", and is often so called in the legends, there was possibly another John the Presbyter or Priest living at Ephesus, mentioned by Papias, who was of course a different person, but also a disciple of Our Lord. This has sometimes caused confusion.

(50)   CONCLUSION: END OF THE APOSTOLIC AGE: ST IGNATIUS OF ANTIOCH

So we have reached the end of our study of the growth of the Church in New Testament times, "built upon the foundation of the Apostles and Prophets, Jesus Christ himself being the chief corner-stone" (Eph. 2. 20, quoted also at the very beginning of this book, Introduction 3). We have followed the work of all the Apostles until the death of the last one, John. We have glanced at the books they have written for us. The Scriptural Revelation is now closed, and we find the Christians looking back to Scripture for their guidance, eager to remain in the tradition of the Apostles, and governed by the successors of the Apostles. The work of the Apostles was done: they had obeyed Our Lord's command (Mt. 28. 19): "Going therefore, teach ye all nations". It was the end of the "Apostolic Age". Now it was for their successors to carry on the work of Christ entrusted to the Apostles. In some places (as in Rome, as we have seen in the Interlude on the Successors of Peter) the work had been taken on by successors long before the death of John, but the "Sub-Apostolic Age" only really begins when the Revelation of the Apostles closes.

Probably the most outstanding figure of this time immediately after the Apostles is *Ignatius*, the second Bishop of Antioch after the departure of St Peter for Rome. He had been a disciple of St John at Ephesus, together with *St Polycarp*, who became Bishop of Smyrna. In the ninth year of the Emperor Trajan, that is in A.D. 107, he was arrested. The Emperor himself, engaged on a war in the East, came to Syria where at Antioch he found that the Christians refused to worship the Roman gods. So Ignatius the Bishop was arrested and questioned by the Emperor. When the Emperor discovered that Ignatius worshipped as the Son of God him who was crucified under Pontius Pilate, he immediately condemned him "to be carried in chains by soldiers to Great Rome, there to be thrown to the beasts for the entertainment of the people". He was taken in a ship which called at all the main ports along the coast of Asia Minor, and at each stop he was met by delegates of all the local Christian communities. He stayed at Smyrna where he saw his friend Polycarp. While making these visits on the way, always in chains, he wrote several letters, especially to communities inland which he could not visit. These seven letters have been preserved, and are among the most valuable documents of the early Church. There is, in addition, an eyewitness's account of Ignatius' journey and final martyrdom, known as the "Martyrium Ignatii", which gives us all these details.

While at Smyrna he wrote to Ephesus (which he had no chance of visiting), to Magnesia (about thirty miles away), to Tralles (about fifty miles away), and to Rome (telling them of his future martyrdom); and while at Troas he wrote to Philadelphia (inland from Smyrna), and back to Smyrna, and finally a letter of farewell and encouragement to Polycarp.

The great interest of these letters is the way in which

Ignatius insists on the Unity of the Church, preserved by unity with the Bishop ("juridical unity") and unity in the Eucharist ("liturgical unity"). His letters therefore form a very important conclusion to our studies on Unity under both these aspects in New Testament times in the Interludes devoted to it.

Ignatius also shows us that the regular Hierarchy as we know it now was completely established in his time, and by the will of Christ, through the Apostles. (The following extracts are given in Dr Brownlow's translation).

He writes (Eph. 3): "Bishops ordained unto the utmost bounds of the earth, are by the will of Jesus Christ. Wherefore it becomes you to run together, according to the will of your Bishop, as also ye do". He insists on obedience to the Bishop (Eph. 5): "Let us take heed therefore that we do not set ourselves against the Bishop, that we may be subject to God". The Hierarchy as a whole is to be honoured (Tral. 3): "Let all reverence the Deacons as Jesus Christ, and the Bishop as the Father, and the Priests ("Presbyters") as the Council of God and the assembly of the Apostles. Without these there is no Church". This passage already shows the distinction between the various parts of the Hierarchy, but also shows how their authority comes from the Apostles.

His exact doctrine of unity, with the Eucharist as the great Sacrament of Unity, is shown here (Philadelphians 4): "Wherefore, let it be your endeavour to partake all of the same Eucharist. For there is but one Flesh of Our Lord Jesus Christ, and one chalice in the unity of His Blood; one Altar; as also there is one Bishop (*i.e.* in one place) together with his Presbytery (*i.e.* his priests), and the deacons my fellow-servants". And again (Eph. 5): "You who are joined to him (your Bishop) as the Church is to Jesus Christ, and Jesus Christ to the Father, so that all things may agree in the same unity! Let no man deceive himself. Whoever is cut off from the Altar, he is deprived of the Bread of God". Here we have the two principles of unity woven together in one thought: unity of government and unity in the Blessed Sacrament.

And the fact that the doctrines contained in these letters were not only accepted as normal by those who received them, but were treasured and followed, shows how the Church as we know her now was the same right back in the times of the Apostles. Ignatius forms a most important link with the Apostles and the times that followed. Of Polycarp also, the friend of Ignatius, we also have many valuable details, recounted by eyewitnesses of his martyrdom; he was burnt to death at Smyrna in about A.D. 155. We also have a letter of his to the Church of Philippi, in which again the Hierarchy of the clergy is taken as an accepted and normal thing.

When we realise this continuity of the Church from the Apostles, through Ignatius and his fellow-bishops whom he visited and wrote to and wrote about, we then can say with more understanding that the Church is not only One, Holy and Catholic, but also in the deepest way Apostolic: "Et in unam, sanctam, catholicam et *apostolicam* Ecclesiam" as we sing in the Credo. And in the Canon of the Mass, before the Consecration, we join ourselves in prayer, in the "Communicantes", first of all with the Mother of God, the Queen of Apostles and Martyrs, and then with Peter and Paul and all the other Apostles, and then with the successors of Peter in Rome, Linus, Cletus, and Clement and finally with many other Bishops and Martyrs. And after the Consecration, in the prayer "Nobis quoque peccatoribus", we ask that to us sinners also may be granted some share and company with the Holy Apostles and Martyrs, among whom are specially mentioned Stephen, Matthias, and Barnabas (of whom we read in the Acts), and Ignatius, into whose heavenly company we ask to be admitted. For the Sacrament of the Eucharist not only binds together all the Christians who partake of it at the same time, but also binds together all the Christians of the past, the present, and the future; by the Eucharist we are brought not only together among ourselves, but brought into unity with the very Apostles themselves and their first devoted followers: "For we, being many, are one bread, one body, all that partake of one bread" (1 Cor. 10. 17).

INDICES

I.—INDEX OF REFERENCES TO AUTHORS
QUOTED OR CONSULTED

NOTES

i. These references are given according to the page in this book where the statement occurs.

ii. Where no figures are given after an author's name, the reference is to the commentary on the passage in question.

iii. Except in the obvious cases of the Breviary, Denzinger, Eusebius, Rouët de Journel's "Enchiridion Patristicum" and St Thomas Aquinas (who all have their usual type of reference), roman capital numbers refer to volumes, and arabic to pages.

iv. For commentaries on the *Acts* we refer chiefly to those of Jacquier (probably the most full and complete there is), Madame Cecilia (a learned work, and probably the most valuable for schoolwork), and the excellent notes and introduction which accompany the translation by Fr Cuthbert Lattey, S.J. in the Westminster Version. These three volumes should be fairly easily available for consultation.

v. The following frequently consulted works are referred to by abbreviations:—

Brev: the Breviary, marked (OP) for Dominican, and (Rom) for Roman where they differ.

Brownlow: the Bishop of Clifton (Dr Brownlow): *The Early History of the Church of God*, CTS 1901 (a very excellent and scholarly study).

CE: *Catholic Encyclopedia*, New York 1910.

Denz: Denzinger: *Enchiridion Symbolorum* (ed. 18–20), Freiburg i.B. 1932.

EB: Encyclopedia Biblica, London 1899 (Non-catholic).

Eusebius: Eusebius of Caesarea, *Historia Ecclesiastica*, A.D. 311–325.

Jacq: Jacquier: *Les Actes des Apôtres*, Paris 1926.

Livius: Livius, C.SS.R.: *St Peter Bishop of Rome*, Burns & Oates 1888 (a very complete and excellent authority).

MC: Madame Cecilia: (Catholic Scripture Manuals) *The Acts of the Apostles*, BOW 1925 (Books I and II bound in one).

233

Pope: Fr Hugh Pope, O.P., *The Catholic Student's "Aids" to the Bible*, revised edition BOW 1926–1938.

STh: St Thomas Aquinas, O.P., *Summa Theologica*.

WV: Westminster Version of the NT in 4 volumes, Longmans 1931–1938.

vi. Other works useful to have at hand, and which also would help the pupils are: Fr Hugh Pope: *The Layman's NT* (S & W 1928), Wood and Harding: *NT History* (Gill 1934), and Fr C. C. Martindale: Princes of his People II: *St Paul* (BOW 1924.)

PAGE

1   Antiquity of the Canon: Cabrol, *Liturgical Prayer, its history and spirit* (BOW 1925) 127 n.

7   Original meaning of ἀπόστολος, Liddell & Scott, s.v.
     On Mt 18 18: Pope, *Layman's NT*
     Apostolate: Dieckmann, S.J., *De Ecclesia* (Freiburg i.B. 1925) I n. 307–308, 312–342.

12   Roman dates: Liddell, *Student's Rome* (London 1885) xiii–xxvii.

13   Vassal kingdoms becoming Provinces, their organisation: Bury, *Student's Roman Empire* (London 1896) 4–83, 116.

14   Jews and Christians: Tucker, *Life in the Roman world of Nero & St Paul* (London 1910) 381–384.
     Pantheon: Brev Nov 1 lectio i.
     Travel: Tucker, *op. cit.* 16–29.

17   Tiberias: EB s.v.
     Emperors: Bury passim.
     Persecutions: Brownlow passim.

18   Procurators: Pope IV 26.

19n. Date of Christ's birth: Pope IV 354 sqq.
     Dionysius Exiguus: CE art. Chronology.
     Herod: Pope IV 10.

20   Greeks in Roman Empire: Tucker, *op. cit.* 32–35.

30   Chronological Tables: Pope IV 28–31 (Lists 25–26).
     Pope V 384–386.
     Brownlow xiii–xiv.
     MC I 27.

33   Necessity of Holy Ghost to understand: MC

34   White garments describe an angel: MC
     Upper Room: Jacq MC

37   v. 9 (Ascension): STh III 57 3.

40   Casting lots: MC
     v. 18 Death of Judas; Jacq: *Beginnings of Christianity* v. 22.

41   Confirmation: STh III 72 1.
     Council of Florence: Denz 697.

II.—SCRIPTURAL INDEX

TO PASSAGES QUOTED

17*

III.—LITURGICAL INDEX

TO QUOTATIONS FROM LITURGICAL TEXTS

IV.—GENERAL INDEX

V.—GREEK INDEX

ἀγάπη, ἡ brotherly love 172
Ἄγνωστος Θεός Unknown God 153
ἀγορά, ἡ market-place 150
ἄγραφον, τό unwritten 179 n.
αἵρεσις, ἡ heresy 73, 189
αἱρέω take 73, 189
ἀναγκάζω compel 136
ἀποκαλύπτω uncover 5
ἀποκάλυψις, ἡ revelation 5
Ἀπόλλων Apollo (Greek god) 164
Ἀπολλώς Apollo 164
ἀπόστολος, ὁ apostle 7
ἀποστέλλω send away 7, 8
Ἄρειος πάγος, ὁ hill of Ares (Areopagus) 152
ἀρετή, ἡ virtue 151
Αὔγουστος Augustus 16
βαπτίζω dip, bathe 34
βάσις, ἡ step, foot, astragalus 62
γραμματεύς, ὁ secretary 165
δέρω skin, flay 76
διακονέω serve 80
διάκονος, ὁ servant, deacon 80
διαμερίζω divide 42
διασπείρω scatter through 24
δόξα, ἡ glory 50
Ἕλλην, ὁ Greek 112
Ἑλληνιστής, ὁ Hellenist 112
ἐξηγέομαι be a leader 32
ἐξήγησις, ἡ exegesis 32
ἐπισκοπή, ἡ supervision 39
ἐπίσκοπος, ὁ overseer, bishop 39
ἡγεμών, ὁ leader 32

Ἰουδαΐζω live as a Jew 136
καθ' ὅλου in general 207
καταφέρω bring down 122
κοινός, ἡ, ὁν common 11, 55
κοινωνία, ἡ communion, fellowship, participation 54, 55, 169, 170, 199
κυβερνήτης, ὁ helmsman 195
νεανίας, ὁ young man 118, 121
οἰκέω inhabit 141
οἶκος, ὁ house 63, 141
οἰκουμένη, ἡ civilised world 141
πεντηκοστός, ἡ, ὁν fiftieth 34
πλήρωμα, τό fulness 56
πρεσβύτερος, ὁ presbyter 134, 179
πρηνής, head foremost 40 n.
πρῶτος τῆς νήσου chief man of the island 195
πρωτοστάτης, ὁ leader 189
ῥαβδοῦχος, ὁ rod-bearer, lictor 149
Σεβαστός Augustus 16
σκεῦος, τό vessel 108
σπερμολόγος, ὁ bird that picks up seed 152
στοά, ἡ portico, arcade 150
στρατηγός, ὁ general, magistrate 149
συνέδριον, τό council 72
σφυδρόν, τό malleolus 62
σφυρόν, τό ankle 62 n.
χειροτονέω appoint, ordain 134
χιλίαρχος, ὁ tribune 189
χριστιανός, ὁ christian 3
ψῆφος, ἡ pebble, vote 122